国家汉办/孔子学院总部
Hanban/Confucius Institute Headquarters

Du Fu

Collection of Critical Biographies of Chinese Thinkers

(Concise Edition, Chinese-English)

Editors-in-chief: Zhou Xian, Cheng Aimin

Author: Mo Lifeng   Wu Guoquan
Translator: Pan Zhidan
Reviser: Thomas Mitchell
Expert: Shi Yunlong

Nanjing University Press

《中国思想家评传》简明读本 － 中英文版 －

主 编 周 宪 程爱民

杜 甫

著 者 / 莫砺锋　　武国权
Mo Lifeng　Wu Guoquan

译 者 / 潘智丹 Pan Zhidan

审 校 / Thomas Mitchell

审 读 / 石云龙

南京大学出版社

Editor: Li Haixia
Cover designed by Zhao Qin

First published 2010
by Nanjing University Press
No. 22, Hankou Road, Nanjing City, 210093
www.NjupCo.com

©2010 Nanjing University Press

Chinese Library Cataloguing in Publication Data
The CIP data for this title is on file with the Chinese Library.

ISBN10: 7-305-06826-3(pbk)
ISBN13: 978-7-305-06826-3(pbk)

Books available in the collection

Confucius
《孔子》
978-7-305-06611-5

Laozi
《老子》
978-7-305-06607-8

Emperor Qin Shihuang
《秦始皇》
978-7-305-06608-5

Li Bai
《李白》
978-7-305-06609-2

Cao Xueqin
《曹雪芹》
978-7-305-06610-8

Du Fu
《杜甫》
978-7-305-06826-3

Zhuangzi
《庄子》
978-7-305-07177-5

Sima Qian
《司马迁》
978-7-305-07294-9

Mencius
《孟子》
978-7-305-07583-4

Mozi
《墨子》
978-7-305-07970-2

总序

General Preface

China is one of the cradles of world civilization, enjoying over five thousand years of history. It has produced many outstanding figures in the history of ancient thought, and left a rich philosophical heritage for both the Chinese people and the entire humanity. The fruit of these thinkers was to establish unique schools that over the long course of history have been continuously interpreted and developed. Today much of these thoughts are as relevant as ever and of extreme vitality for both China and the rest of the world. For instance, the ideal of " humaneness" and the concept of " harmony" taught by Confucius, the founder of Confucianism, have been venerated without ceasing by contemporary China as well as other Asian nations.

Ancient Chinese dynasties came and went, with each new dynasty producing its own scintillating system of thought. These rare and beautiful flowers of philosophy are grounded in the hundred schools vying for attention in pre-Qin times and the broad yet deep classical scholarship of Han and Tang times and in the simple yet profound occult learning of the Wei and Jin dynasties together with the entirely rational learning of Song and Ming Neo-Confucianism. The fertile soil of religious belief was Buddhism's escape from the emptiness of the sensual world and Daoism's spiritual cultivation in the search for identification with the immortals. The founders of these systems of thought included teachers, scholars, poets, politicians, scientists and monks— they made great contributions to such disparate cultural fields in ancient China as philosophy, politics, military science, economics, law, handicrafts, science and technology, literature, fine arts, and religion. The ancient Chinese venerated them for their wisdom and for following moral paths, and called them sages, worthies, saints, wise men, and great masters, etc. Their words and writings, and sometimes their life experiences, constitute the rich matter of ancient Chinese thought distilled by later generations. The accomplishments of Chinese thought are rich and varied, and permeate such spiritual traditions as the harmony between humans and nature, the unification of thought and action, and the need for calmness during vigorous action, synthesizing the old and innovating something new.

Nanjing University Press has persisted over the last twenty years in publishing the 200-book series, *Collection of Critical Biographies of Chinese Thinkers*, under the general editorship of Professor Kuang Yaming, late honorary president of Nanjing University. This collection is the largest-scale project of research on Chinese thinking and culture undertaken since the beginning of the twentieth century. It selected more than 270 outstanding figures from Chinese history, composed their biographies and criticized their

中国是世界文明的发源地之一，有五千多年的文明史。在中国古代思想史上，涌现出了许许多多杰出的思想家，为中华民族乃至整个人类留下了丰富的思想遗产。这些思想成果独树一帜，在漫长的历史中又不断地被阐释、被发展，很多思想对于今天的中国乃至世界而言，仍然历久弥新，极具生命力。比如，儒家学派创始人孔子"仁"的理念、"和"的思想，不仅在当代中国，在其他亚洲国家也一直备受推崇。

古代中国朝代更迭，每一个朝代都有灿烂夺目的思想文化。百家争鸣的先秦诸子、博大宏深的汉唐经学、简易幽远的魏晋玄学、尽心知性的宋明理学是思想学术的奇葩；佛教的色空禅悦、道教的神仙修养是宗教信仰的沃土；其他如经世济民的政治、经济理想，巧夺天工的科技、工艺之道，风雅传神、丹青不老的文学艺术……都蕴涵着丰富的思想。这些思想的创造者中有教师、学者、诗人、政治家、科学家、僧人……他们在中国古代的哲学、政治、军事、经济、法律、工艺、科技、文学、艺术、宗教等各个文明领域内贡献巨大。古代中国人尊敬那些充满智慧、追求道德的人，称呼他们为圣人、贤人、哲人、智者、大师等，他们的言论、著作或被后人总结出来的经验构成了中国古代思想的重要内容，在丰富多彩中贯穿着天人合一、知行合一、刚健中和等精神传统，表现出综合创新的特色。

南京大学出版社坚持20余年，出版了由南京大学已故名誉校长匡亚明教授主编的《中国思想家评传丛书》，这套丛书共200部，是中国20世纪以来最为宏大的中国传统思想文化研究工程，选出了中国历史上270余位杰出人物，为他们写传记，

intellectual accomplishments; all in all, it is a rigorous and refined academic work. On this foundation, we introduce this series of concise readers, which provides much material in a simple format. It includes the cream of the crop of great figures relatively familiar to foreign readers. We have done our best to use plain but vivid language to narrate their human stories of interest; this will convey the wisdom of their thought and display the cultural magnificence of the Chinese people. In the course of spiritually communing with these representative thinkers from ancient China, readers will certainly be able to apprehend the undying essence of thoughts of the Chinese people.

Finally, we are deeply grateful for the support from Hanban/ Confucius Institute Headquarters, and the experts from home and abroad for their joint efforts in writing and translating this series.

Editors
November, 2009

评论他们的思想成就，是严肃精深的学术著作。在此基础上推出的这套简明读本，则厚积薄发，精选出国外读者相对较为熟悉的伟大人物，力求用简洁生动的语言，通过讲述有趣的人物故事，传达他们的思想智慧，展示中华民族绚烂多姿的文化。读者在和这些中国古代有代表性的思想家的心灵对话中，一定能领略中华民族思想文化生生不息的精髓。

最后，我们衷心感谢国家汉办/孔子学院总部对本项目提供了巨大的支持，感谢所有参与此套丛书撰写和翻译工作的中外专家学者为此套丛书所做的辛勤而卓有成效的工作。

编者

2009年11月

目录
Contents

2 Contents ❧

一　意气风发的青少年时代

Chapter Ⅰ　An Exuberant Youth

China is a nation of poems.

For China, the 8th century A.D. marked a period of unparalleled poetic creativity. Many famous poets lived during this time, of whom Du Fu and his senior contemporary Li Bai are considered representative figures. Historians consider them the two brightest stars in the vast galaxy of Chinese poetry.

Du Fu's style name was Zimei. His ancestors were from Duling in Jingzhao (now Xi'an in Shaanxi). It was said that in ancient times, the region of Duling was a manor of the kingdom of Dubo, and was later established as Du County during the Qin Dynasty. Later, Emperor Xuan of the Han Dynasty was buried there, and his tomb was therefore called *Duling* (or the "Tomb of Du"). Not far from Duling was the tomb of Emperor Xuan's wife, Empress Xu. As it was somewhat smaller, her tomb was called *Shaoling* (meaning the "smaller Duling"). Because Du Fu's ancestors had a small holding near Shaoling, Du Fu once stayed there while seeking office in Chang'an. This is why Du Fu often called himself "An Old Village Man of Shaoling" in his poems, which earned him the nickname *Du Shaoling* (or "Du of Shaoling") in later generations. The last official title Du Fu held was Vice Director of the Ministry of Public Works, so people also called him *Du Gongbu*, meaning "Du of the Ministry of Works." These nicknames are considered *zuncheng*, respectful forms of address.

In the first year of the reign of Tang Emperor Ruizong (712 A.D.), Du Fu was born in Yaowan Village, which was two miles east of Gongxian County on the southern coast of the Yellow River (now the south of Gongyi City in Henan). Du Fu was born into a family of government officials. His father Du Xian, who at the time was in his early thirties, had been appointed magistrate of Fengtian County (now Qianxian County in Shaanxi). His mother was born in the Cui family in Qinghe, a well-known noble family.

Like other scholars of the Tang Dynasty, Du Fu was fond of praising his ancestors' achievements and virtues, therefore, let's start with his family. The Du family's respect for culture and tradition had produced generations of upstanding Confucian scholars and officials. Throughout Du Fu's life, he was always proud of being born in a family endowed with such intellectual values. He often expressed his admiration for his ancestors in poetry, especially for two of his ancestors, Du Yu and Du Shenyan.

Du Yu was Du Fu's thirteenth forefather. During the Three Kingdoms Period, he was a minister in the Western Jin Dynasty and a brilliant general in the war against Eastern Wu. After the destruction of Eastern Wu, he served as a local official in areas south of the Yangtze River. During this time, his political achievements included constructing irrigation systems and

中国是一个诗的国度。

公元八世纪是这个古老诗国诗歌创作的鼎盛时代。这一时代诞生并成就了许多著名诗人。杜甫与比他大十一岁的李白（并称"李杜"）是其中的代表，也是整个中国诗歌史浩瀚星河中最璀璨的两颗星辰。

杜甫，字子美，其祖上是京兆（今陕西西安）杜陵人。据说杜陵一带在古代是杜伯国的领地，秦置杜县，后来汉宣帝刘询葬在此处，他的陵墓就被称为杜陵。杜陵旁边是宣帝许皇后的墓，稍小一点，所以称少陵。杜甫的祖先在少陵附近留有一点产业，杜甫成年后在长安求职时曾住在那里，因而他常在诗中自称少陵野老，后人也就据此称他为"杜少陵"。杜甫最后的官衔是检校工部员外郎，故世人又称他"杜工部"。这些都是对他的尊称。

唐睿宗太极元年（712），杜甫出生于黄河南岸巩县城东二里的瑶湾村（今河南巩义市南）。杜甫的家庭是一个官宦家庭，父亲杜闲此时已三十出头，曾做过奉天（今陕西乾县）县令，母亲出身于门第高贵的清河崔氏。

杜甫和唐代的其他读书人一样，喜欢讲述自己祖先的功德。那么我们也就从他的家族说起吧。杜氏家族有着良好的文化传统，世代都有人读书做官，并且谨守着儒家的信条，从来没有背离过。杜甫长大后，一直为有这样的家庭文化传统而自豪，他常常在诗文中夸耀自己的两位祖先——杜预和杜审言。

杜预离杜甫远了点，是杜甫的十三世祖。他是西晋的大臣，曾在三国时对东吴的战争中立下赫赫战功。灭吴之后，他在江南任地方官期间，又主持兴修水利，发展生产，颇有政绩。他

increasing production. In addition, he was knowledgable in many fields, dabbling in such diverse areas as politics, economics, military affairs, law, calendar systems, arithmetic, engineering and so on. The breadth of his learning earned him the nickname "Du the Arsenal." It is worth noting that his thirty- volume works *Annotations of Zuo's Tradition of the Spring and Autumn Annals* is the earliest and most authoritative annotated version of *Zuozhuan* in existence today. His annotations were later included in Commentaries and Subcommentaries of *The Thirteen Classics*, the most important collection of Confucian classical works. Because of Du Yu's military and literary excellence having reached remarkable achievements in both fields, he was well-respected by later generations. Such an ancestor was an ideal Confucian role-model for Du Fu. When he was thirty, Du Fu composed an essay to commemorate Du Yu, praising Du Yu's outstanding achievements and fame, at the same time showing that he would follow Du Yu as his life model, and "would not forget his roots or act against the doctrine of benevolence." Throughout his life, Du Fu was a man of clear principles and strong passion, declaring himself to be "an upright and outspoken man with a strong hatred of evil practices" and "a man whose primary concern all the year round was for the people." This can be attributed to his fine family cultural tradition as well as the influence of notable ancestors as Du Yu.

Another ancestor that Du Fu held in high esteem was his grandfather Du Shenyan. Du Shenyan was a successful candidate in the highest imperial examination during the reign of Tang Emperor Gaozong. Though his political record and personal character didn't leave much to be desired, he was well-known for his literary gifts. Even while young, his popularity was on par with Li Qiao, Cui Rong and Su Weidao. They were collectively referred to as the "Four Friends of Essays." Later, he used poems to communicate with Shen Quanqi and Song Zhiwen, contributing a great deal to the establishment of modern poetic forms. Du Fu highly praised his grandfather's poetic talents. He considered his poems to be a family tradition, saying, "My grandfather surpassed all the other ancient poets" (" To Brother Monk Lvqiu of Shu"). He also said to his son, "Poetry is our family business" (" On the Birthday of Zongwu").

Though Du Fu's father Du Xian may not have been as prominent as his ancestors, he did receive a government stipend so that his family could live a rather easy life, rich enough to provide good conditions for the growth and education of the young Du Fu as well as for his future travels. The eldest son of Du Xian and Cui died young, which caused them great sorrow; Cui herself passed away several years after giving birth to her second son, Du Fu. After that, Du Xian married Lu, who gave birth to Du Fu's four younger brothers:

还博学多术，在政治、经济、军事、律令、历法、算术、工程等方面都有涉猎，因而被人们称为"杜武库"。特别值得一提的是，他的《春秋左氏经传集解》三十卷是现存最早、最具权威性的《左传》注本，后被收入最重要的儒家经典著作汇编《十三经注疏》中。这样一位能文能武、功业和著作都流芳后世的祖先在杜甫心目中简直是儒家的理想典型，因而备受杜甫推崇。三十岁的时候，杜甫专门写文章纪念杜预，高度颂扬了杜预的功业和名望，并表示自己"不敢忘本，不敢违仁"，要以杜预作为自己的人生楷模。杜甫一生爱憎分明，感情强烈，自称"嫉恶怀刚肠"、"穷年忧黎元"，这与他良好的家庭文化传统以及杜预等人事迹的影响是分不开的。

杜甫极为推崇的另一个祖先是他的祖父杜审言。杜审言是唐高宗朝的进士，平生在政治上作为不大，人品也不很高，但他的文采在当时享有盛名，年轻时代就同李峤、崔融、苏味道齐名，称"文章四友"，后来与沈佺期、宋之问唱和，对今体诗形式的确立颇有贡献。杜甫对祖父的诗歌才能推崇备至，把他的诗学成就看成是家庭的传统，说："吾祖诗冠古。"（《赠蜀僧闾丘师兄》）又对自己的儿子说："诗是吾家事。"（《宗武生日》）

杜甫的父亲杜闲虽不如祖上官职显赫，但也一直做官食禄，家境还是富裕的，这为少年杜甫的成长、读书和日后的漫游，提供了良好的条件。杜闲和崔氏生的大儿子不幸早夭，生下第二个儿子杜甫后没几年，崔氏也去世了，杜闲又娶了卢氏为妻。

Du Ying, Du Guan, Du Feng and Du Zhan, as well as a younger sister, who married into the Wei family when she grew up.

For most of his childhood, Du Fu was left in the care of his second aunt who lived in the eastern capital, Luoyang. This kind aunt provided loving care to Du Fu through his many illnesses. Once Du Fu and his cousin were caught up in an epidemic at the same time, his aunt asked a witch what to do. She said, "The child will be all right if he is placed at the southeast corner of the house." Du Fu's aunt moved her own son away from the southeast corner and put Du Fu there instead. Du Fu soon recovered, but his cousin's condition worsened until he finally died. Du Fu would never forget his aunt's sacrifice for him. Later, after his aunt had passed away, Du Fu specially mentioned this altruistic act in the inscription on the memorial tablet of her tomb. Du Fu had a sensitive disposition and a sympathetic heart, which had a lot to do with the loss of his mother at an early age and his encounter with a kind and affectionate aunt.

Born into a family of Confucian scholars, Du Fu started composing poems when he was very young. He wrote, "I had developed an agile mind and a bold writing style by the age of seven / That I could chant the poem on phoenixes the moment I opened my mouth" ("Grand Tour"). Phoenixes are auspicious heavenly birds that often appear in legends, representing light and happiness in Confucian culture. It is thus clear that Du Fu had exceptional poetic creativity, even as a child. From the time he was young, he never stopped writing poems, working harder and harder and yielding more and more great poems. Such brilliant artistic achievements enabled him to become one of the greatest poets in China's ancient history. Du Fu's poems share many similarities with those of his grandfather, Du Shenyan. These similarities show that Du Fu not only learned from and imitated his grandfather in areas such as syntax, organization and structure, but also was influenced by him in terms of poetic framework and imagery. Du Fu not only carried on Du Shenyan's tradition of five-character verse, but also achieved much by writing a great many excellent poems in the regulated and five-character verse form.

During his childhood, Du Fu received sound literary and artistic training.

By the time of Du Fu's life, the Tang Empire had existed for nearly a hundred years, built on a solid foundation of national strength, cultural advancement, convenient transportation and frequent communication with foreign countries. Owing to a healthy and mature national consciousness, the Tang people were courageous enough to accept foreign cultures with an open mind. As a result, music and dance from the Western Regions became

卢氏后来为杜甫生了四个弟弟，颖、观、丰、占，还有一个妹妹，长大后嫁给了韦氏。

童年的很多时间里，杜甫都寄养在东都洛阳的二姑家里。善良的姑母对待杜甫十分慈爱，使体弱多病的杜甫得到了悉心照料。有一次杜甫和表兄弟同时染上时疫，姑母问女巫怎么办，女巫说："把孩子放在房屋的东南角就没事了。"姑母便把亲生儿子从东南角移开，把杜甫安顿在那里。杜甫的病果然从此就好了，而表兄弟的病却一天一天加重，最后竟死了。这件事让杜甫终身难忘。后来姑母去世时杜甫在墓志中专门提到它。杜甫生性敏感而又富有同情心，这与他早年失去母亲而又遇到慈爱的姑母有很大关系。

生于诗书门第的杜甫很小就开始作诗了："七龄思即壮，开口咏凤凰。"（《壮游》）凤凰是传说中一种吉祥的神鸟，也是儒家文化中光明和美好的象征，可见杜甫从小作诗便立意不凡。在后来的日子里，杜甫从未中断过创作，并且越写越勤奋，越写越好，以其高度的诗歌艺术成就成为我国古代最伟大的诗人之一。在诗艺上，杜甫与杜审言一脉相承，不仅在句法、章法等方面有向祖父学习和模仿的痕迹，而且在诗歌意境的构思和意象的塑造方面也受到了杜审言的影响。杜甫继承了杜审言注重五言律诗的创作传统，并把它发扬光大，用联章律诗和五言排律的形式创作出了许多优秀诗篇，取得了巨大的成就。

童年的杜甫不仅接受了良好的文学教育和训练，而且还接受了多方面的艺术熏陶。

到杜甫的时代，唐帝国已经持续发展了将近百年，国力强盛，文化发达，交通便利，中外交流频繁。由于民族心智的健康和成熟，唐人敢于以开放的心灵，对外来文化进行兼收并蓄，因此，西域民族的音乐和舞蹈大量涌入。"剑器"、"浑脱"是

extremely popular. "*Jianqi*" and "*Huntuo*" were two kinds of vigorous dances imported from there. Where the former focused primarily on battle scenes, the latter attracted audiences by bold and rigorous moves. The two dances were later incorporated into a new dance—Dashing Demeanous Sword Dance. Being accustomed to listening to slow and dignified court music as well as such soft music as "Gathering Lotus Seeds," the people of Tang became so obsessed by that. They were not only popular among the commoners, but were also taught by special dancers in the Imperial Theatre. In the first year of the Kaiyuan reign, Lady Gongsun achieved popularity as the best sword dancer in the Imperial Theatre. At the age of six, Du Fu went with his family to watch her dance in Yancheng, Henan Province. It left such a lasting impression on the young Du Fu that he could still clearly visualize the dance of Lady Gongsun in his mind when he watched her students performing sword dances 50 years later.

Luoyang functioned as an auxiliary capital for the Tang Empire, in addition to the main capital at Chang'an. As it was located to the east of Chang'an, it was called the "Eastern Capital," a gathering place for princes, dukes, aristocrats, poets and men of letters. Since Luoyang was less than a hundred miles from Du Fu's home in Gongxian County, young Du Fu often followed his older family members to visit the residences of nobles and officials, where he was able to appreciate the performances of many artists. Du Fu watched several of Li Guinian's performances, the most famous singer of that time, whose sweet and moving songs left a lifelong impression on him.

In addition to music, painting of the Tang Dynasty also had a great influence on Du Fu. At the age of twenty, Du Fu once traveled to Waguan Temple in Jiangning (now Nanjing in Jiangsu). In this temple displayed a portrait of Vimalakirti, painted by the well-known painter Gu Kaizhi during the Jin Dynasty. It was said that as Gu Kaizhi painted, people donated large amounts of money to Waguan Temple just to watch him add the finishing touches. Du Fu traveled to the temple especially to admire this portrait of Vimalakirti. He was so overwhelmed with admiration for this great master's skill and so fascinated by the painting that his eyes were glued to it. Because of his love of the painting, he obtained a copy from a friend whose family name was Xu and took it with him everywhere he went, so that he could take it out and admire it from time to time.

Du Fu studied calligraphy from the age of nine, producing numerous calligraphy works throughout his life. As a child, he copied the works of Yu Shinan, a calligrapher from the early Tang Dynasty, who learned from the great

西域传来的两种健舞，前者表现战争的场面，后者则以粗犷大胆的动作吸引人，二者后来结合形成一种新的舞蹈——剑器浑脱。听惯了凝重迟缓的雅乐和轻柔婉转的"采莲曲"等音乐的唐人对这些健舞十分着迷，因而不但民间流行，宫廷的教坊中也有人专门传授。开元初年，教坊中精于剑器浑脱舞的，首推公孙大娘。杜甫六岁的时候曾在河南郾城随家人一道欣赏了她的舞蹈。这次的观舞经历给少年杜甫留下了极为深刻的印象，以至于五十年后，当他看到公孙大娘的弟子再次舞起剑器浑脱时，眼前又清晰地浮现出公孙大娘当年的舞姿。

唐帝国除了首都长安外，还有一个辅助的首都在洛阳，距杜甫巩县的家不过百里之遥。因为洛阳在长安东边，故称"东都"。这里云集着不少的王公贵族和诗人墨客，日渐长成的杜甫经常随着前辈出入一些达官贵人的宅邸，欣赏了许多艺人的表演。有几次，杜甫正好赶上当时著名的歌手李龟年的演唱，那美妙动听的歌声同样给他留下了终身难忘的印象。

除了音乐之外，唐代的绘画艺术也对杜甫有很大的影响。杜甫二十岁时曾游江宁（今江苏南京）的瓦棺寺。这座寺庙里有晋代著名画家顾恺之的维摩诘画像。相传当年顾恺之作画时，人们为了参观他最后的点睛之笔，曾为瓦棺寺捐了一百万的巨资。杜甫特意到瓦棺寺来欣赏这幅维摩诘画像，他为大师精湛的画艺而倾倒，如痴如醉，看个不够，并从当地一位姓许的朋友那里弄到了这幅画的摹本带在身边，时时欣赏。

杜甫还练习书法，从九岁开始就写大字，创作的书法作品装满了一袋子。唐初的书法家虞世南是学晋代大书法家王羲之

calligrapher Wang Xizhi of the Jin Dynasty.

As all kinds of art are interrelated, it came as no surprise that the artistic flourishing at the height of the Tang Dynasty inspired Du Fu's artistic talents in many ways. His environment was perfect for artistic growth and had a definite and direct influence on his increasing artistic sensibility as well as his poetic composition.

As Du Fu grew up, his once poor health improved greatly. By the age of fourteen or fifteen, he had grown to be a lively and strong boy.

> Though I still had a childish heart at the age of fifteen,
> I was as strong as a roving calf.
> When the dates in front of the yard became ripe in August*,
> I would climb up and down the trees thousands of times a day.
>   ("Collection of Hundreds of Worries")

Since he was both intelligent and fond of learning, he had already finished school by the age of fifteen. With his brilliant literary talent, he soon stood out from his peers, rising to early prominence in the literary world of Luoyang. Later, Du Fu recalled that Li Yong, the greatest literary giant of the time, requested to meet him; that the poet Wang Han wished to become his neighbor; that the famous intellectuals Cui Shang and Wei Qixin, successful candidates in the highest imperial examination, compared him to the famous historian Ban Gu and the writer Yang Xiong of the Han Dynasty. This appreciation by his seniors greatly enhanced young Du Fu's ambition, strengthening his self-confidence, and giving him a sense of superiority and faith in the future.

Knowing that the Sui Dynasty, which held power before the Tang Dynasty, was overthrown by peasant uprisings, the second Tang Emperor Li Shimin stated the following regarding the destruction of Sui: "The monarch is like a boat tossed upon the waters of the people; the waters not only carry the boat afloat, but also have the power to overturn it." Therefore, after Li Shimin's succession to the throne, he enacted numerous progressive administrative measures, such as carrying out land equalization system to narrow the gap between the rich and the poor, reforming tax laws to ease burdens on the people, and promoting imperial civil examinations to enlist intellectuals. He also built water reservoirs, developed production, and increased commercial trade. At the same time, he built up the military, defeated the Tujue and Tuyuhun tribes who had posed a constant threat to the safety of people in the north of China, and opened trade routes to the Western Regions.

的，杜甫小时候曾临摹过他的书法。

各种门类的艺术是相通的，盛唐时代艺术的繁茂发展，从多方面刺激着少年杜甫的艺术细胞，给他以丰富的营养，这对于他日后形成敏锐的艺术感受力、从事诗歌创作无疑有着直接的影响。

杜甫一天天地长大了。他小时候多病的身体也强壮起来，十四五岁时，已经成长为活泼健壮的少年：

忆年十五心尚孩，健如黄犊走复来。

庭前八月梨枣熟，一日上树能千回。

——《百忧集行》

由于他聪明好学，这时已经学业初成，文采出众，从同辈少年中脱颖而出，在洛阳文坛上崭露头角。杜甫后来回忆说，当时的大文豪李邕都想要见他一面，诗人王翰希望能和他做邻居，中过进士的名士崔尚和魏启心甚至把他比作汉代著名的史学家班固和文学家杨雄。前辈的赏识增强了少年杜甫进取的精神和强烈的自信心，他傲气的眼神充满了优越感和对未来的自信。

唐以前的隋朝是被农民起义推翻的，唐太宗李世民从隋朝灭亡的历史教训中总结出一个道理："舟所以比人君，水所以比黎庶；水能载舟，亦能覆舟。"因而他继位之后，制定了一些进步的措施，如推行"均田制"以缩小贫富差距，改革税法以减轻人民负担，实行科举以网络知识分子。并兴修水利，发展生产和商业贸易。同时建立起强大的军事力量，打败了长期威胁中国北方的少数民族突厥和吐谷浑，打通了通往西域之路。

---

* in Chinese lunar calendar.

All these measures sped up economic growth of the society, ushering in an unparalleled golden age of prosperity generally called the "Reign of Zhenguan." After the reign of Emperor Taizong, several other emperors continued these efforts for dozens of years, which further promoted social productivity. In August when Du Fu was born, the Xuanzong Emperor, Li Longji, took the throne. In the early years of his reign, Emperor Xuanzong did his best to make the country prosperous by basing his appointments on merit and being humble enough to accept admonition. As a result, the Tang Empire reached the height of its prosperity under his reign during the Kaiyuan era, which came to be called the "Golden Age of Kaiyuan." It was an age of even greater economic prosperity than the "Reign of Zhenguan." Du Fu once illustrated the social conditions at that time in his poem "Recalling the Past" :

> In the golden days of the Kaiyuan era,
> In even the smallest county there lived over ten thousand households.
> The rice was so ripe with grease and the maize so white,
> That the people's barns and the officials' granaries were both full.

The Tang Dynasty's vast territory and booming foreign trade broadened the people's horizons and developed their imaginations while national stability and economic prosperity enhanced the people's self-confidence. It was in just such an atmosphere that Du Fu entered his adolescence. In the ancient times, it was a common practice for young men of good living conditions to travel around to enrich their experiences and broaden their understanding of the world. By the Tang Dynasty, this practice had become more prevalent, and the young Du Fu was no exception. Since he was twenty years old, he had travelled for ten years, first to Wu and Yue in the south (now Zhejiang and the south of Jiangsu) and then to Qi and Zhao (now Shandong and the south of Hebei). Like other people of his age, he was seldom weighed down by worry, sorrow, or disappointment; quite the contrary, he radiated vigor, excitement, and hunger for improvement.

In the eighteenth year of the reign of Kaiyuan (730 A.D.), nineteen-year-old Du Fu traveled north to cross the Yellow River, seeking refuge from floods in Luoyang. He traveled as far as Xunxia in the Jin region (now Yishi in Shanxi), where he became acquainted with future regional governors Wei Zhijin and Kou Xi . After a short stay there, he returned to Luoyang.

The next year, he started a four-year journey to Wu and Yue. He set out by canal from Luoyang, crossing the Yangtze River and coming to Jiangning.

这些措施使得社会经济迅速发展，出现了"贞观之治"的空前
繁荣。太宗以后经过其他几位皇帝几十年的惨淡经营，社会生
产力进一步发展。杜甫出生那一年的八月，唐玄宗李隆基即位。
早期的唐玄宗励精图治，任人唯贤，善于纳谏，他统治下的唐
帝国在开元年间达到隆盛的顶点，史称"开元盛世"。这是一
个经济上比"贞观之治"更加繁荣富足的时代。杜甫在《忆昔》
中描写了当时的社会面貌：

> 忆昔开元全盛日，小邑犹藏万家室。
>
> 稻米流脂粟米白，公私仓廪俱丰实。

广阔的疆域和对外贸易的繁荣，扩大了国人的视野和想象
力，国家的稳定和经济的富足，增强了国人的自信心。杜甫就
是在这样一种氛围中拉开了他青年时代的序幕。古人为了增加
阅历、增长见闻，有条件的男青年都有漫游四方的习气。唐代
这一风气更加盛行，青年杜甫也不例外。他从二十岁开始，进
行了十年的漫游：先南下吴越（今江苏南部、浙江），后北上
齐赵（今山东、河北南部）。和同时代其他人一样，他的精神
世界中很少有担心、哀伤和失望，通体散发出一种蓬勃、昂扬、
向上的气息。

开元十八年（730），十九岁的杜甫为了躲避洛阳的水灾，
北渡黄河，远行到晋地的郇瑕（今山西猗氏），结识了后来做
了刺史的韦之晋和寇锡，不久就回来了。

第二年，他开始了为时四年的吴越之游。他从洛阳水路出
发，沿着运河，渡过长江，来到江宁。江宁曾经是三国时吴国、

Jiangning was once the capital city of six dynasties, beginning with the Kingdom of Wu during the Three Kingdoms Period, then continuing with the Eastern Jin Kingdom as well as the Song, Qi, Liang and Chen kingdoms of the Northern and Southern Dynasty period. After enjoying the historical sights of this ancient capital and admiring the portrait of Vimalakirti by Gu Kaizhi in the Waguan Temple, Du Fu continued his travels along the Yangtze River, finally arriving at Gusu (now Suzhou in Jiangsu). Gusu was a place of beautiful scenery and legendary stories. During the Spring and Autumn Period, the Wu Kingdom established its capital at Gusu. The founder of the Wu Kingdom was Taibo, the eldest son of Taiwang of Zhou (also known as Duke Danfu). Because Taibo's father intended to let his third son inherit the throne, Taibo gave up his claim on the throne and escaped to the south with his second brother Zhongyong, there founding the Wu Kingdom. Later, a young prince of the Wu Kingdom named Guang thought that he had the right to the throne, so he prepared a banquet and invited King Liao. At the banquet, he asked an assassin to hide a dagger inside a fish and kill the king while he was eating. Guang then announced himself King of Wu, called King Helv of Wu in history. After his death, King Helv was buried with three thousand famous swords in the Tiger Hill in the northwest of Suzhou city. It was said that a white tiger crouched on the tomb three days after it was finished. Later, Emperor Qin Shihuang tried to open the tomb to retrieve the swords, leaving a deep trough in the giant rock, which later became the famous Sword Pond. When Du Fu visited Helv's tomb, it was covered with lush wild shrubs; he also visited the Sword Pond and Changzhou Garden, where King Wu once went hunting and where lotus flowers now filled the pond, giving off sweet fragrance. He walked through the grand Changmen Gate and paid homage to Taibo's Temple, thereby showing his consciousness of not only Taibo's mortality, but also Taibo's humility in yielding his own position to the more virtuous and talented. In this region of Wu, there once lived another important historical figure, Zhu Maichen of the Han Dynasty. Even though his wife abandoned him when he was poor, he still invited her and her new husband to his official residence to live when he later became Prefect of Kuaiji (now Shaoxing in Zhejiang). His ex-wife was so ashamed that she committed suicide. When Du Fu visited this place, he could not help but remember this story.

After leaving Gusu, Du Fu continued his travels south, following the route that Emperor Qin Shihuang took for his eastern journey, entering the region of Yue by crossing the Qiantang River. There he recalled the story of King Goujian of Yue in the Spring and Autumn Period, who slept on firewood,

东晋及南北朝时期宋、齐、梁、陈六个朝代的首都，杜甫在这里游览了六朝古都的名胜古迹、瞻仰了瓦棺寺顾恺之的维摩诘画像之后，继续沿着长江而下，来到姑苏（今江苏苏州）。姑苏是一个风光旖旎而又充满各种传说故事的地方。春秋时吴国曾在此定都。吴国的始祖是太伯，他本是周太王（古公亶父）的长子，因为其父想让三儿子季历继位，太伯便主动放弃王位继承权，和二弟仲雍避往南方，成为吴国的始祖。吴国的王族中后来有一个叫光的青年，认为王位应该是自己的，就摆酒席请国王僚来赴宴。在宴席上，他安排刺客专诸把匕首藏在鱼腹之中，在给吴王僚进食时趁机杀了他。光便自立为吴王，史称吴王阖闾。阖闾死后葬于苏州城西北的虎丘山，有三千柄名剑作为陪葬品。相传他的墓修好三日，便有白虎蹲踞其上。后来秦始皇发冢求剑，在巨岩上劈开一道深邃的壕沟，这便是著名的剑池。杜甫参观了埋没在萋萋荒草中的阖闾墓，观看了剑池和吴王曾经游猎过的长洲苑——那里荷花满池，散发着芳香。杜甫还穿过雄壮的阊门，向北拜谒了太伯庙，对他避位让贤的德行表达了深深的敬仰。吴地还有一个历史人物——汉代的朱买臣，他贫贱时妻子离婚另嫁，后来朱买臣当了会稽（今浙江绍兴）太守，把前妻及其后夫接到官舍来住，前妻惭愧难当，便自杀了。杜甫游览吴地时，不禁也想起了这个故事。

离开姑苏，诗人继续南下，沿着秦始皇东巡的路线，渡过钱塘江进入越地。诗人在此缅怀春秋时越王勾践卧薪尝胆、枕

tasted gall, and lay on a spear to wait for daybreak. He toured around Kuaiji, the capital city of the Yue Kingdom and climbed Kuaiji Mountain to visit Yu's Cave, rumored to be the place where Yu of Xia hid his books. He praised the fair skin of the maidens of Yue and felt the clear, cool water of Jianhu Lake in May. Despite the breadth of his travels, his lifelong regret was never being able to visit Japan.

In the twenty-third year of the Kaiyuan reign (735 A.D.), Du Fu ended his four-year-long travel to Wu and Yue, returning to his hometown of Gongxian County to prepare for that year's highest imperial examination. In the Tang Dynasty, less than one percent of candidates were selected. Though Du Fu was a man of brilliant intellect, he was still unable to succeed. Despite his failure, Du Fu was not disheartened, for he soon set out to travel again to the north, visiting the regions of Qi and Zhao. At that time, Du Fu's father was an official in charge of war in Yanzhou of Shandong, so he was able to visit his father while touring there.

The Qi and Lu regions, where Yanzhou was located, was a land of long-standing cultural tradition. As it was the birthplace of Confucianism, there were numerous historical sites. Qufu, the hometown of Confucius, the founder of Confucianism, was located here, as was Mount Tai, the Eastern Sacred Mountain which was considered the first of the Five Sacred Mountains. After climbing Mount Tai, Du Fu composed the grand poem "Gazing at the Sacred Mountain."

> What does the first Sacred Mountain look like?
> It lies in the Qi and Lu regions, lands of unending green.
> With all nature's magical beauty gathered here,
> Its towering peak splits dusk and dawn on its north and south sides.
> Looking down, layers of clouds sweep before my chest;
> Looking up at the distant returning birds, I strain my eyes.
> One day, I will climb to the peak of this mountain,
> To overlook all the other smaller ones with a single glance.

The first line of this poem is a question that provides momentum for the unexpected development of the whole piece. The green mountain scene of Mount Tai is depicted in the second line, which describes its stretching ranges that can be seen from anywhere in the Qi and Lu regions. The third line means that nature has gathered together all its most miraculous and graceful natural splendor, emphasizing the beauty of Mount Tai. The fourth line says that the mountain divides day from night so that the south and north of the mountain are in different states at dusk and dawn, thereby praising the towering height of

戈待旦的事迹。他游览了越国的首都会稽，登上会稽山探访了传说是夏禹藏书的地方——禹穴。他赞美越地的女孩儿皮肤白皙，感到五月的鉴湖水清凉怡人。他一生一直有一个遗憾，就是没有东渡日本，以尽游兴。

　　开元二十三年（735），杜甫结束了为期四年的吴越之游，回到老家巩县，准备参加这年的进士考试。唐代的进士考试录取率不到百分之一，虽然杜甫才华横溢，但最终还是落榜了。不过这次落榜并没有给年轻的诗人造成心理打击，他很快就再次出发，向北去漫游齐、赵。当时杜甫的父亲在山东兖州任司马，他去看望父亲，并在这一带游历。

　　兖州所在的齐鲁大地，具有悠久的文化传统，是儒家学说的发源地，附近的名胜古迹很多。这里有儒家学说的创始人孔子的故乡曲阜，也有被尊为五岳之首的东岳泰山。杜甫登临泰山，写下了气魄雄伟、语言警拔的《望岳》：

　　　岱宗夫如何？齐鲁青未了。

　　　造化钟神秀，阴阳割昏晓。

　　　荡胸生层云，决眦入归鸟。

　　　会当凌绝顶，一览众山小。

本诗首句发问，领起全篇，起势突兀。二句说泰山青碧的山色在整个齐鲁大地都能看到，极言泰山绵延之广。第三句说大自然把神奇秀丽的景色都集中到这里了，极言泰山之秀丽。第四句说山峰分开了白昼和黑夜，山南山北，晓昏不一，极言泰山

Mount Tai. The fifth and sixth lines describe how the poet's mind surged with the misty air of the mountain as he looked up into the sky. He strained his eyes gazing far into the distance at the birds flying back to the mountain. The last two lines describe what the poet saw and felt as he climbed to the peak and looked down on the mountains below. The poet borrowed Confucius' famous lines to express his high aspiration and heroic spirit: "Climbing to the top of the East Peak, Lu seemed small to Confucius /Climbing to the top of Mount Tai, the whole world below appeared insignificantly small."

In the twenty-ninth year of the Kaiyuan reign (741 A. D.), Du Fu ended his travels and returned to his hometown. By that time, he was already thirty years old.

In the northwest region of Yanshi County (now Yanshi in Henan), east of Luoyang was a mountain called Shouyang, at the foot of which there was a garden named Luhun Village built by Du Fu's ancestors. Du Fu's forefather Du Yu and his grandfather Du Shenyan were both buried there. Before the Cold Food Festival of that year, Du Fu built several cave dwellings and paid his respects to Du Yu and his other ancestors at their tombs before marrying the daughter of Yang Yi, the deputy minister of agriculture. The new couple spent a period of peaceful time in the newly built cave dwellings, which laid a foundation for a lifetime of deep affection as they passed through good times and bad ones. As their happy life began in Luhun Village, Du Fu often mentioned it with nostalgic longing.

Nevertheless, Du Fu did not content himself with family life and carefree travels. The achievements of his ancestors inspired him to the point that his fiery heart was filled with lofty aspirations. He actively involved himself in the literary world of Luoyang, making friends with other writers through exchanging poems as well as gaining fame and recognition by visiting prominent officials and eminent personages. The intrigues he witnessed in this bustling city greatly depressed him, creating a stark contrast to his carefree wanderings of the past eight to nine years. As soon as he met Li Bai, he couldn't help pouring out his heart-felt sadness. At that time, Du Fu thought Li Bai was finally able to escape and win freedom, though in fact Li Bai had been driven out of the capital city by conspiring courtiers close to the emperor. Du Fu praised Li Bai's talent and wanted to follow him to gather herbs for making immortality pills and to visit Taoist gods of immortality.

Li Bai (701 ~ 762 A. D.), who had the style name Taibai and poetic name Qinglian Jushi, was a great and talented poet. During the early Tang Dynasty, his poems were well-known both in and out of the court. He was summoned to the capital by Xuanzong of Tang in the first year of the Tianbao reign (742 A. D.),

之高。第五、六两句写诗人仰视天空，心胸随山中弥漫的云气而激荡，极目远眺归山的飞鸟，眼眶都要裂开了。最后两句写登上顶峰俯视群山的所见所感，借用孔子"登东山而小鲁，登泰山而小天下"的名句，表达了诗人远大的抱负和豪迈的气概。

开元二十九年（741），诗人结束漫游，回到他的家乡，这时他整整三十岁了。

洛阳东面的偃师县（今河南偃师）西北，有一座首阳山。山下有杜甫祖上留下来的一个庄园，叫陆浑庄。杜甫的远祖杜预和祖父杜审言都葬在这里。这年寒食节来临之前，诗人在这里修筑了几间窑洞，拜祭过杜预等先人的陵墓之后，他和司农少卿杨怡的女儿结婚了。一对新人在新建的窑洞里度过了一段平静的时光。此后，夫妻二人一直感情深厚，同甘苦，共患难，直到白头。陆浑山庄见证了他们最初的幸福生活，因而杜甫后来常常带着美好的回忆提起这里。

然而他并没有沉溺于家庭生活和游山玩水之中。祖先的功业和声名激励着他，建功立业的雄心壮志在他三十岁火热的胸腔中激荡着。他活跃在洛阳文坛上，与文人进行诗文交往以求获得声誉，与达官贵人交游以求被引荐。在这鱼龙混杂的繁华都市，他看到了人们之间的钩心斗角。这使得快意漫游了八九年的杜甫感到很郁闷。所以当他一见李白，便忍不住倾倒出胸中的苦闷。当时，李白虽然是被皇帝周围的人赶出京城，但杜甫却觉得李白是"脱身"而得到自由了。他赞扬李白的才华，想要跟他一起去采药炼丹，求仙访道。

李白（701～762），字太白，号青莲居士，是一位伟大的天才诗人。他的诗歌在当时朝野闻名，因而于天宝元年（742）

but wasn't given any important position. His proud and free-spirited personality made things worse by arousing the hatred and jealousy of Xuanzong's two court favorites, Lady Yang Yuhuan and Eunuch Gao Lishi. Due to their slandering remarks, Li Bai was alienated from the emperor just after more than a year. In the spring of the third year of the Tianbao reign (744 A.D.), Li Bai left Chang'an for the Eastern Capital Luoyang, vowing indignantly that he would never bow and scrape to men of high office again. That April, he met with Du Fu in Luoyang, a meeting between two brilliant poets that would happen only once a millinium. Their time together was very pleasant; they traveled together to Wangwu Mountain in autumn to visit the dwelling of the deceased Taoist monk Hua Gai. As Hua Gai had already died, they only paid a visit to the cleanroom where he had tried to make pills of immortality before his death. After that, Du Fu left for Liangsong (now Shangqiu in Henan). After paying a visit to some relatives and friends, Li Bai also came to Liangsong to meet with Du Fu. There they met with Gao Shi, who had traveled along the northern frontiers and had won his fame by writing frontier poems. Liangsong was a prosperous place in the Tang Dynasty, so the three of them drank and composed poems together, visiting Guchui Tower in Songzhou County and coming to Shanfu County (now Shanxian County in Shandong) in winter, where they climbed up Shanfu Tower. Du Fu so admired the literary talent of these two poets, both over ten years older than him and already renowned far and wide, that he wrote poems in their honor.

In the fourth year of the Tianbao reign (745 A.D.), Gao Shi went southward to the region of Chu (now Hunan), and Li Bai and Du Fu traveled northward to Qizhou (now Jinan in Shandong). Li Bai received the "Taoist magic figure" from Heavenly Master Gao in Ziji Monastery, there becoming a registered Taoist priest, while Du Fu visited the great literary master Li Yong, who had always wanted to meet Du Fu. Since some of Li Bai's family were staying temporarily in Rencheng City of Lu Prefecture (now Jining in Shandong), he traveled there to visit them. Du Fu was also invited there after he returned to Yanzhou. In Rencheng City, they exchanged experiences through poetry, sought talented men and friends, visited Mr. Fan who lived in seclusion in the north of the city, and climbed up Dongmeng Mountain to visit the Taoist priests Dong Lianshi and Yuan Yiren. Du Fu intended to go back to the west in winter, so the two friends parted at the stone gate in the east of the city. They were very reluctant to bid farewell to each other, and Li Bai composed a parting poem. Though from that time on, the two great poets lived far apart from each other and would never see each other again, their friendship lasted forever and never changed.

被唐玄宗征召入京，但唐玄宗并没有重用他。李白傲岸疏放的性格又遭到唐玄宗最宠爱的两个人物——贵妃杨玉环和太监高力士——的嫉恨。由于他们的谗毁，只过了一年多，李白便被皇帝疏远了。天宝三载（744）春，李白怀着"安能摧眉折腰事权贵，使我不得开心颜"的激愤离开长安，前往东都洛阳。四月就在洛阳遇到了杜甫。这是两颗璀璨的明星在诗国夜空中一次难得的相遇，是文学史上一段千年等一回的佳话！这次见面十分愉快。秋天，他们一起来到王屋山，拜访著名的道士华盖君，由于华盖君已死，他们只凭吊了他生前炼丹的净室。接着，杜甫前往梁宋（今河南商丘）。李白访过亲友后也来梁宋与杜甫会合。他们在这里碰到了曾去过北方边塞并以写边塞诗著称的高适。唐代的梁宋很是繁华，三人一起饮酒赋诗，登览了宋州的古吹台，又于冬天来到单父县（今山东单县），登上这里的单父台。面对两位年长自己十多岁且早已诗名远播的大诗人，杜甫对他们的诗才十分钦佩，写诗予以赞美。

　　天宝四载（745），高适南下楚地（今湖南），李、杜北上齐州（今山东济南）。在齐州，李白到紫极宫领受了高天师的"道箓"，成了记录在册的道士；杜甫则拜访了大文豪李邕，满足了后者早就想结识自己的愿望。李白因为有家小寄住在鲁郡的任城（今山东济宁），接着便去探望，杜甫重回兖州后，也应邀前往。他们切磋诗艺，寻贤访友，拜访了隐居城北的范居士，又登上东蒙山访道于董炼师和元逸人。冬天，杜甫要西归，他们便在城东的石门分手，两个人恋恋不舍地分别，李白还写了一首送别诗。此后，这两位伟大的诗人就天各一方，再也无缘一见，然而他们的友谊却历久不衰，终生不渝。

杜甫画像
Portrait of Du Fu

二　旅食京华的悲辛

Chapter Ⅱ　Bitter Life in the Capital

In the fifth year of the Tianbao reign (746 A.D.), Du Fu came to Chang'an.

As the capital city of the Tang Empire, Chang'an was the political and cultural center of the whole country and was also one of the most magnificent and prosperous metropolises in the world. During the Tianbao reign, Chang'an reached its height of prosperity, with a population of over a million people. Du Fu came to know some people of power and influence in Chang'an, such as Prince Ruyang Li Jin and the imperial son-in-law Zheng Qianyao. Li Jin had a special status, for he was the son of Li Xian, the eldest brother of Emperor Xuanzong Li Longji. He not only looked just like Taizong Li Shimin, but he also excelled at poetry and calligraphy, carrying himself with scholarly bearing. In accordance with the Chinese tradition that the eldest son should succeed the throne, Li Xian should have had the right to the throne. However, he willingly gave up this right, enabling Xuanzong, who was the third by age, to succeed smoothly to the throne. Because of this, Xuanzong was very thankful to him. He later bestowed the posthumous title of "Resigning Emperor" on him and gave Li Jin a high position of responsibility. Du Fu spent a great deal of energy composing a poem for Li Jin, thereby becoming acquainted with him. The imperial son-in-law Zheng Qianyao was a nephew of Zheng Qian, a close friend of Du Fu. Probably for the sake of Zheng Qian, Du Fu became a frequent visitor in the imperial son-in-law's home, often strolling through the gardens and taking part in banquets there. In addition, Du Fu also made friends with poets such as Wang Wei and Cen Shen.

Because he was preparing for the upcoming imperial examination, Du Fu did not return home in Spring Festival of that year. He spent the Festival's Eve playing gambling games with a group of people at an inn in Chang'an. The examination was held in the sixth year of the Tianbao reign (747 A.D.), and it was presided by Prime Minister Li Linfu, an uneducated and untalented man who often misread words. To make matters worse, he was also a hypocritical and malignant conspirator whose successful official career was a result of his skill in flattery. After taking the office of prime minister, he pushed out the more liberal-minded Prime Minister Zhang Jiuling, fabricating charges against and persecuting many upright people. In order to suppress talented men and centralize power to himself, he gave the secret order that all the scholars taking part in this examination should be dismissed, so all the examinees failed, including Du Fu and another great poet named Yuan Jie. He dared to submit a congratulatory memorial to Xuanzong, proclaiming "that no talented person was left outside the court." This fraud made Du Fu feel so disappointed, grievous and indignant, that he wrote the following lines: "It is too late to help

天宝五载（746），杜甫来到了长安。

作为唐帝国的首都，长安是全国的政治、文化中心，它还是当时全世界最壮丽繁华的一个大都会。天宝年间长安繁盛到了顶点，人口超过百万。杜甫在长安结识了一些有权势的人物，如汝阳王李琎、驸马郑潜曜等。李琎的身份有点特殊，他是当朝皇帝唐玄宗李隆基的大哥李宪的儿子，长得很像唐太宗李世民，善诗文、工书法，颇有儒雅之风。按照中国长子继位的传统，李宪本应该做皇帝的，可是他却主动放弃这个权力，使得排行第三的唐玄宗得以顺利继位，因而唐玄宗很感谢他，日后谥他为"让皇帝"，也给了李琎很高的职位。杜甫精心构思，写了一首诗献给李琎，从此就与这个很有身份的王公相识了。驸马郑潜曜则是杜甫的一个亲密朋友郑虔的侄儿，可能是因为郑虔的缘故，杜甫成了郑驸马府中的常客，常常有机会游览府中的园林，参加驸马的宴会。此外，杜甫还和王维、岑参等诗人交往。

为了迎接即将到来的制举考试，这年春节他没有回家。除夕之夜他是和一帮人在长安的一家客舍里玩赌博游戏度过的。天宝六载（747），制举考试进行了。考试由宰相李林甫主持。李林甫是个不学无术的人，因为常常认错字而留下了不少笑话，但他又是一个"口蜜腹剑"的阴谋家，由于善于溜须拍马而官运亨通。任宰相后，他排挤掉比较开明的宰相张九龄，诬陷、迫害了很多正直人士。为了压制人才、独揽大权，他授意将参加此次考试的士人全部黜落，致使包括杜甫和另一位大诗人元结在内的所有应举者都落榜了，而他竟然还向唐玄宗上表祝贺，说是"野无遗贤"。这场骗局使杜甫感到失望和悲愤，"致君时

the emperor / It is meaningless to harbor ill will for past wrong deeds" ("To Brother Xiao Shi, Director of the Document Section"). These lines were indeed a true portrayal of Du Fu's feelings. Five or six years later, he still felt so bitter about this that he exclaimed indignantly that he had fallen prey to Li Linfu, the dictatorial conspirator, making his already hard life even more miserable.

For Du Fu, this was not only failure in the examination, but also loss of an important chance to realize his goals. To some extent, this meant a significant change to his life's course and the beginning of tragedy. From that time on, Du Fu ended his romantic career and embarked on a life journey of frustration, sadness and bitterness.

In the ninth year of the Tianbao reign (750 A.D.), Wei Ji, Du Fu's old family friend who had often visited him in Luhun Village, took office in Chang'an as a minister's assistant. Du Fu wrote a poem to him hoping to be introduced to the political world; however, Wei Ji was unable to help him. Afterwards, Du Fu sent another poem to a Hanlin academician named Zhang Ji, son-in-law of Xuanzong. He even wrote a poem to Xianyu Zhongtong, the local head official of the capital, asking him to seek help from the Prime Minister Yang Guozhong, but still received no satisfactory reply. Zhang Ji once defamed Li Bai and also betrayed his country during the later An Shi Rebellion. Since Xianyu Zhongtong had helped out Yang Guozhong when Yang was poor, he later became Yang's trusted subordinate. The two of them collaborated with each other, rashly launching a war against Nanzhao, which ended in a crushing defeat with over two hundred thousand casualties that they concealed and did not report. None of these were upright people, so when Du Fu sought their help, he was like a deathly ill person who turned in desperation to any doctor he could find.

As Du Fu was a good friend of two frontier poets, Gao Shi and Cen Shen, he had some understanding of military life. "The First Five Frontier Poems" and "The Later Nine Frontier Poems" all showed his familiarity with military life. He loved fine horses, composing many poems about them in which he expressed his own sentiments of charging over the battlefield and fighting the enemy to win honor. Because he dreamed of following in the footsteps of his friend Gao Shi and joining the army, he sent poems to officers in the field. In the thirteenth year of the Tianbao reign (754 A.D.), he wrote a poem to Ge Shuhan, the governor of Hexi, hoping to be recruited as his military advisor. He asked an assistant of Ge Shuhan named Tian Liangqiu to forward the poem for him, so he specially wrote a poem for Tian Liangqiu as well, but this effort was also for naught.

已晚，怀古意空存"（《赠比部萧郎中十兄》），这是他当时心情的真实写照。直到五六年后，杜甫想起这件事，还是沉痛不已，气愤地说自己栽在李林甫这位阴谋独断的奸相手里，使得本来就很艰难的日子变得更加辛酸了。

对于杜甫来说，这不单纯是一次考试的失败，而是失去了一次重要的施展抱负的机会。在某种程度上来说，这意味着他人生轨迹的重大改变，也是他人生悲剧的开始，杜甫从此就结束了他的浪漫生涯，开始了坎坷悲辛的人生之旅。

天宝九载（750），与杜甫家有世交并曾多次到陆浑山庄探访过杜甫的韦济到长安任尚书左丞，杜甫便写了一首诗给他，希望得到引荐，然而韦济似乎也没有什么办法帮助他。杜甫又向玄宗的女婿——翰林学士张垍——赠诗，甚至向京兆尹鲜于仲通赠诗，托他向宰相杨国忠求助，然而都没有得到满意的答复。张垍曾经谗毁过李白，后来又在安史之乱中叛国投敌。鲜于仲通在杨国忠贫贱时曾周济过他，后来成了杨的心腹，他和杨国忠相互勾结，轻率地发动了对南诏的战争，招致大败，死伤二十多万，而又隐瞒不报。这些人都不是什么正派人物，杜甫向他们求援，真是有点"病急乱投医"了。

杜甫与从军边塞的诗人高适和岑参都是好朋友，他自己对军队生活也很留心，从他写的《前出塞五首》和《后出塞九首》中都可以看出他对军事生活的熟悉。他喜欢骏马，数首咏马诗中都寄托着自己驰骋疆场、杀敌立功的豪情。他曾想过像他的朋友高适一样，走从军这条路，于是也给军队里的人物投赠诗歌。天宝十三载（754），他写诗给河西节度使哥舒翰，希望对方能收录自己入幕府参谋军事。他是托哥舒翰的一位判官田梁丘转呈这首诗的，为此专门给田梁丘也写了一首诗，不过这件事后来也没有什么结果。

Du Fu also wrote *Fu* prose to the emperor directly. *Fu* was a literary style that enabled the author to elaborate his ideas and express himself to the fullest. As it was suited for describing grand, spectacular and complex scenes, it satisfied the emperor's craving for greatness and success. Because of this, *Fu* became Du Fu's first choice when writing for the emperor. In the sixth year of the Tianbao reign (747 A.D.), Du Fu happened to pass by the royal menagerie and saw the mighty, swift, and ferocious royal dog, so he decided to write a *Fu* piece entitled "On the Royal Dog." In the first lunar month of the ninth year of the Tianbao reign (750 A.D.), Xuanzong was preparing to hold a ritual on Mount Hua, the Western Sacred Mountain, by building an altar and offering sacrifices to Heaven. Du Fu wrote a *Fu* piece for the occasion, entitled "On Crowning the Western Sacred Mountain," but because the emperor chose not to perform the ritual, it was never presented to him. In September of the same year, Du Fu wrote the *Fu* prose "On Vulture," as well as a memorial about his submission, both of which were earnest and imploring in tone, but still unable to move the emperor. In the first month of the next year, the emperor held three consecutive major sacrificial ceremonies, for which Du Fu composed three major *Fu* pieces on court rituals, namely "The Emperor Offering Sacrifices to Heaven in Taiqing Palace," "The Emperor Offering Sacrifices to His Ancestors in the Royal Ancestral Temple" and "The Emperor Offering Sacrifices to Both Heaven and Earth in the Southern Outskirts." With these poems, he finally aroused the attention of Xuanzong, who asked him to wait in Jixian Academy for a future appointment. The emperor also ordered the prime minister to examine Du Fu's essay writing abilities, which made his reputation skyrocket.

Jixian Academy was also known as the Jixiandian Academy of Classical Learning, and its primary function was writing public notices, as well as proofreading and sorting classical works. As such, it employed quite a few scholars. When Du Fu went there to take the examination, many officials came to watch. Du Fu rubbed the ink stick, laid down his paper and composed his essay right where the prime minister did his office work. The examination went smoothly and Du Fu, feeling proud and excited, still remembered the experience even when he was old. However, the court still did not pay him any real attention, for it just wanted to put his name on the list of candidates for vacancies; the examination was nothing but a formality. Du Fu would have to wait again for an appointment.

Because of the failure of his official career and lack of economic support, Du Fu lived a very hard life in Chang'an; he had to "Knock at the door of the rich in the morning / And follow their fat horses in the evening / In order to get

　　杜甫还直接向皇帝献过赋。赋是一种能让作者尽情铺陈抒写的文体，由于适合描写宏大壮观、纷繁复杂的场面而迎合了帝王好大喜功的心理，于是成为杜甫向皇帝投赠的首选文体。天宝六载（747），杜甫因为偶然的机会参观了皇家的兽坊，见到了威武迅猛的天狗，于是作了一篇《天狗赋》。天宝九载（750）正月，唐玄宗准备在西岳华山举行筑坛祭神的封禅活动，杜甫便写了《封西岳赋》，后来由于皇帝罢封而没有献上。同年九月，杜甫写了一篇《雕赋》，并写了一篇言辞恳切"伏唯哀怜"的《进雕赋表》，但献上去之后没能打动皇帝。次年正月，皇帝·连举行了三次大的祭祀活动，杜甫便作了《朝献太清宫赋》、《朝享太庙赋》和《有事于南郊赋》这"三大礼赋"以投献朝廷。这次终于引起了玄宗的注意，让他在集贤院等待进一步的安排，并命宰相亲自考试杜甫写文章的本领，这使得杜甫一时名声大噪。

　　集贤院即集贤殿书院，职能主要是撰写文告，校理经籍，其中不乏能文之士。杜甫到那里考试的时候，许多官员前来观看。杜甫就在宰相办公的地方研墨铺纸，落笔成义。考试顺利通过了，杜甫十分兴奋，直到晚年还为此事自豪。但其实朝廷并不真正重视他，考试的程式走完了，最后的结果只是把他列入到候补的名册中，等待任用。

　　由于仕途不顺，经济上又没有来源，杜甫在长安的生活日益窘迫，过着"朝扣富儿门，暮随肥马尘。残杯与冷炙，到处

leftovers for a living / Hide in his heart all his pain and bitterness" ("A Twenty-Two Rhyme Poem to Wei Ji"). He was even reduced to buying government subsidized rice like the poor people. Facing starvation, he turned depressed and resentful. He even began to doubt the Confucian ideals in which he had always believed, uttering the uncharacteristic and radical words: "What is the use of Confucianism to me / Since both Confucius and Daozhi have turned into dirt?" ("A Song Written in Drunkenness") Daozhi was a well-known bandit in ancient times, generally considered to be the prototypical villain by the ancients. By putting Daozhi's name together with Confucius, Du Fu was saying that there was no difference between them because they both turned into dirt after death; this was an extremely melancholy and indignant use of irony.

Of course, life's repeated disappointments and the gradual deterioration of his mood were not enough to truly demoralize Du Fu. On the contrary, it led him to calmly examine the social reality in which he lived.

Though the Tianbao reign (742 ~ 755 A.D.) was sometimes lumped together with the Kaiyuan reign as the "Golden Age of the Kaiyuan Era," in fact, the empire's inner conflict during this time was festering beneath a veneer of surface prosperity. After achieving prosperity in the early part of his reign, Xuanzong had gradually become addicted to a luxurious and opulent life, losing his spirit of enterprise and indulging in pleasures such as cockfights, playing instruments, singing and dancing in the imperial harems. In the twenty-eighth year of the Kaiyuan reign (740 A.D.), he even violated family protocol by taking his daughter-in-law Yang Yuhuan away from his son and turning her into his own concubine. Since then, his lust for luxurious life raged out of control like water breaking through a dike. In the seventh year of the Tianbao reign (748 A.D.), he granted an additional title of "General of the Flying Cavalry" to Eunuch Gao Lishi and speedily promoted Yang Guozhong, the cousin of Lady Yang, just because he was good at extorting money from the people. He even appointed him to over fifty positions within one year. Xuanzong also rashly launched repeated wars against Tubo and Nanzhao, causing hundreds of thousands of casualties. What's more, he particularly favored and trusted the northern tribesman An Lushan, a dishonest man who took advantage of others; trusting him was as foolish as letting a jackal or wolf into one's home. Despite all this, the vast majority of poets were still caught up in the romantic atmosphere of the height of the Tang Dynasty, even though they should have been most sensitive to the signs of the times. As a result, many of them composed poems about the pleasures of wine and boisterous singing, about their thoughts and feelings living in seclusion in the wilderness,

潜悲辛"(《奉赠韦左丞丈二十二韵》)的悲苦生活。他已经沦落到与贫民为伍去购买减价官米的地步。面临着饿死的威胁，他的精神状态也日益苦闷、愤激，甚至对自己一向引以为豪且坚持不懈的儒家思想有了怀疑，说出了"儒术于我何有哉，孔丘盗跖俱尘埃"(《醉时歌》)的诡激之语。盗跖是古代有名的大盗，是古人心目中典型的坏人。杜甫把他和圣人孔子并称，说他们死后都化为了尘土，没什么区别，这实在是一种极其悲愤的反话。

当然，生活和情绪的巨大落差并未能使诗人真的消沉，反而刺激了他的思想，他开始渐渐以冷静的态度审视他所生活在其中的社会现实。

天宝（742～755）年代虽然有时也被与此前的开元（711～741）年代一起并称为开元盛世，但其实在繁荣的表面下面，帝国内部隐藏的矛盾已不断孕育、滋生和激化。唐玄宗经过前期统治的繁荣之后，逐渐骄奢淫逸，不思进取，沉溺于后宫的斗鸡、击坤、歌舞等享乐。开元二十八年（740），他又违背人伦，抢夺了儿媳妇杨玉环，后来又把她立为自己的贵妃，从此骄奢之心更是如水决堤，不可收拾。天宝七载（748），给宦官高力士加了"骠骑大将军"的头衔，而杨贵妃的堂哥杨国忠竟然因为善于搜刮民财，而得到快速的提拔，一年中担任了五十余项官职。玄宗还轻率地发动了多次对吐蕃和南诏的战争，死亡数十万人。他还宠信善于偷鸡摸狗、投机钻营的胡人安禄山，那简直就是养了一只豺狼。而这时候的诗人群体，作为对时代气息最为敏感的知识阶层，却还陶醉在盛唐时代的浪漫氛围中，他们中间大多数人的作品或表达纵酒高歌的惬意，或抒发隐逸

and about the heroic spirit of military life on the frontier. They rarely wrote poems reflecting the existing crisis facing the empire.

Only Du Fu seemed to have a clear understanding of the times, and his poems gradually drifted away from the idealism and romanticism of the poetry at the height of the Tang Dynasty. This transition can already be seen in his poem "The Song of Eight Drinking Gods," which described the life of scholars in Chang'an during the waning years of the Kaiyuan reign and the early period of the Tianbao reign.

> Zhizhang rode his horse as if he were sailing on the river.
> His eyes blurred, he fell into a well and slept in the water.
> The Prince of Ruyang would drink three bottles before paying respect to the emperor.
> Seeing a cart of distiller's yeast along the way, he could not help but drool.
> How he wished he could be granted the Wine Well as his manor.
> Li Shizhi spent ten thousand coins on wine each day,
> Drinking as a whale swallowing the water of all rivers,
> But he only drank with high class drinkers, staying away from those with bad manners.
> Zongzhi was a handsome young man, debonair and unrestrained.
> Holding a wine cup and casting a contemptuous eye at the blue sky,
> He looked like a jade tree standing against the wind.
> A faithful believer who fasts continuously, sitting before an embroidered image of Buddha,
> Su Jin often ran away from his meditation just to get his drink.
> Li Bai could compose a hundred poems after drinking a bottle of wine.
> In the wineshops of the market of Chang'an, he often went to sleep.
> Even when the emperor asked him to get on a boat,
> He would refuse, calling himself the drinking god.
> Before practicing calligraphy, Zhang Xu would drink three cups,
> And then, taking off his hat before princes and dukes,
> He wielded his writing brush on the paper like cloud and smoke.
> After drinking five bottles, Jiao Sui would brim with energy and vitality,
> Delivering brazen speeches that shocked all those who listened.

Eight prominent men of that time were depicted in this poem: He

山水的情怀，或描写从军边塞的豪迈，而对帝国存在的危机则反映得很少。

只有杜甫开始对时代有了清醒的认识，逐渐从盛唐诗坛的理想主义和浪漫主义群体中游离出来。这个转变在他写的反映开元末天宝初长安士人生活的《饮中八仙歌》中就已有所表现：

知章骑马似乘船，眼花落井水底眠。

汝阳三斗始朝天，道逢麹车口流涎，恨不移封向酒泉。

左相日兴费万钱，饮如长鲸吸百川，衔杯乐圣称避贤。

宗之潇洒美少年，举觞白眼望青天，皎如玉树临风前。

苏晋长斋绣佛前，醉中往往爱逃禅。

李白斗酒诗百篇，长安市上酒家眠。天子呼来不上船，自称臣是酒中仙。

张旭三杯草圣传，脱帽露顶王公前，挥毫落纸如云烟。

焦遂五斗方卓然，高谈雄辩惊四筵。

诗里写了当时的八个人物：贺知章、李琎、李适之、崔宗

Zhizhang, Li Jin, Li Shizhi, Cui Zongzhi, Su Jin, Li Bai, Zhang Xu and Jiao Sui. All of these eight people once lived or held offices in Chang'an. When Du Fu arrived there, some of them had already passed away or had left, so Du Fu depicted their drunkenness from memory. These eight people were all brilliant figures at the height of the Tang Dynasty who had one thing in common: their love of drink. Because of this, they were often called the "Eight Drinking Gods." However, their uncouth manners and wild drinking were, in fact, not merely an expression of their joyous mood. For example, when Li Shizhi was forced out of the court by Li Linfu and had to resign his post as prime minister, he felt so lonely and indignant that he wrote the poem "On Resigning as Prime Minister" to voice his complaint, committing suicide soon after. Li Bai was alienated from Xuanzong due to the slandering remarks of others, "so he started to indulge himself in wandering and drinking to make himself confused and disoriented....He wrote many *Fu* prose pieces and hundreds of poems about banished immortals, most of which expressed his depression" ("Preface to the Cottage Collection" by Li Yangbing). Nevertheless, unable to change their innate natures, they tried to erase sadness and frustration from their hearts by maintaining a romantic and free-spirited lifestyle (including excessive drink), being unable and unwilling to open their eyes to bitter reality. But Du Fu, as a clear-headed observer, had come to realize the abnormal state of mind of the "Eight Drinking Gods." The difference between him and the " Eight Drinking Gods" can be summarized as the difference between one sober man and eight drunken ones.

One autumn day during the eleventh year of the Tianbao reign (752 A.D.), five poets, Du Fu, Gao Shi, Xue Ju, Cen Shen and Chu Guangxi, climbed up the tower in Ci'en Temple in the southeast quarter of Chang'an, there composing a poem each. Except for Xue Ju's poem which was lost, the other four poets' poems were all preserved. Du Fu's poem goes like this:

> **Climbing the Tower in Ci'en Temple with Five Gentlemen**
> The tower rose high up into the sky.
> A strong wind blew with no end.
> For a man without broad understanding,
> Climbing up the tower would bring great sorrow.
> Then I understood the force of Buddha,
> Powerful enough to go beyond the limit of one's mind.
> Climbing as if through caverns of dragons and snakes,
> I finally came out from under the dark props of the tower.
> The Big Dipper was in the north,

之、苏晋、李白、张旭和焦遂。这八个人物都曾在长安为官或生活，当杜甫到达长安的时候，他们中有的已死去，有的离开了长安，杜甫用追忆的形式描写了他们的醉态。这八个人都是盛唐时代的优秀人物，他们都有一个共同特点，就是好饮酒，因而被人们称为"饮中八仙"。但实际上他们痛饮沉醉的狂态并不完全是欢快心情的体现，比如李适之当时因受李林甫排挤而罢相，孤独愤激，写了《罢相》诗以发牢骚，并且不久就自杀了。李白受到谗谤而被玄宗疏远，"乃浪迹纵酒，以自昏秽，……朝列赋谪仙之歌凡数百首，多言公之不得意"（李阳冰《草堂集序》）等等。但他们在惯性的支配下，仍然以充满浪漫情调的举止（如痛饮）来消解心底的惆怅失意，而没有能够也不情愿睁大眼睛清醒地正视现实。而杜甫则开始以一个清醒的旁观者的身份审视"饮中八仙"的非正常精神状态，他与"八仙"的关系简直可以归结为：一个醒的和八个醉的！

天宝十一载（752）的一个秋日，杜甫、高适、薛据、岑参和储光羲五位诗人登上长安城东南慈恩寺里的宝塔，并每人赋诗一首。除了薛据的诗已佚外，其他四人的诗都留存下来了。其中杜甫的诗是这样的：

同诸公登慈恩寺塔

高标跨苍穹，烈风无时休。
自非旷士怀，登兹翻百忧。
方知象教力，足可追冥搜。
仰穿龙蛇窟，始出枝撑幽。
七星在北户，河汉声西流。

The Milky Way led to the west,
God Xihe was driving the chariot of the sun,
And God Shaohao was preparing for the autumn season.
The peaks of the Mountains in Qin region rose and fell as if broken.
The Jinghe River and Weihe River were indistinguishable.
Looking down, I saw only a dim mass,
Unable to distinguish Chang'an from the rest.
Turning back, I called to Yu Shun,
Only to find clouds of Cangwu in great sorrow.
How valuable it was for King Mu of Zhou to have a feast
With Queen Mother of the West at Jasper Lake in the Kunlun
Mountains!
Calling mournfully, the swans were about to fly away,
Not knowing where to stay.
Just watch the wild geese that live in the sunshine.
They all know how to make life fine.

At that time, Gao Shi and Cen Shen were living leisurely in the capital, while Chu Guangxi was in office as a supervising official, a very low position of only the eighth rank. These poets were all depressed and frustrated, but Du Fu's living conditions were far worse. The poems of Cen Shen and Chu Guangxi both emphasized the great height of the tower and the broadness and remoteness of the view from the top, with the goal of symbolizing the greatness of Buddhist doctrines and power. Their poems suggested that they wished to escape to the pure land of Buddhism. Though Gao Shi's poem expressed his wish to serve the country, his first concern was for his own individual future, without reflecting the grim social reality of the time.

Du Fu's poem was quite different. It is true that like the others, he exaggerated the height of the tower in order to reiterate the topic, saying that it towered into the blue sky so high that from the top, one could look straight at the Big Dipper, hear the sound of water in the Milky Way, and move close to the God Xihe and God Shaohao, suggesting that it was the Buddha's power that helped to build the tower so high. But the poem did not merely stop at the theme of Buddhism; instead, it related the scenes he saw with the social reality of the time. In Du Fu's mind, filled with hundreds of worries, the scenes below him were painted in dismal colors. "A strong wind blowing with no end" was no doubt a description of a mountaintop, but it was also a symbol of volatility and impending disorder. The four lines following the line "The peaks of the Mountains in Qin region rose and fell as if broken" described the scene which

羲和鞭白日，少昊行清秋。

秦山忽破碎，泾渭不可求。

俯视但一气，焉能辨皇州。

回首叫虞舜，苍梧云正愁。

惜哉瑶池饮，日晏昆仑丘。

黄鹄去不息，哀鸣何所投。

君看随阳雁，各有稻粱谋。

高适和岑参当时在京闲居，储光羲时任监察御史，官阶很低，仅为从八品上。几位诗人都抑郁不得志，而杜甫的处境更为窘迫一些。岑参和储光羲的诗都把重点放在描写塔之高耸和景物之广远，借以象征和衬托佛家教义之高和法力之大，表示要逃到佛家净域中去。高适诗虽然表达了为国效劳的志愿，但着眼点只是个人前途，而没有反映当时的社会现实。

杜甫则不同，他虽然为了应题，夸张地写了塔之高，说它跨越青天之上，站在塔顶能平视北斗七星，能听到银河水声，能接近为日神驾车的羲和和司秋之神白帝少昊，并表明是佛教的力量使塔建得如此之高。但他并没有停留在仅写佛教主题上，而是将眼前景物与整个社会现实联系起来。在胸怀百忧的诗人看来，一切景物都蒙上了一层惨淡的颜色。"烈风无时休"固然是高处的应有之景，但又何尝不是时局飘摇、天下将乱的征兆？"秦山忽破碎"以下四句写景，诗人感到：高山忽然破碎，

made the poet feel that high mountains had collapsed suddenly, that the river was unclear, and that looking far and wide, one saw only dark clouds and gloomy fog, unable to locate the royal palace. It was not unlike the scene in which "a strong wind sweeping through the tower heralds a rising storm in the mountains." The last eight lines moved from describing scenery to delivering moral. The two lines starting with "Turning back" used Yu Shun to symbolize Taizong of Tang, the wise and enlightened ruler of ancient China's idealized society. Cangwu, the burial place of Yu Shun, was used to symbolize Zhaoling Tomb of Taizong, to express nostalgia for the golden age of the Tang Dynasty. The two lines starting with "How valuable" used the legend of King Mu of Zhou and Queen Mother of the West who toured and feasted together on Jasper Lake to satirize Xuanzong and Lady Yang, who indulged themselves in feasting, touring and sexual pleasures. The two lines starting with "Calling mournfully" used the call of the noble swans to express the indignation of virtuous people who had no shelter after loosing their posts. The two lines starting with "Just watch" employed the metaphor of wild geese, a kind of migratory bird, to reprimand the shamefulness of the evil villains who fawned on the rich and the powerful in order to gain wealth and power. It can be seen from this that though the four poets composed poems on the same topic in the same place at the same time, that is, the later years of the Tianbao reign when the great Tang Empire was gradually moving to its decline and fall, only Du Fu sensed the crisis of the national fate and expressed it in his poem, indicating that he was the first to drift away from the romantic and lofty poetic style of the height of the Tang Dynasty.

From then on, realism became Du Fu's major style. He focused on lower-class people whose lives were growing harder and harder, at the same time turning on the upper-class aristocrats who were leading increasingly unscrupulous and immoral lives. In the poem "On War-Chariots," written in the tenth year of the Tianbao reign (751 A.D.), Du Fu made a severe attack on the militaristic policy adopted during the Tianbao reign that promoted "endless expansion of the frontiers," causing the blood of the people to flow like rivers. This showed his deep sympathy for those kind people who were driven to death, their bones being buried in distant and inaccessible lands.

"The Tour of Beautiful Ladies," written in the twelfth year of the Tianbao reign (753 A.D.), satirized the Yang brother and sisters. The three female cousins of Lady Yang were conferred the titles of Duchess of Han, Duchess of Guo and Duchess of Qin respectively, and her cousin Yang Guozhong succeeded to the office of prime minister after the death of Li Linfu in the

河流清浊不分，放眼望去一片愁云惨雾，找不到皇宫在哪里。这真是一种"山雨欲来风满楼"的景象。最后八句，由写景而转为寓意。"回首"两句用虞舜这位中国古代理想社会中的有道明君象征唐太宗，用虞舜的埋葬地苍梧象征太宗的陵墓昭陵，深切缅怀大唐帝国的全盛时代。"惜哉"两句又以周穆王和西王母游宴于瑶池的传说以讽刺沉湎于宴游淫乐中的玄宗和杨妃。"黄鹄"两句，借天鹅这种高贵飞禽的哀鸣，写贤士失职而无所归依的悲愤。"君看"两句用雁这种候鸟作比，斥责奸邪小人趋炎附势而谋取富贵之无耻。由此可见，在大唐帝国已经暗暗走向衰亡的天宝后期，当这四位诗人同时同地根据同一主题做诗时，只有杜甫感到了国家命运的危机并且形诸诗歌，这说明杜甫最早从浪漫高华的盛唐诗坛中游离出来了。

从此，杜甫的创作开始以写实为主要倾向。他的目光既对准了日益陷于苦难的下层人民，也对准了日益荒淫无耻的上层贵族。在天宝十载（751）左右所写的《兵车行》中，他对天宝年间"开边未已"以至"血流成海"的穷兵黩武政策进行了严厉的抨击，对被驱往死地的善良人民和他们的父母妻儿以及抛骨绝域的冤魂表示了深切的同情。

作于天宝十二载（753）的《丽人行》则是讥刺杨氏兄妹的。杨贵妃的三位堂姊于天宝七载（748）分别被封为韩国夫人、虢国夫人和秦国夫人，其堂兄杨国忠则于天宝十一载

eleventh year of the Tianbao reign (752 A.D.). The Yang brother and sisters had great power and influence and indulged in unrestrained immoral activities; Yang Guozhong even committed adultery with the Duchess of Guo. It was warm and sunny on the third day of the third month of the twelfth year of the Tianbao reign (753 A.D.). As it was Shangsi Festival, all the people in Chang'an put on their holiday best and went to the suburbs to play on the green grass, to soak in the spring sun, and to drink and feast. According to the traditional custom, they would go to the Qujiang River to wash away bad luck and ominous fate and to pray for safety and happiness. Suddenly, a group of soldiers rushed shouting through the crowd, throwing the people into tumult. The soldiers cleared a path for a long fleet of carriages following after them. It was a grand procession, with colorful flags flapping in the wind and royal carriages inlaid with gold and silver shining in the sun. There was a pavilion facing the river nearby. In front of the pavilion, the ground was covered with magnificent carpet, with royal guards standing on sentry duty. There the fleet of carriages stopped, and several noble ladies slowly got off. Each of them glowed with beauty and radiance. They looked like fairy maidens, with their jade pendants tinkling and their belts floating lightly. Judging by their dresses and guards, they were none other than Lady Yang and her sisters. Laughing, the Yang sisters walked into the elaborately furnished tent and leisurely sat down in front of the table. Then, servants fetched dish after dish from the carriages, setting the table with dainties of every kind. At the same time, the royal band played sweet, enchanting music. In addition, young eunuchs dressed in yellow rode speedy horses, bringing one batch of food after another, presented continuously by eunuchs working in the royal kitchen. However, these noble ladies had no intention of taking so much as a bite, as they were already bored of the dainty foods. They didn't even touch their chopsticks, and the chefs' efforts came to nothing. From amongst the crowd, Du Fu watched all this in dismay. Suddenly, he saw another team of men and horses arriving. With attendants crowding around, this procession was so large that the whole roadway was blocked. Towards the middle of the procession, riding on a horse of great stature, there was a minister wearing an official hat. The onlookers whispered that it was the Prime Minister Yang Guozhong. Yang Guozhong dismounted from the horse, strode across the magnificent carpet without respect for anybody, and joined in the ladies' feasting. Separated by the stern guards, people could only hear the laughter of the men and women coming from the pavilion.

It was a fresh day on the third day of the third month,

（752）李林甫死后继任右相。杨氏兄妹权势熏天、荒淫无度，杨国忠甚至与虢国夫人私通。天宝十二载（753）三月三日，风和日丽。这一天是上巳节，长安城里的士民百姓纷纷穿上节日的盛装，到郊外踏青、游春、饮宴，他们要按照传统的风俗到曲江边洗去晦气和不祥，祈求来日的平安和幸福。突然，人群中起了一阵骚动，只见一群士兵吆喝着冲进人群中，清出一条大道，士兵后面跟着一个长长的车队，彩旗飘扬，仪仗隆重，镶金嵌银的宫车在阳光下闪闪发光。不远处，有一座临江的亭台，亭台前铺着华丽的地毯，有皇宫的卫队在周围站岗。车队在这里稳稳停下，几位贵妇从车上缓缓下来，仪态万方，光彩照人，玉佩声响，罗带轻扬，宛如仙女一般。从她们的服饰和卫队就能看出，这正是杨贵妃和她的几位姐姐。杨氏姊妹们说笑着走进早已搭好的帐幕，在桌前款款落座，侍从们就立刻从车上拿出一个个食盒，在桌上摆满了山珍海味。又有皇家乐队演奏着婉转的音乐，听得人神摇魂荡。还有许多穿着黄衣服的小太监骑着快马，一批一批地向这里运送着食品，然后由御膳房的太监络绎不绝地呈上去。可是吃腻了山珍海味的贵妇们一点都不想吃，她们连筷子都没有动一下，害得厨师们空忙一阵。杜甫在人群中远远望着这一切，突然，他看见又有一队人马过来，前呼后拥，声势浩大，占满了整条要道。队伍正中，一个冠冕堂皇的官人骑在高头大马上。人们都说，这就是当朝宰相杨国忠。杨国忠下了马，旁若无人地跨过锦绣的地毯，加入到先前到来的贵夫人的宴饮中，隔着森严的护卫，人们只听见亭台里传出一阵阵的男欢女笑来：

　　三月三日天气新，长安水边多丽人。

So many pretty ladies in Chang'an gathered to the rivers.
In their makeup, they looked elegant and dignified.
With fine and delicate skin, they were well-proportioned in stature.
Their dresses shone in the late spring,
Embroidered with gold peacocks and silver kylins.
What ornaments did they wear in their hair?
Jade and flower-like ornaments hanging over their temples.
What could be seen on their back?
Skirt belts with jewels that suited their waists well.
They were sisters of Lady Yang of the imperial harem,
Who were granted titles of Guo and Qin.
The camel humps were carrying jade pots,
And crystal plates were holding sliver fish.
Chopsticks of rhinoceros horns stopped in the air,
And knives with bells were wielded wildly in vain,
For the ladies were disinterested by the food.
The eunuchs galloped on horses without stirring up dust,
Busy bringing delicacies from the imperial kitchen.
The music played by the flutes and drums was so moving,
And numerous attendants crowded on important roads.
A man on a horse walked so leisurely behind.
He got off the horse and walked across the magnificent carpet,
unmindful of others.
Willow catkins fell down like snow, turning everything white.
The blue bird flew away with a red handkerchief in its mouth.
The Prime Minister was extremely powerful and arrogant,
So don't come close or he will be irritated.

In this poem, the poet deliberately and openly went into detailed and elaborate description of the appearance, clothes, and food of the Yang brother and sisters, which contained implied irony. The last four lines, on the other hand, resorted to direct satire. Willow catkins turn into duckweeds when they fall into water, and big duckweeds are called clover ferns. Therefore, willow catkins and clover ferns are, in fact, the same thing. The poet used willow catkins to satirize the incest between the Yang brother and sister. The blue bird was said to be messenger of Queen Mother of the West, so it became another name for messengers. The image of a blue bird holding a red handkerchief in the mouth suggested that the Yang brother and sister secretly conveyed amorous feelings to each other. The two lines "The Prime Minister was extremely powerful and

态浓意远淑且真，肌理细腻骨肉匀。

绣罗衣裳照暮春，蹙金孔雀银麒麟。

头上何所有？翠微匎叶垂鬓唇。

背后何所见？珠压腰衱稳称身。

就中云幕椒房亲，赐名大国虢与秦。

紫驼之峰出翠釜，水晶之盘行素鳞。

犀箸厌饫久未下，鸾刀缕切空纷纶。

黄门飞鞚不动尘，御厨络绎送八珍。

箫鼓哀吟感鬼神，宾从杂遝实要津。

后来鞍马何逡巡，当轩下马入锦茵。

杨花雪落覆白蘋，青鸟飞去衔红巾。

炙手可热势绝伦，慎莫近前丞相嗔。

这首《丽人行》故意用工笔重彩对杨氏姊妹兄弟的容态、服饰和肴馔一一作正面描写，暗含讽刺。结尾四句则转入直接讽刺。杨花落水化为萍，萍之大者为蘋，故而杨花、蘋为一物，诗人借杨花覆蘋来讽刺杨氏兄妹的乱伦。青鸟是传说中西王母的使者，后用为传递消息者的代称。青鸟衔巾暗示杨氏兄妹暗中传情达意。"炙手可热势绝伦，慎莫近前丞相嗔"两句对杨国忠

arrogant / So don't come close or he will be irritated" profoundly satirized Yang Guozhong's arrogant, aggressive, shameless and disgusting manner.

"On War-Chariots" and "The Tour of Beautiful Ladies" were both important milestones in Du Fu's literary career, and a key step in the evolution of Tang poetry. They exposed and criticized the profound social problems hidden beneath the surface prosperity of the Tang Empire during the transitional period which began its decline. They also sharply satirized the shamelessness and criminal behavior of the relatives of Lady Yang. In terms of artistic form, these two poems displayed Du Fu's brilliant achievements in the composition of *Yuefu* folk songs. Like other poets of the same age, when Du Fu composed poems in the folk song genre, he used topics passed down from the ancient times, which posed a problem because the content didn't always conform to the narrow range of topics, limiting the expressive power of the poems. Du Fu courageously reformed this poetic style by discarding the old folk song topics and starting the practice of "naming poems by their content without following the old topics" ("Preface to the Ancient Topics of Folk Songs" by Yuan Zhen, from volume 23 of *Changqing Collection of Yuan Zhen*). This means that he created a new title according to the poem's content. In doing so, his *Yuefu* folk songs corresponded more closely with their titles, allowing them to more freely reflect reality with greater expressive power.

"Poets must pass through hardship before being able to produce great poetry." Like many poets, Du Fu often expressed his resentment towards society through his poems, using them to depict his bitter experiences. But what made Du Fu truly great, was that he did not stop at conveying his own feelings and experiences, but directly related his own fate to the misfortune of the common people and to the crisis facing his nation. This made his poems convey a more profound, far-reaching, and realistic meaning. The earliest traces of this characteristic can be found in the poems Du Fu wrote in the latter end of his ten-year stay in Chang'an. For example, in the autumn of the thirteenth year of the Tianbao reign (751 A.D.), Chang'an suffered heavy rain and flooding, but because Prime Minister Yang Guozhong concealed this from Xuanzong, no one dared to mention the disaster. Many of the poems written by Du Fu during this period reflected the true conditions of that time, such as "To Cen Shen on the Ninth," and the three poems named "Sighing on the Autumn Rain," in which Du Fu expressed heartfelt sympathy for the fate of the people suffering from the disaster.

In the winter of the thirteenth year of the Tianbao reign, due to the lack of food, Du Fu sent his family to Fengxian (now Pucheng in Shaanxi), to live

盛气凌人、恬不知耻的丑态做了深刻的讽刺。

《兵车行》和《丽人行》是杜甫创作道路上的一个里程碑，也是唐诗发展过程中的一个关键。它们对唐帝国由盛转衰过程中掩盖在繁荣表面下的社会问题和矛盾进行了深刻的揭露和批判，也对气焰正盛的外戚贵族的无耻和罪行进行了尖锐的讽刺。在艺术形式上，这两首诗也表现出杜甫乐府诗创作的巨大成就。杜甫从前和同时代的诗人，在用乐府这种体裁来写时事的时候，用的都是古代流传下来的题目，这样就出现了文不对题的情形，也影响到诗歌的表现力。杜甫则以巨大的勇气进行了创新，他摆脱乐府旧题，采取"即事名篇，无复依傍"（元稹《乐府古题序》，《元氏长庆集》卷二三）的办法，根据诗歌内容自拟新题，这就使得他的乐府诗做到了文题一致，因而在反映现实时十分自如、灵活，表现力很强。

"诗穷而后工"，同许多诗人一样，杜甫也常常在诗歌中抒发自己的愤懑心情，反映自己的悲苦遭遇。但杜甫的伟大之处在于，他不仅仅停留在抒写一己的感情和遭遇上，而是把自己的命运同广大人民的不幸和国家的危机灾难有机地结合起来，从而使诗歌具有更加深刻而广泛的现实意义。这一特点在杜甫长安十年后期的诗作中就已反映出来，如天宝十三载（751）秋，长安淫雨成灾，宰相杨国忠却百般欺瞒玄宗而导致无人敢言灾情。杜甫在这一时期写的一些诗生动地反映了当时的真实情况，如《九日寄岑参》和《秋雨叹》三首中都对受灾人民的命运表达了无限的同情。

天宝十三载冬，杜甫因京师乏食，把家小送往奉先（今陕

temporarily at the public residence of the county government, returning by himself to Chang'an. In the early summer of the following year, he left for Baishui (now Baishui in Shaanxi) to visit his uncle Cui Xu, then returning with Cui Xu to Fengxian to see his family in September. In October, Du Fu went back to Chang'an, and was appointed as a county official in Hexi. However, not willing to bow and scrape to the local flunky, he refused the office. Later, he was appointed as a military assistant in the Right Flank Guards. As it was a position under the eighth rank which required little work, Du Fu decided to take the office. Before long, he went to see his family in Fengxian and there wrote five-character poem entitled "Feelings Expressed in Five Hundred Words after Traveling from the Capital to Fengxian County." The poet revealed his aspiration with a note of self mockery: "How foolish I was ! / I thought I could match Ji ❶ and Qi ❷ ." Though much of his effort was in vain, he never betrayed his dream of caring for the people: "I'm always worrying about the people all year round / That I keep sighing with anxiety in my heart." When he passed by Lishan Mountain, he thought of Xuanzong and Lady Yang, who were enjoying themselves to their heart's content and living a luxurious life in Huaqing Palace while the people were struggling against death from hunger and cold. At this thought, all sorts of feelings welled up in his heart, causing him to burst out with the bitter denouncement: "The portals of the rich reek of wasted meat and wine / While skeletons of the poor frozen to death lie by the roadside." By the time he arrived home, he found his youngest son had starved to death, which pierced his heart with grief. When he further thought of those people who had lost their land, of the soldiers who had been sent to the remote frontiers, and of the great hardships they faced, his heart was weighed down with sorrow. The theme of the poem was the expression of the poet's feelings, with long narrative, descriptive and argumentative passages woven in, so that scenery and sentiment were successfully blended into an integral whole. He always put himself in the place of others and associated his own misfortune with the fate of the nation and the people. Because of the profound revelations of the national plight found in Du Fu's poems, Wang Sishi, the literary critic of the Qing Dynasty, referred to them as "poetic history." This was a new characteristic of Du Fu's poetry. From then on, Du Fu moved firmly towards a career of composing poems to reflect reality.

西蒲城），寄寓在县署公舍里，只身返回长安。第二年初夏，他往白水（今陕西白水）省视舅氏崔顼，九月与崔同往奉先探望家小。十月，杜甫回到长安，被任命为河西县尉。为了避免向乡里小儿折腰，他没有接受。接着改任右卫率府兵曹参军，这是一个从八品下的闲职，杜甫接受了。不久，他前往奉先探视家小，写下了五古名篇《自京赴奉先县咏怀五百字》。诗人以自嘲的口吻披露自己的志向："许身一何愚，窃比稷❶与契❷。"虽然一事无成，但关心百姓的志向始终不改："穷年忧黎元，叹息肠内热。"他路经骊山，想到唐玄宗与杨贵妃等人正在山上的华清宫尽情享乐，挥霍无度，而百姓却饥寒交迫地挣扎在死亡线上，心中百感交集，迸发出"朱门酒肉臭，路有冻死骨"的血泪控诉。等他回到家中，发现幼子已经饿死，更是心如刀割。当他进一步想到那些失去田产的百姓和征戍远方的士兵，想到他们承受着更为深重的灾难时，更是忧积如山。全诗以"咏怀"为主线，中间穿插着大段的叙事、描写和议论，情景交融，浑然一体，并处处推己及人，把自己个人的不幸和国家、人民的命运联系起来，从而以其对整个国家形势的深刻反映被清代的文学批评家王嗣奭称为"诗史"。这是杜甫诗歌中一个新的特点。从此，诗人就朝着以诗歌反映现实的方向坚定地迈进了。

❶ 译者注：稷，周代祖先。
❷ 译者注：契，殷代祖先。
❶ Translator's note: Ji-the ancestor of Zhou Dynasty.
❷ Translator's note: Qi-the ancestor of Yin Dynasty.

《丽人行》诗意画，描绘宫廷后妃宫女出游的场景
Painting of *The Tour of Beautiful Ladies*

三　赋到沧桑句便工

Chapter Ⅲ　Gathering Experience and Developing
　　　　　　Writing

In November of the fourteenth year of the Tianbao reign (755 A.D.), the An Shi Rebellion broke out just as Du Fu was heading to Fengxian county to visit his family.

An Lushan (705 ~ 757 A.D.) and Shi Siming (705 ~ 761 A.D.) were both men of Turkic-Sogdian origin, born in Yingzhou. They had known each other from the time they were young and had been business partners after growing up. An Lushan was once caught by Governor Zhang Shougui of Youzhou for stealing sheep. However, because the governor found him strong, handsome, and eloquent, An was exempted from the death penalty, and was even appointed along with Shi Siming to work as kidnapping officers, responsible for catching Khitan people alive. Due to their great service in catching Khitans, they were later promoted by Governor Zhang as assistant generals; An Lushan was even adopted as his son. Once, An Lushan was reckless in attacking rebel forces, causing him to suffer a crushing defeat. According to the law, such an act should have warranted the death penalty. But because Governor Zhang did not have the heart to kill him, he had An Lushan escorted to the capital to allow the emperor to make the final decision. As Governor Zhang expected, the warlike Emperor Xuanzong appreciated his talent, granting him pardon despite of the prime minister's objection. After returning to Youzhou, An Lushan went to great lengths to win Xuanzong's favor; he bribed officials, trapped and killed tribal chiefs, and falsely reported his military achievements, winning himself the position of General of the Flying Cavalry. Later, he was also appointed as Governor of Fanyang, the north of the Yellow River and in change of the Pinglu army, which enabled him to seize military and political control of the three regions. He was also adopted by Lady Yang as her son, so he even had free access to the palace.

Though on the surface An Lushan was simple and honest, in fact, he had always harbored rebellious motives, making substantial preparations over the course of nearly ten years. Though Yang Guozhong had repeatedly tried to convince Emperor Xuanzong of An Lushan's rebellious motives, the emperor always turned a deaf ear. This incurred hatred from An Lushan and aroused his vigilance so that he hastened his rebellious plot. In November of the fourteenth year of the Tianbao reign (755 A.D.), when he felt that the time was ripe for action, he conspired with Shi Siming to raise the An Shi Rebellion, supposedly to suppress Yang Guozhong. This caused an eight-year war, plunging the people into the abyss of misery and bringing such a blow to the Tang Empire that it would never be able to recover.

Claiming to be two hundred thousand strong, the rebel troops rose in revolt in Fanyang and marched directly towards the Eastern Capital Luoyang.

天宝十四载（755）十一月，就在杜甫往奉先县探望家人的时候，安史之乱爆发了。

安禄山（705～757）和史思明（705～761）都是营州的混血胡人，两人自幼便相识，长大后又合伙做生意。一次，安禄山因偷羊被幽州节度使张守珪抓住，张见他长相肥壮，有些模样，言语也异于常人，便免其死罪，让他和史思明一起，做了专门抓契丹人的捉生将。由于捉生有功，后来张守珪提拔安、史二人做了偏将，并收安禄山为义子。有一次，安禄山在讨伐叛军的战争中恃勇轻进，一败涂地，按律当斩。张守珪却不忍杀他，便将他押送到京师让皇帝处理。好武的唐玄宗果然爱其材力，不顾宰相反对，赦免了安的死罪。安禄山回幽州后，小心经营，他通过贿赂官员、诱杀少数民族酋长和谎报战功等伎俩，获得玄宗宠信，做到骠骑大将军。后来他又同时做了范阳节度使、河北采访使，领平卢军，实际上控制了三镇的军政大权。他还被杨贵妃认为"义子"，能自由地出入于宫廷。

表面愚憨忠厚的安禄山，实际上怀着叛逆之心，并已在将近十年的时间里做了大量的准备。杨国忠多次对玄宗说安禄山有反意，玄宗却总不听。但这却引起了安禄山的警觉和仇恨，因而加快了谋反的步伐。天宝十四载（755）十一月，他看到时机已经成熟，便以讨伐杨国忠为名，勾结史思明，发动了安史之乱。一场绵延了八年、导致生灵涂炭并使大唐帝国从此一蹶不振的战乱从此开始了。

号称二十万的叛军，从范阳起兵，采用游牧民族单兵突进

They employed the military tactics of nomadic tribes, using a single point of attack without trying to outflank the enemy and without covering the flanks. Since most of the Tang troops were stationed along the frontiers, the Central Plains garrisons were lacking, so the rebels were met with minimal resistance, and were soon able to capture Luoyang. In the first lunar month of the next year, An Lushan established his own dynasty, claiming to be Emperor of Yan. At the same time, his troops pressed on towards the "East Gate of Chang'an," Tongguan Pass (now in Shaanxi province), thus menacing the capital. On the ninth of June, at the suggestion of Yang Guozhong, Emperor Xuanzong ordered the old and infirm Ge Shuhan to command the troops stationed at Tongguan Pass. Though their morale was low, they were to hold the pass and repel the enemy's attack. They suffered a crushing defeat and Ge Shuhan surrendered to An Lushan after being captured.

While this was happening in February, Du Fu left home for Chang'an to take office, but he returned to Fengxian soon in April to escort his family north to Baishui County to seek refuge with his uncle Cui Xu. In June, Tongguan Pass was lost, and the people inside the pass fled in disarray. Meanwhile, Du Fu left Baishui with his family and traveled further north. They traveled with Du Fu's great grandnephew Wang Li's family. They walked for a long time through the turmoil and chaos of war, when suddenly Wang Li found Du Fu missing. As he was a very kind-hearted man, he went back alone, shouting as he went, in search of Du Fu. After much effort, he finally found Du Fu, who had strayed from his family and gotten lost in a wilderness of fleabane and wormwood. He let Du Fu ride on his own horse and, with a knife in one hand and the reins in the other, protected Du Fu as he caught up with Du's family.

As the Du's continued their journey, it rained for days on end, making the road extremely slippery. What's more, the family was short of food and clothing, they were cold and hungry, and they had to guard against the attacks of tigers and wolves. Words could not express the hardships they faced. Later, they came to a place called Tongjiawa near Fuzhou, seeking refuge at the home of Du Fu's friend Sun Zai. At the sight of them, Sun Zai at once lit the lamps and invited them in. He attended to them warmly, inviting them to eat and bathe. He even cut paper to call back the spirit of the dead for Du Fu.

The Du's continued their journey after a few days rest in Su Zai's home. Passing by Huayuan (the local authority is now situated in the southeast region of Yaoxian County in Shaanxi) and Sanchuan (the local authority is now situated in the south of Fuxian County in Shaanxi) and making their way through the torrential floods caused by days of heavy rain, they finally arrived at Fuzhou (now Fuxian County in Shaanxi).

的军事战术，没有迂回，也不用左右侧翼掩护，单一主力迅猛进攻，直接向东都洛阳进军。由于唐政府的军队大多驻扎在边塞，中原守备空虚，叛军长驱直入，很快就占领了洛阳。第二年正月，安禄山在洛阳建立政权，自称大燕皇帝，他的部队则进逼长安的东大门潼关（今属陕西），威胁长安。到了六月九日，在杨国忠的唆使下，唐玄宗命年老体病的哥舒翰率领斗志松懈的潼关守军出关迎敌，结果遭受大败，哥舒翰被俘，并投降了安禄山。

这期间杜甫曾于二月离家到长安就职，但很快就于四月回到奉先，携家北行到白水县投靠舅舅崔顼。六月，潼关失守，关内百姓纷纷逃亡，杜甫于是携家离开白水，继续北行。他们同重表侄王砅一家同行，兵荒马乱中，走了很久，王砅突然发现杜甫不见了，心地善良的他于是只身返回，一边呼喊一边沿路寻找，好不容易才在蓬蒿荒野之中找到了与大家失散的杜甫。他把马让杜甫骑着，自己一手提刀，一手牵着缰绳，终于保护杜甫赶上了家人。

杜甫一家继续赶路，一路上连日大雨，路滑难行，全家人缺吃少穿，又冷又饿，还得提防虎狼的袭击，真是苦不堪言。他们来到鄜州附近一个叫同家洼的地方，杜甫在这里有一个朋友孙宰，便去他家投宿。孙宰一看，赶紧点起灯来把他们请进门，热情地招呼他们吃饭洗漱，还为杜甫剪纸招魂。

在孙宰家歇息了几天后，杜甫一家继续北行，经过华原（治所在今陕西耀县东南）、三川（治所在今陕西富县南），穿过连日淫雨引起的滔滔洪水，终于来到鄜州（今陕西富县）。

On the fourth morning after Tongguan Pass was lost, which was the thirteenth of June in the fifteenth year of the Tianbao reign (755 A.D.), escorted by troops led by Chen Xuanli, Emperor Xuanzong took Lady Yang, Yang Guozhong, some members of the royal family, as well as several ministers and eunuchs, fleeing secretly from Chang'an to Shu by moonlight. When they reached Mawei Station in Xingping, the soldiers were ordered by Chen Xuanli to mutiny, killing Yang Guozhong and forcing Emperor Xuanzong to strangle Lady Yang to death. After the incident at Mawei Station, Emperor Xuanzong and his party continued westward until they arrived at Chengdu on the twenty-eighth of July. At the same time, the crown prince Li Heng left Mawei Station for Shuofang directly and arrived at Lingwu (now Lingwu in Ningxia) on the ninth of July. He announced to ascend the throne on the twelfth of July, changing the title of the imperial reign to Zhide, becoming known in history as Emperor Suzong.

Having heard the news that Suzong had ascended the throne, Du Fu settled his family in Qiangcun Village northwest of Fuzhou City and set out alone for Lingwu, nearly a thousand miles away. Soon after his departure, however, he was captured by the rebels and taken to occupied Chang'an. Fortunately, he was dressed in plain clothes, and his official rank was so low that he did not suffer the same fate as the other officials, palace maids, and eunuchs captured by An Lushan, who were sent from Chang'an to Luoyang.

As Du Fu was being escorted to Chang'an, on an autumn night when the bright moon was shining in the sky, he expressed his longing for his wife and young children, forced to flee from place to place in the chaos of war, in a poem entitled "The Moonlit Night."

> In the moon at Fuzhou tonight
> She watches alone in our room.
> What a pity that my children far away
> Know not why she misses me in Chang'an.
> Her cloud-like hair is wet in the scented mist;
> Her jade-like arms are shining in the cold light.
> When will we sit together against thin curtains,
> Gazing at each other with tears in the moonlight.

The techniques used in this poem were very unique. At the time, poems about people generally began with the poet's own emotions, but this poem did exactly the opposite. It began with the subject, describing how much his wife in Fuzhou missed him. He knew that his young children couldn't understand

潼关失守后的第四天凌晨，即天宝十五载（755）六月十三日，唐玄宗慌忙带着杨贵妃、杨国忠和部分亲近的皇亲国戚、大臣和宦官，由陈玄礼率领的部队护送，趁着夜色偷偷离开长安逃往西蜀。他们走到兴平的马嵬驿时，士兵在陈玄礼的指引下，群起哗变，杀死了杨国忠，并逼玄宗缢杀了杨妃。马嵬驿事变后，唐玄宗一行继续西逃，于七月二十八日到成都，太子李亨则从马嵬直奔朔方，于七月九日抵达灵武（今宁夏灵武），十二日宣布即位，改元至德，是为肃宗。

杜甫听到肃宗即位的消息，便把家人安顿在鄜州城西北的羌村，只身投奔相隔近千里的灵武。没想到刚出发不久，就被叛军逮住，押往已经沦陷的长安。幸亏他身着布衣，又官职低微，才没有像其他官吏一样，连同安禄山搜捕来的宫女和宦官一道被送往洛阳。

杜甫被押到长安，在一个明月当空的秋夜，他无限思念在战乱中漂泊的弱妻幼子，于是写了一首《月夜》：

今夜鄜州月，闺中只独看。

遥怜小儿女，未解忆长安。

香雾云鬟湿，清辉玉臂寒。

何时倚虚幌，双照泪痕干。

这首诗手法极有特色。一般的怀人诗大多从自己的思绪写起，这首诗却反其道而行，从对方的角度入手，写鄜州的妻子思念自己。他又想到小儿女们也还不懂得妻子的"忆长安"，

why his wife longed for him in Chang'an, describing her watching the moon and thinking of her husband alone, emphasizing his wife's deep affection for him. Du Fu imagined his wife's appearance at that moment: her hair, loose as clouds, bathed in scented mist, and her arms, as white as jade, bathed in cold moonlight. What a moving image of a woman watching the moon while missing her husband! The last two lines evoked another interesting image, that of the couple's future reunion, when they would lean against gossamer curtains and recall how they missed each other at this place and this moment. Then they would regard each other with tears shining in their eyes. The whole poem contained a complicated stream of thoughts and one fascinating idea after another, showing deepest affection and sincere concern in an implicit and restrained way.

As Du Fu was not kept under strict guard, he still had considerable freedom to move about, allowing him ample opportunity to witness the miserable conditions in Chang'an after his capture. One day, Du Fu saw a nobleman's son who had survived the attack, weeping on the roadside. When questioned, he was reluctant to tell his own name, only hoping that someone would take him in as a servant. He told the poet that he had been hiding in thickets of thorns for nearly a hundred days, so that his whole body was covered with bruises and cuts. Du Fu comforted him, telling him that the rebels would surely be defeated. The poem "Grieving for a Nobleman's Son" used the experience of this nobleman's son to elucidate the terrifying and bloody atmosphere of Chang'an, while expressing the poet's confidence and desire that the rebels would be defeated.

The atrocities of the rebels aroused the resistance of people and officials from all regions, and there was continuous fighting against their rule. Supported by the scholar Li Mi, general Guo Ziyi, and Li Guangbi, who all gathered one after the other to Lingwu, Emperor Suzong advanced into Pengyuan (now Ningxian County in Gansu), preparing to attack to the east. In October, the new Prime Minister Fang Guan led troops to fight against the rebels at Chentaoxie in the east of Xianyang. Due to tactical mistakes, they were soon defeated by the rebels, suffering some forty thousand casualties. Two days later, because Emperor Suzong had sent Eunuch Xing Yan'en to encourage the troops to fight, Fang Guan led the remaining soldiers to fight the rebels at Qingban, suffering another disastrous defeat. Angry and sorrowful, Du Fu wrote two poems.

Grieving over the Battle at Chentao
In the first month of winter, the sons of good folks from every

所以妻子只有一个人望月思夫，更加突出了妻子苦忆之深情。诗人设想此刻妻子的样子：蓬松如云的发髻膏沐着清香的夜气，玉一样洁白的双臂映照着清寒的月光，那是一幅多么动人的望月怀人图啊。末尾两句又翻出一层奇想，设想夫妻将来团聚了，再倚着透明的帷幕，来回忆此时此刻的相离相思之苦，那时候四目相对，两人的眼中一定都闪烁着晶莹的泪光。全诗思致曲折，奇想迭出，写得情真意切而又含蓄蕴藉。

由于并没有被严加看管，行动还算自由，杜甫得以目睹了长安沦陷后的各种惨状。有一天，杜甫遇到一位虎口余生的王孙在路边哭泣，当人们问起他时，他不肯说出自己的姓名，只恳求有人收他作奴仆。他告诉诗人，自己已经在荆棘丛中逃窜上百日了，浑身伤痕，体无完肤。杜甫诚恳亲切地劝慰他要小心珍重，并鼓励他说叛军一定会被平定。《哀王孙》通过这位王孙的遭遇，以小见大，反映了长安恐怖血腥的气氛，也表达了诗人对平叛的信心和希望。

叛军的暴行激起了各地民众和官吏的抵抗，不断有人起而杀敌。肃宗也在先后到达灵武的文士李泌以及大将郭子仪和李光弼的拥护下，进驻彭原（今甘肃宁县），准备东征。十月，新任宰相房琯领兵与叛军战于咸阳东面的陈陶斜，由于战术不当，一战即溃，死伤四万人。两日后，由于肃宗派宦官邢延恩催战，房琯再率余部与叛军战于青坂，又遭大败。杜甫悲愤填膺，写下两首诗：

悲陈陶

孟冬十郡良家子，血作陈陶泽中水。

county
　　Shed their blood at Chentao, pooling into puddles like water.
　　No sound could be heard in the open field under the clear sky,
　　For forty thousand righteous soldiers had died that day.
　　Gangs of rebels returned, their arrows covered with blood.
　　Drinking and singing their songs, they made merry in the city.
　　Facing the north, the people of the capital wept aloud,
　　Yearning night and day for the arrival of government troops.

Grieving over the Battle at Qingban
At the Eastern Gate of Qingban are stationed our troops,
　　Watering their horses in the pond of Taibai Mountain on cold days.
　　The elite rebel troops press so far westward with each passing day
　　That lone squads of cavalrymen dare to rush forward with bows.
　　The mountains are covered with snow, the rivers are frozen, and the
world is bleak.
　　The blue beacon fire still burns, and white bones lie everywhere.
　　How can I send a message to our troops
　　To tell them to wait until next year and not make haste.

　　In the poems, though the battles were not described directly, emphasis was given to the bloody, corpse-ridden aftermath of the battles, as well as the arrogance of the rebel soldiers. The poems were also meant to warn the officers and soldiers to fight with caution. This shows that Du Fu kept his wits about him, even in times of fury and distress.

　　When winter came to occupied Chang'an, Du Fu wrote grievingly that "No news came from any prefecture / So I could do nothing but sit in anxiety and write in the air" ("Watching Snow").

　　With the arrival of spring, his mood became even darker.

　　Though the capital is seized, we still have control of the land;
　　Though it is spring in the city, grass and trees grow in clumps.
　　I'm in such grief that I shed tears when I see blooming flowers.
　　I'm startled to hear chirping birds.
　　Now that the war has lasted for months,
　　A letter from home is worth ten thousand gold.
　　My white hair has grown so sparse and short from scratching
　　That it could no longer hold even a hairpin.

　　　　　　　　　　　　　　　　　　　　　　("A Spring View")

野旷天清无战声，四万义军同日死。

群胡归来血洗箭，仍唱胡歌饮都市。

都人回面向北啼，日夜更望官军至。

悲青坂

我军青坂在东门，天寒饮马太白窟。

黄头奚儿日向西，数骑弯弓敢驰突。

山雪河冰野萧瑟，青是烽烟白人骨。

焉得附书与我军，忍待明年莫仓卒。

诗中没有具体描述战斗过程，而是着重渲染战后血流成河、尸横遍野的惨状和叛军的嚣张气焰，并告诫官军谨慎应战。可以看出诗人虽在悲愤之中却能冷静思索。

冬天到了，在沦陷的长安，诗人艰难地唱着："数州消息断，愁坐正书空。"（《对雪》）

到了春天，他的心情更加伤感：

国破山河在，城春草木深。

感时花溅泪，恨别鸟惊心。

烽火连三月，家书抵万金。

白头搔更短，浑欲不胜簪。

——《春望》

Facing the ruined and wasted capital, Du Fu was so overcome with sadness that he shed tears when seeing blooming flowers and was startled when hearing chirping birds. As the war went on with no end in sight, letters from home could not arrive, causing Du Fu such homesickness and bitterness that he kept scratching his head until it was covered with white hair, so sparse and short that it wasn't able to hold the hairpin used to bind up his hair. This poem expressed such deep emotions and employed such sharp imagery to describe how one would feel in such a situation that it could bring tears to one's eyes.

One day at dusk, Du Fu came to the bank of the Qujiang River. Seeing the tightly locked palace gate and the young green cattails and willow twigs, the poet couldn't help thinking of the old days when Emperor Xuanzong and Lady Yang, attended by a crowd, were on their spring outing at the side of the Qujiang River. Now, however, it was a totally different picture: "Where is the lady with clear bright eyes and beaming white teeth? / She has become a roaming ghost stained with blood, unable to return / The clear Weihe River flows east to Jiange / There has been no news since their departure" ("Grieving by the Riverside"). At this thought, the poet sobbed in his heart before giving way to a flood of tears, expressing sympathy for the tragic fate of Li Longji and Yang Yuhuan while mourning for the golden days of the Kaiyuan and Tianbao eras.

In the first lunar month of the second year of the Zhide reign (757 A.D.), An Lushan's son An Qingxu murdered his father and seized the throne. In February, Emperor Suzong captured Fengxiang, and then the government troops and rebel troops were locked in a confrontation in the western suburbs of Chang'an. In Chang'an, the people all thought that Chang'an would soon be retaken, but despite their long wait, there was no sign of major activity by the government troops. In April, Du Fu made a courageous escape from Chang'an. He risked his life traveling along treacherous paths, crossed the battle lines, and finally arrived at Fengxiang, having been through all kinds of hardships and difficulties.

"I called on the emperor in hemp shoes / With both my elbows poking out of the sleeves" ("Pouring out My Feelings"). These two lines aptly described Du Fu's pathetic appearance when calling on Emperor Suzong. On the sixteenth of May, Emperor Suzong appointed Du Fu as Commissioner of the Left. Though a seemingly low position (under the eighth official rank), the person in this position shouldered great responsibility as he was supposed to provide advice to the emperor. The poet accepted this position with grateful

诗人面对残破而荒芜的国都，感时伤世，见到花开也掉泪，听到鸟鸣也惊心。战乱不息，家书难至，思念和痛苦让他不停地搔头，直搔得满头白发又少又短，连束发的簪子也插不住了。这首诗再现了典型环境中的典型感受，感情深沉，形象鲜明，意境感人，催人泪下。

一个黄昏，诗人来到曲江边。看到宫门紧锁，蒲柳新绿，不禁想起当年众人簇拥着玄宗和贵妃在曲江边游春的情形，而现在则是："明眸皓齿今何在，血污游魂归不得。清渭东流剑阁深，去住彼此无消息。"（《哀江头》）诗人内心呜咽，老泪纵横，这是对李、杨悲剧命运的同情之泪，也是对开、天盛世的悼念之泪。

至德二载（757）正月，安禄山的儿子安庆绪杀死其父，宣布即位。二月，唐肃宗进驻凤翔，官军和叛军在长安西郊形成对峙局面。长安城内，士民都以为长安克复在即，可是等了好久，却没有什么大的动静。到了四月，杜甫便以极大的勇气逃出长安。他冒着生命危险，沿着崎岖的小路，穿过两军对峙的前线，历尽艰辛，到达凤翔。

"麻鞋见天子，衣袖露两肘。"（《述怀》）这就是杜甫拜见肃宗时的狼狈模样。五月十六日，唐肃宗任命杜甫为左拾遗。此职虽低（从八品下），却要常常向皇帝提出建议和意见，责

tears, but was soon involved in the political whirlpool of the Fang Guan incident, which almost caused his own death.

Fang Guan once studied on Yiyang Mountain near Luhun Village for ten years in his youth, and was a friend of Du Fu before gaining official rank. While being a local official, he showed both talent and love toward his subjects. When Emperor Xuanzong entered Shu, he heard the news and went to meet him. He was then ordered to go to Lingwu to attend the crowning of the Suzong the emperor. Later, he was appointed as prime minister by Emperor Suzong, volunteering to command troops to suppress the revolt. But as he was originally a scholar, he was not familiar with military tactics. After the first defeat, he was not able to maintain his own correct stand that "they should be prudent and bide their time" when Emperor Suzong sent the eunuch to supervise the battle, which eventually caused another defeat. At the same time, Fang Guan's political enemies took advantage of the conflict between Emperor Xuanzong and Suzong, father and son, to fabricate charges against him, saying that he was only loyal to Emperor Xuanzong but secretly against Emperor Suzong. In May, someone accused Fang Guan's parasitic guest Dong Tinglan of accepting bribes, so Emperor took the chance to remove him from his office. Seeing that Fang Guan suffered from unjust punishment, Du Fu, then newly appointed Commissioner of the Left, determined to submit a memorial to the emperor, stating with indignation that he should not remove a minister from office due to minor negligence. Emperor Suzong flew into a rage at these remarks, ordering the Three Departments to interrogate him. Thanks to a rescue by Prime Minister Zhang Hao, he was exempted from punishment.

This incident made Du Fu regretful for his whole life, so in the statement of thanks he wrote to Emperor Suzong after being exempted from punishment, he appeared to express thanks to the emperor but was, in fact, defending himself. Many years later, he mentioned this time and again in his poems, claiming that "he felt shameful for all his life as he was unable to succeed in presenting the memorial to the emperor" ("The Funeral Oration for the Deceased Prime Minister, Revered Fang of Qinghe").

This incident also caused Emperor Suzong to distance himself from Du Fu, so in the early eighth leap month, he let Du Fu return to Fuzhou to visit his family. Du Fu borrowed a horse from General Li Siye and set out with only one servant. He trudged across mountains and rivers all the way, covering over seven hundred miles, arriving in the evening. His wife and children had not thought that they would ever see their husband and father return alive, their shock and excitement leading them to shed tears of joy. Even his neighbors

任很重大。诗人感激涕零地接受了这个官职，随即便卷入房琯事件的政治漩涡，险遭杀身之祸。

房琯少年时代曾在陆浑伊阳山读书十年，与杜甫是"布衣交"，做地方官期间，有为而又爱民。玄宗入蜀，他闻风前往，又奉命到灵武册立肃宗。被肃宗任命为宰相后，他主动要求带兵平叛。但他本是一介书生，于军旅战事不太熟悉。一战而败后，在肃宗派太监督战时，又不能坚持自己原先"持重以伺之"的正确主张，导致再败。同时，房琯的政敌又利用玄宗和肃宗父子之间的矛盾，诬陷房琯，说他只忠于玄宗而对肃宗不利。五月，又有人告发房琯的门客董庭兰招纳货贿，肃宗于是借此罢去他的相位。新任左拾遗的杜甫，看到房琯遭受的处罚过重，便毅然上书，言辞激烈地陈说不应为细过而罢黜大臣。唐肃宗勃然大怒，命三司推问，幸亏宰相张镐营救，才免其罪。

这件事让杜甫终身遗憾，在被免罪后，他写给皇帝的谢状中，表面上感谢肃宗，实际上为自己表白和辩解。多年以后，他还在诗文中一再提起此事，称自己"伏奏无成，终身愧耻"。（《祭故相国清河房公文》）

这件事也招致了肃宗对杜甫的疏远，到了闰八月初，便让他回鄜州探家。杜甫向将军李嗣业借了一匹马，带着一个仆人便上路了。一路上跋山涉水，经过七百多里的路程，终于在一天傍晚到家了。妻子儿女想不到经过这么大的战乱，还能见自己的亲人活着回来，又惊又喜，眼泪直流。邻居们也爬到墙头

climbed on top of the courtyard wall to see, sighing with wonder and sniffling back tears. That night, he and his wife gazed silently at each other in the candlelight, feeling as though they were dreaming.

Though reunited with his family after long separation, Du Fu was sad that he could only muddle on from day to day at such an old age, being unable to bring happiness to his family even though he was back home. The elders brought wine to comfort him, telling him that no one was working in the fields and that production had virtually halted, as the young and strong had all been drafted to fight in the war. After hearing these words, Du Fu composed a sad poem: "I looked up with a deep sigh after singing / Only to find all the people present weeping" ("Three Poems Written in Qiang Village" , No. Three).

Looking back on what he had experienced on the journey from Fengxiang to Qiangcun Village and reflecting on the fate of China, Du Fu wrote another long five-character poem entitled "Traveling to the North" after he wrote the poem called "Feelings Expressed in Five Hundred Words after Traveling from the Capital to Fengxian County." This poem contained a hundred and forty poetic lines, using detailed imagery to reflect social life during the An Shi Rebellion. The poem can be roughly divided into five stanzas.

The twenty lines of the first stanza were set before the poet's departure, mainly describing the poet's love for the imperial palace and his concern for China.

> On the first day of the eighth leap month,
> In the autumn of the second year of the new reign,
> I, Du Fu, was about to travel to the north
> To visit my family, weighed down by anxiety and pain.
> The country was in hard times at the time,
> So the government and the people had no time for leisure.
> I was humbled that because of His Majesty's clemency,
> I was allowed to return to my humble home.
> Bidding a farewell to His Majesty in the palace,
> I was seized with fear, reluctant to take my leave.
> Lacking competence in offering advice,
> I was still afraid that His Majesty would make careless mistakes.
> His Majesty was the only one who could truly recover the country,
> So I hoped he would do his utmost in directing the state.
> The rebels were making trouble,
> Making me resentful and sorrowful.

上来看，纷纷感叹着，歔欷着。晚上，夫妻二人在烛光下相对无言，觉得好像是在梦中一样。

虽然见到了久别的亲人，但是诗人却感慨自己年龄老大，为情势所迫而苟且偷生，回到家里也带不来欢乐和趣味。父老们携酒来慰问他，诉说着青壮年都被征去打仗、田地无人耕种、生产遭到破坏的情形。杜甫听了，悲歌一曲，"歌罢仰天叹，四座泪纵横"。（《羌村三首》其三）

回顾从凤翔到羌村一路的经历，又思考着国家的命运，杜甫写下了继《自京赴奉先县咏怀五百字》之后的另一首长篇五言古诗——《北征》。这首长达一百四十句的诗歌，通过具体的形象描写，真实地反映了安史之乱中的社会生活面貌，其内容大致可分五段：

第一段二十句，主要写临行前恋阙忧国的心情：

皇帝二载秋，闰八月初吉。

杜子将北征，苍茫问家室。

维时遭艰虞，朝野少暇日。

顾惭恩私被，诏许归蓬荜。

拜辞诣阙下，怵惕久未出。

虽乏谏诤姿，恐君有遗失。

君诚中兴主，经纬固密勿。

东胡反未已，臣甫愤所切。

Wiping my tears, I was so unwilling to leave
That I was still listless on my way home.
As heaven and earth were all torn by war,
When would my worries end?

The poet's loyalty showed forth in his writing. Du Fu respected Emperor Suzong, worried that the emperor would make careless mistakes in his reign. As the nation was faced with a crisis at the moment, it would have been the perfect time to concentrate one's efforts on the nation and realize one's own ambition, but Du Fu was forced to leave the capital. As a result, his feelings of love, worry, sorrow and pain were all jumbled together as he left, and there was nothing he could do about it. This heart-rending expression of emotion at the beginning of the poem immediately makes readers shed tears of sorrow.

The thirty-six lines of the second stanza described Du Fu's observations as he traveled, giving detailed description to the devastation that the war had brought to vast rural areas of China. What the poet described was a scene of such misery that it strikes readers right to the heart.

Slowly, I walked on paths crisscrossing in the field,
Meeting few people on such a desolate day.
Those I met were wounded men,
Moaning and bleeding on their way.

Moreover, the poem also described the horrible scene of the battlefield in the moonlight, a description that sends cold shivers down one's spine.

Owls were hooted in yellow mulberry trees,
And wild mice burrowed.
Passing by the battle fields at night,
I saw white bones bathed in cold moonlight.

This led Du Fu to reflect on the cruelty of war, so he described the heavy casualties of the battle at Tongguan Pass and the slaughter that the people of the region of Qin suffered after the defeat.

At Tongguan Pass, there once were millions of troops,
Who suddenly disappeared as if they'd vanished into thin air.
As a result, half the people in the region of Qin
Were slaughtered and reduced to refuse.

In this stanza, the poet also added description of grass and trees on the mountains.

挥涕恋行在，道途犹恍惚。

乾坤含疮痍，忧虞何时毕？

诗人的一片赤心跃然纸上。杜甫敬爱他的皇帝唐肃宗，担心皇帝在执政上有所疏漏。此时国难当头，正是为国出力实现抱负的时刻，自己却要离开京城，临行之际，依恋、担心、忧愁、痛苦的心情交织在一起，但又无可奈何。一开篇就让读者黯然泪下。

第二段三十六句，写沿途观感，具体描绘了战乱给广大农村造成的巨大破坏。诗人碰到的是一幕幕悲惨的景象，令人触目惊心：

靡靡逾阡陌，人烟眇萧瑟。

所遇多被伤，呻吟更流血。

此外，还描写了月下战场的恐怖景象，令人毛骨悚然：

鸱鸟鸣黄桑，野鼠拱乱穴。

夜深经战场，寒月照白骨。

由此诗人想到战争的残酷，描写了潼关之战的惨重伤亡和战败后秦地百姓所遭受的屠杀：

潼关百万师，往者散何卒！

遂令半秦民，残害为异物。

此段还插入对山间草木的描写：

> The mountain fruit trees were slender and many;
> Oak and chestnut trees grew in clumps.
> Some were as red as cinnabar;
> Others were as black as pitch.
> So long as they received rain and dew,
> They would bear fruit, be they bitter or sweet.

The colorful natural scenery was a stark contrast with the miserable social life, lamenting that man's life was more miserable than that of grass and trees.

The thirty-six lines of the third stanza described the bittersweet scene of Du Fu's returning home. His wife was dressed in patched clothes. His daughters wore short clothes made of coarse cloth on which was sewn an old embroidery depicting ocean waves; however, the embroidered patterns of sea waves, God Tianwu and purple phoenixes had been made upside down awkwardly. His sons, who had always been his pride and joy, turned away with tears as soon as they saw their father.

> When I arrived at my cottage, a year had passed.
> I saw my wife in a patch-covered dress.
> The wind in the pine trees whistled as I wailed,
> And the sad spring stream would echo when I wept.
> The sons I have favored most
> Had pale skin as white as snow.
> Seeing their father, they turned away to cry,
> Their dirty feet wearing no stockings.
> Two daughters were standing before the bed,
> Their mended clothes hardly covering their knees.
> The scene of sea waves on the sewn cloth was split,
> For the old embroidered cloth was not mended straight.
> The patterns of Tianwu and purple phoenixes
> Were seen to be upside down on their coarse clothes.

This detailed description was filled with concern and self-reproach. It recorded the misfortune that the war had brought to his family, which was representative of the lives of millions of families at that time.

As the head of the family, Du Fu did not forget to buy daily necessities for his wife and children, which livened the home atmosphere.

> Opening my package, I produced face powder and eyebrow liner,
> Showing the quilts and bed curtains I had brought for my family.

> 山果多琐细，罗生杂橡栗。
>
> 或红如丹砂，或黑如点漆。
>
> 雨露之所濡，甘苦齐结实。

自然风物的多彩和社会人生的悲惨构成强烈的对比，蕴涵着人命不如草木的深沉感叹。

第三段三十六句，写回到家后的悲喜之状。妻子穿着打满补丁的衣服。女儿穿的粗布短衣上缝补着绣有海景波涛的旧衣料，那旧衣料上绣的波涛、天吴、紫凤等图案都被弄得上下颠倒，东倒西歪。平生所娇惯的儿子，见了父亲反而背过脸去哭：

> 经年至茅屋，妻子衣百结。
>
> 恸哭松声回，悲泉共幽咽。
>
> 平生所娇儿，颜色白胜雪。
>
> 见耶背面啼，垢腻脚不袜。
>
> 床前两小女，补绽才过膝。
>
> 海图坼波涛，旧绣移曲折。
>
> 天吴及紫凤，颠倒在裋褐。

这一段细腻的描写，笔端饱含着关切与自责，真实地记录了战乱给家庭带来的不幸，而这只是当时千千万万家庭的一个缩影。

身为家长，杜甫没有忘记给妻子儿女买些日用品，于是家庭气氛活跃了：

> 粉黛亦解苞，衾裯稍罗列。

After applying cosmetics, my thin wife's face shone again
While my playful daughters combed their own hair,
Trying to learn everything their mother did:
Combing hair in the morning and applying make-up with ease.
They tried rouge and powder for some time,
Making their eyebrows look broad and messy.
They pulled my beard, pestering me with questions,
But how could I have the heart to scold them?
Recalling the grief I felt when Chang'an was seized by rebels,
I'd rather take pleasure in listening to such chatter.

His wife and daughters were busy enjoying the cosmetics Du Fu bought for them. As time went on, his children were no longer afraid of him, vying with each other to pull their father's beard and pestering him with questions. Du Fu did not scold them. Recalling the anxiety and distress that he couldn't return home from Chang'an despite his homesickness, he felt that listening to his children making noises was indeed a kind of pleasure. The war may have reduced the Du family to destitution, but their reunion brought some small happiness to them, even if it was fleeting and mingled with tears. Du Fu was able to capture these details and give them vivid, specific and exquisite description. The ability to grasp details and to reveal social life by describing trivial matters was one significant feature of Du Fu's realistic poems.

The twenty-eight lines of the fourth stanza were a commentary on the current political situation, consisting of three aspects. First, he worried about the government's decision to beseech the troops of Huihe for aid in suppressing the rebellion. Huihe was a nomadic tribe living in the northwest. In September of the second year of the Zhide reign (757 A.D.), the court raised troops from Huihe. Khan Huairen of Huihe ordered his son Yehu to lead over four thousand crack troops to Fengxiang. Du Fu thought that there might be future trouble though Huihe troops were indeed brave and reliable, so he said, "As a chilly wind swept from the northwest / Misery and desolation came along with Huihe troops." This showed that Du Fu gave thorough consideration to political affairs. Later, it turned out that his worry was confirmed by the fact that Huihe troops plundered wealth without restraint after helping the Tang Empire recover its two capitals, bringing great calamity to the people. Second, he reiterated that the court should rely on its own troops to suppress the rebellion: "The government troops should penetrate into the enemy's rear area / And save their strength so as to launch a joint attack with the Huihe troops." In this way, not only the Western Capital and Yiluo could be

瘦妻面复光，痴女头自栉。

学母无不为，晓妆随手抹。

移时施朱铅，狼藉画眉阔。

问事竞挽须，谁能即嗔喝？

翻思在贼愁，甘受杂乱聒。

妻子和女儿们忙着享用杜甫买回来的化妆品，时间一长，儿女们也不怕他了，争先恐后地扯着爹爹的胡须问这问那。杜甫也不呵斥他们，回想起陷贼长安时思归不得的愁苦，感到听儿女们的吵嚷真是一种乐趣。遭受战乱变得一贫如洗的家庭也因亲人团聚而带来一点欢笑，即使这笑是短暂的，而且是带泪的笑，杜甫也能敏锐地捕捉到，并且描写得十分细致、具体而又传神。能抓住细节，以小见大地反映社会生活，这正是杜甫现实主义诗歌的一大特色。

第四段二十八句，是对时局的议论，包括以下三个方面：一、对朝廷向回纥借兵平叛表示忧虑。回纥，是生活在西北地区的一个游牧民族。至德二载（757）九月，朝廷向回纥借兵，回纥怀仁可汗派儿子叶护率精兵四千余人到达凤翔。杜甫认为回纥兵固然有勇可用，但也怕会留下后患，故云："阴风西北来，惨澹随回纥。"这说明杜甫考虑政事很周全。后来事实果然应验了杜甫的忧虑，回纥军队在帮助唐王朝恢复两京以后，大肆掠夺财物，给人民带来深重灾难。二、朝廷应主要依靠自己的军队平息叛乱，"官军请深入，蓄锐可俱发"，不仅可以迅

be soon recovered, but the two prefectures of Qing and Xu could also be seized, and even remote places such as Hengshan and Jieshi could be recaptured. Third, he asserted categorically that it was time for a counterattack, saying, "It is time that misfortune visited the tribesmen of the north / It's time to seize these men." This meant that the rebels were due for misfortune, and the court should seize the chance. These suggestions evidenced Du Fu's active participation in court affairs, so they could be considered as memorials written in the form of poems, specifically reflecting that "he was afraid that the emperor might be negligent."

The twenty lines of the fifth stanza recalled some of the measures that the Tang Empire took after the outbreak of the An Shi Rebellion, explaining that the Tang Empire would be able to prosper by applying lessons of the past to the present and by understanding the will of the people. The poem praised Chen Xuanli's decision to force the emperor to step down at Mawei Station. It also praised Emperor Xuanzong, because he was able to accept the inevitable and ordered Lady Yang to commit suicide, thus removing the source of disaster. This difficult decision was something that many ancient emperors had not the heart to accomplish. In addition, the common people supported the Tang Empire, looking forward to the time when the emperor would return to the capital. All of this showed that there was hope for the future prosperity of the Tang Empire. With a wise monarch, loyal ministers and the people's support, the idea expressed in the last two lines that "The bright career started by Emperor Taizong / Would have a brilliant future" seemed to be very natural. The poem ended on a strong positive note, giving people great encouragement.

This long poem vividly revealed the social reality of the time, from the court politics of upper society to the commoners' plight of lower society. Because of this, it is considered to be "poetic history." The poem broke away from the tradition of most Chinese classical poems, in which descriptions of landscape and emotion were the main means of expression. Instead, it integrated many forms of expression, such as narration, description, emotion, and logic, all into one piece. This lack of set form and demonstration of great flexibility started the poetic tradition of the Tang and Song dynasties, that one should write poems as if writing an essay.

In September of the second year of the Zhide reign (757 A.D.), leading 150 thousand Tang troops and troops from the Western Regions and Huihe, the chief commander Li Chu and assistant commander Guo Ziyi recaptured the Western Capital Chang'an, then pressed their advantage and recovered the Eastern Capital Luoyang on the eighth of October. Before the battle, Emperor Suzong

速收复西京和伊洛，而且可以攻下青、徐二州。恒山、碣石等边远之地也可收复。三、断言反攻之势已成，"祸转亡胡岁，势成擒胡月"，叛军的厄运已经到来，朝廷应抓住时机。这些建议体现了作为谏官的杜甫对朝政积极参与的精神，可以看作是用诗写成的奏疏，是"恐君有遗失"的具体体现。

第五段二十句，回顾了安史之乱爆发后唐王朝所采取的一些措施，通过古今对比、人心归向来说明唐王朝一定能够中兴。杜甫在诗中高度赞扬了陈玄礼发动的马嵬兵谏，也赞扬玄宗在紧要时刻能接受兵谏，赐死贵妃，铲除祸根，做出了古代帝王做不到的事。而天下百姓也都心向大唐，日夜盼望皇上复京。这都表明唐朝中兴有望。主明、臣忠、民心归附，三者并具，所以结尾二句"煌煌太宗业，树立甚宏达"，就显得水到渠成。全诗以时代的最强音作结，具有巨大的鼓舞力量。

这首长诗牛动展现了安史之乱中上至朝廷政治、下至百姓生活的广泛内容和社会现实，堪称一代"诗史"。全诗突破了中国古典诗歌以写景和抒情为主要表现手法的特点，熔叙事、描写、抒情、议论等多种表达方法于一炉，灵活多变，不拘一格，开中唐及宋人以文为诗的先声。

至德二载（757）九月，天下兵马元帅李俶、副元帅郭子仪，率领唐军及西域、回纥之兵十五万人，收复了沦陷一年零三个月的西京长安，并乘胜前进，于十月八日收复东都洛阳。

signed a contract with Huihe stipulating that the land and people of the recaptured cities would belong to the Tang Empire, while the gold, silk, and young children would belong to Huihe. As a result, after Luoyang was recovered, Huihe's commander-in-chief Yehu led his troops to "accept" clothing by plundering and looting for three days, causing great harm to the people.

Upon hearing the news that the Tang troops had won victory after victory, and that Emperor Suzong had returned to the capital, Du Fu wrote several poems, such as "Twenty Rhymes on the Happy News that the Tang Troops were Closing in on the Rebels' Territory" and "Three Poems about the Retaking of the Capital," all of which were filled with joy in imagining the scene of the Tang troops' victory. In November, he took his wife and children back to Chang'an. Since Du Fu was filled with joy, the scenery along the way put him in a peaceful mood. Du Fu had once traveled from Chang'an to Fengtian to visit his father Du Xian during the Tianbao reign. He had passed by the Zhao Tomb of Emperor Taizong of Tang and wrote the poem "Passing by Zhaoling Tomb," giving comprehensive praise to Emperor Taizong's outstanding statecraft and brilliant military exploits. This time he passed by the Zhaoling Tomb again, so he wrote the poem "Passing by the Zhaoling Tomb Again," expressing his fervent hope for the prosperity of the Tang Empire.

Having returned to Chang'an, Du Fu took the office of Commissioner of the Left again.

In December, the former emperor Xuanzong returned to Chang'an from Chengdu where he had fled. The Tang government then granted many titles to officials of merit in Chengdu and Lingwu, at the same time investigating officials who had surrendered to the rebels. Officials who had surrendered to the rebels and who had accepted posts given by the rebels were divided into six ranks for punishment. Among Du Fu's friends, Wang Wei had accepted a post from the rebels, but he had also written a poem entitled "Regarding the Green Pond" to express his yearning for the Tang Empire, a poem which became popular in Lingwu. At that time, his younger brother Wang Jin suggested that he resign from his office to atone for his brother's crime. As a result, Suzong showed mercy on Wang Wei, so he was only demoted and served as deputy chief censor, responsible to the crown prince. Du Fu's old friend Zheng Qian had sent secret memorials to Lingwu at the time of Luoyang's capture, but his punishment was more severe than that of Wang Wei. He was only exempted from capital punishment, and was banished to the remote region of Taizhou (now Linhai in Zhejiang) to act as an official in the census registration department there. Zheng Qian left in such a hurry that Du Fu had no time to

战前，唐肃宗与回纥订立了"克城之日，土地、士庶归唐，金帛、子女皆归回纥"的条约，所以收复洛阳后，回纥统帅叶护便引兵"接受"布帛，大肆抢掠三天，人民大受其害。

杜甫在羌村听到唐军接连胜利以及肃宗回京的消息，先后写下了《喜闻唐军已临贼境二十韵》和《收京三首》等诗，满怀喜气地展望唐军胜利的情景。十一月，他便带领妻子儿女返回长安。诗人心中充满了喜悦，一路上所见之景在他看来都呈现出太平气象。诗人曾于天宝年间从长安赴奉天探望父亲杜闲时，路过唐太宗的陵墓昭陵，写下《行次昭陵》，全面地赞颂了唐太宗的文治武功。这次又路过昭陵，便写下《重经昭陵》，对盛唐的中兴给予热望。

杜甫回到长安后，继续任左拾遗。

十二月，太上皇唐玄宗从逃亡之地成都回到长安。唐政府大封成都、灵武扈从的功臣，同时追查陷贼官员的问题，对于投降叛军及接受伪官者，分六等定罪。杜甫的朋友中，王维虽接受了给事中的伪职，但他曾写过一首以怀念唐王朝为内容的《凝碧池诗》并传到灵武，此时他的弟弟王缙又提出愿意削去自己官职替兄长赎罪，因而肃宗对他宽大处理，仅贬为太子中丞。杜甫的故友郑虔在陷于洛阳时就有密章达于灵武，但此次定罪却远比王维重，他仅免于死，被远谪至台州（今浙江临海）任司户参军。郑虔仓促上路，杜甫来不及送行，于是写了一首

send him off, so he wrote a seven-character verse to bid farewell.

> The venerable Mr. Zheng's talent was not recognized though he was graying on the temples.
>
> Such being the case, he often called himself the old painter after getting drunk.
>
> Banished to a faraway place, he grieved to have received such severe punishment.
>
> Being too old, he was doomed to die just as the nation recovered.
>
> He began on his long journey in such a hurry
>
> That I came too late to see him off, being held up by an unexpected matter.
>
> Though it is time that we part forever in this life,
>
> I am sure we still resume our friendship after death.
>
> ("A Poem Written to Zheng Qian, Who was Banished to Taizhou for Falling into the Hands of Rebels and Whom I Failed to See off in Person")

This poem showed the poet's loyal devotion to his friend who was in dire peril, the emotions being so sincere as to move one to tears. Later, Du Fu often missed this old friend who was banished to the bank of the East Sea.

Once Chang'an was recovered, both the emperor and the ministers were able to relax somewhat. One day, Jia Zhi, Drafter in the Secretariat, wrote a poem while on his way to *Daminggong* (the Palace of the Great Brightness) to go to court. Du Fu, Wang Wei and Cen Shen all wrote poems in reply. These poems described the court as peaceful and prosperous. However, the chaos of war still menaced the empire, mercenaries hired from the Western Regions were still stationed in the capital, and the rebel troops were still wreaking havoc all over the country. Under such circumstances, it was improper to write poems to heighten the peaceful atmosphere, for the contents of such poems did not accurately reflect the state of the nation. Perhaps, like Emperor Xuanzong, Emperor Suzong and many of the ministers, Du Fu was too optimistic about the current situation.

Though his position was low and insignificant, Du Fu felt very proud to be in the presence of the emperor. Every night, he worried about going to court the next morning to give council to the emperor, causing him to toss and turn the whole night and keep asking the time. It may have been that Du Fu was so dutiful that he felt a great deal of mental pressure. He once wrote a poem on the wall of the Chancellery where he worked, saying that he felt very restless because he was nothing but a feeble scholar who was granted a post at an old

七律送别：

> 郑公樗散鬓成丝，酒后常称老画师。
>
> 万里伤心严谴日，百年垂死中兴时。
>
> 苍惶已就长途往，邂逅无端出饯迟。
>
> 便与先生应永诀，九重泉路尽交期。
>
> ——《送郑十八虔贬台州司户伤其临老陷贼之故阙别
>
> 情见于诗》

此诗以赤诚之心对待危难中的朋友，感情真挚，催人泪下。之后，杜甫常常怀念这位被发落在东海之滨的老友。

长安收复，君臣得以喘息。一日，中书舍人贾至往大明宫上朝，写了一首诗，杜甫便与王维、岑参一起作诗唱和。这些诗将朝中景象描写得一派升平，欣欣向荣。但是，在刚刚经受乱离、京城还驻扎着借来的西域军队、叛军还在全国肆虐的情况下，诗歌这样渲染升平气象，其内容显然不符合国家的实际情况。杜甫此时或许和唐玄宗、唐肃宗以及许多朝臣一样，对形势估计得太过乐观了。

虽然官职低微，但作为能够目睹天颜的近臣，杜甫感到很荣耀。晚上想着第二天一早要上朝进谏，竟然彻夜不眠，并且频频问讯时刻。也许是太过忠于职守，杜甫的心里产生了一定的压力，他在自己工作的门下省墙壁上题诗说：我这个迂腐衰

age by mistake. He felt very ashamed that he didn't give any advice which the emperor could adopt to benefit the state affairs, and despite holding the position of rectifying deviations and making up deficiencies, he was unable to perform any deed to repay the emperor's favor.

In the court at that time, below the peaceful surface, a new power struggle was in full swing. It was the factional fighting between the old ministers who followed Emperor Xuanzong to the region of Shu, and the newly appointed high officials who followed Emperor Suzong to Lingwu.

Emperor Suzong did not ask Emperor Xuanzong's consent before ascending to the throne, but rather informed him of it afterwards. Since Emperor Xuanzong returned from Shu to the capital, he had been living in Xingqing Palace in the east of the imperial city. As elders and passers-by often came there to pay respects, Emperor Suzong felt rather uneasy. In addition, the eunuch Li Fuguo went about sowing discord, causing the conflict between father and son to gradually reveal itself. Soon, Emperor Suzong allowed Li Fuguo to move Emperor Xuanzong's residence by force to Xinei, to separate him from his subjects. Right after that, the trusted followers around Emperor Xuanzong, including Eunuch Gao Lishi, were exiled, and Princess Yuzhen and Lady Ru Xianyuan, who had been keeping Xuanzong company, were also sent away. Thereafter, Emperor Suzong chose new palace maids for Emperor Xuanzong. From then on, Emperor Xuanzong grew unhappier day by day, finally dying of grief in the first year of the Baoying reign (762 A.D.). Despite finally being rid of his rival, Emperor Suzong was met with misfortune, dying of illness mere thirteen days after Xuanzong.

Due to the lies spread by Li Fuguo and Emperor Suzong's favorite concubine Lady Zhang Liangdi, the emperor felt suspicious and jealous of Emperor Xuanzong's old ministers. Consequently, men such as Fang Guan, Jia Zhi and Yan Wu became the targets of harsh measures. After finding an excuse to remove Fang Guan from his office as prime minister in May of the second year of the Zhide reign (757 A.D.), Emperor Suzong also removed Jia Zhi from his office as a mid-level official at the legislative bureau and appointed him as Governor of Ruzhou (now Linru in Henan) in the first year of the Qianyuan reign (758 A.D.). Though Du Fu risked his life by seeking refuge with Emperor Suzong, and had received promotion at his hand, he still enraged the emperor for having rescued Fang Guan and was consequently abandoned by Suzong. In addition, he was very friendly towards Emperor Xuanzong's old ministers, including Jia Zhi and Yan Wu, so according to the new officials appointed by Emperor Suzong, he belonged to the faction of the old ministers. Because of this, he fell into politically embarrassing circumstances with no

朽的书生在老大的年纪被朝廷错误地授了一个官职，内心十分彷徨；身任纠偏补缺的官职，却没有一句谏言被皇帝采纳以补益朝政，并报答君恩之重，自己感到十分惭愧。

当时的朝廷，在和平景象的背后，正在进行着一场权力和政治利益的重新配置，那就是随玄宗入蜀的旧臣和随肃宗赴灵武的新贵之间的派系斗争。

当初肃宗在灵武即位，事先并未征得玄宗的同意，而是在自行宣布即位后才通知玄宗。玄宗自蜀回京后，住在皇城东边的兴庆宫，常常有父老路人瞻望拜呼，这令肃宗颇为不安，加上宦官李辅国挑拨，父子之间的矛盾逐渐显露出来。不久，肃宗听任李辅国带人将玄宗强行迁居于西内，与臣民隔绝。紧接着，玄宗周围的亲信高力士等人都被流放，陪伴玄宗的玉真公主、如仙媛也被打发出去，肃宗重新为玄宗挑选了一批宫人。至此，玄宗日渐不乐，两年后，即宝应元年（762），便郁郁而终。可是，终于可以安下心来做皇帝的肃宗并不幸运，仅仅在玄宗去世十三天后，他也病逝了。这是后话。

当时，在李辅国和宠妃张良娣的挑拨下，肃宗对玄宗的旧臣如房琯、贾至、严武等人心生猜忌并加以打击。自至德二载（757）五月，借故罢除房琯的宰相职务后，乾元元年（758）春，又免去贾至中书舍人的职务，出为汝州（今河南临汝）刺史。杜甫虽在安史之乱中冒死只身投奔肃宗，是被肃宗提拔的近臣，但他又为营救房琯而触怒肃宗，因而受到肃宗冷落。他又与玄宗旧臣贾至、严武等人友善，所以在肃宗任命的新贵眼中，他实际上是属于旧臣一派。这样他就在政治上陷入前途无

future or prospects. By then he was nearly fifty years old, but he was still among the officials of lower status. Because of his low pay, he had difficulty supporting his family's life in the capital, let alone fulfilling his ambition of "assisting the emperor to become a monarch as wise as Yao and Shun."

The inability to realize his goals, the gloomy political prospects, and the loss of dignity due to poverty all troubled Du Fu, making him question life and become disappointed with politics and uninterested in being an official. He sighed bitterly that "the life of a man is such misery" ("Living Close Together: To Bi Yao").

Because of this, he took to drinking to drown out his sorrows: "Come to meet me for a drink today / I have but three hundred bronze coins as the pay" ("Living Close Together: To Bi Yao"). When he had no money left, he sold his clothes to buy wine; he even began to accumulate drinking debts. He would sit by the side of the Qujiang River for a long time, pondering on the ups and downs of human life. In court, he became known as "a white-haired man in drunken and sleepy state" ("A Poem to Revered Mr. Min in Jiangning as Xu Ba was on His Way There"). He even expressed his desire to resign, saying that his perpetual drunken stupor was improper. He bemoaned his old age, regretting not to have left the court to live in seclusion earlier.

In short, most of the poems Du Fu wrote while serving as Commissioner of the Left in Chang'an revealed his frustration at being a low official in the capital, showing the arduousness of his journey to reconcile his idealism with the harsh reality of the world around him. He had devoted his whole heart to becoming an official in the capital, not realizing until he was finally close to the emperor that being an official was not what he had thought it would be. He felt that he did not belong in the capital, nor in the unpredictably changing court at all. The vast and mighty mountains and rivers had always been his lifeblood. He had always had the whole nation and all the people under heaven at heart. His world was made up of the lives of commoners, forged on the long journey of seeking truth.

Because he cared for all under heaven, he felt reinvigorated as he thought on the future of the nation and on the battlefields at the frontier. At the moment, the Tang troops' situation on the battlefield of the frontier was heartening. After losing Chang'an and Luoyang, An Qingxu had to lead the remnants of his defeated army in retreat to Yecheng (now Anyang in Henan). In December of the second year of the Zhide reign (757 A.D.), Shi Siming finally surrendered. Upon hearing the news of victory sent from the frontier, Du Fu's gloomy mood vanished, and he wrote a seven-character ancient verse

望而又处境尴尬的境地。他这时已年近五十，但却沉于下僚，不要说实现"致君尧舜上"的理想抱负，因为薪水微薄，加上全家都住在京城，连生活都捉襟见肘。

理想无法实现，政治光景暗淡，生活贫穷而没有尊严，这些情况困扰着杜甫，使他对人生感到困惑，对政治感到失望，对做官感到无趣，发出了"男儿性命绝可怜"（《逼仄行赠毕曜》）的悲叹。

他于是借酒浇愁："速宜相就饮一斗，恰有三百青铜钱。"（《逼仄行赠毕曜》）没钱了就典衣买酒，甚至到处欠下了酒债。他久久地坐在曲江池畔，思考着人生进退的道理。在官府中他也是"头白昏昏只醉眠"（《因许八奉寄江宁旻上人》）。他甚至表示要辞职，说自己整天地醉酒，与世情相违，自叹年岁已老，为没能早日归隐而感到悲伤。

总之，杜甫在长安任左拾遗期间所写的大部分诗歌，反映了他作为一个下级京官在政治失意中的真实处境，传达出在理想和现实的矛盾中他所经历的艰难曲折的心路历程。为了在京城做官以实现理想，他曾投入了无比巨大的热情和心血，然而，当他真正成为皇帝近臣的一员时，才发现做官并非他所想象的样子。或许，他本来就不属于京城，不属于那波谲云诡的朝廷。他的禀赋来自于广阔伟丽的山川，他的心里装着整个国家和天下的苍生，他的天地在广大的人民中间，在那艰难曲折的漫漫求索之路上。

正因为胸怀天下，当他把目光投向整个国家的未来和前线的战场时，他的精神又振作起来。这时，唐军在前线的战况颇为可喜，收复长安、洛阳以后，安庆绪率残部退守邺城（今河南安阳）。到了至德二载（757）十二月时，史思明奉表归降。前方的捷报传到京城，冲散了杜甫心头的愁闷，写下了七言古

entitled "Cleaning Weapons and Horses."

> The generals have recovered the regions east of Huashan Mountain,
> And news of victory pours in day and night.
> It's said that as soon as a small boat goes by in the river,
> The rebels' lives would be no longer safe in the coming battle
> And that soon only Yecheng City would be left unconquered.
> If Governor of Shuofang was given power, he'd accomplish great feats.
> Huihe troops riding fine steeds are seen everywhere in the capital.
> In the Grape Palace, they are allowed to feed meat to themselves.
> Though it's a relief that the royal power has recovered from Bohai Sea to Mount Tai,
> I often recall the days when the royal procession passed by the Kongtong Mountains.
> Music of homesickness has been played by the pipes for three years.
> There every bush and tree looks like an enemy.
> Prince Cheng has grown more prudent though a great feat has been achieved.
> Prime Minister Guo has such forethought that few could surpass him.
> Minister Li has sober judgement like a bright mirror.
> Minister Wang has such open and lofty bearing as that of autumn.
> These great generals were born for the times.
> They've fulfilled their duty of saving the state from disaster.
> People fleeing to the east no longer need to recall the taste of perch fish,
> And those wanting to return to the south can find places to settle.
> With ministers and officials, spring has come back to the palace,
> Forming a perfect match of the lovely spring scene.
> The emperor and the crown prince are often seen
> To extend their greetings to the former emperor at dawn.
> Those who curry favor with the emperor and his concubines
> Are granted power as princes and dukes.
> They should understand they are blessed to have their authority,
> Owing to the emperor's favor rather than their own talent.
> Prime Minister Xiao is still in office in Central Shaanxi,

诗《洗兵马》：

> 中兴诸将收山东，捷书夜报清昼同。
> 河广传闻一苇过，胡危命在破竹中。
> 祗残邺城不日得，独任朔方无限功。
> 京师皆骑汗血马，回纥喂肉葡萄宫。
> 已喜皇威清海岱，常思仙仗过崆峒。
> 三年笛里关山月，万国兵前草木风。
> 成王功大心转小，郭相谋深古来少。
> 司徒清鉴悬明镜，尚书气与秋天杳。
> 二三豪俊为时出，整顿乾坤济时了。
> 东走无复忆鲈鱼，南飞觉有安巢鸟。
> 青春复随冠冕入，紫禁正耐烟花绕。
> 鹤禁通霄凤辇备，鸡鸣问寝龙楼晓。
> 攀龙附凤势莫当，天下尽化为侯王。
> 汝等岂知蒙帝力，时来不得夸身强。
> 关中既留萧丞相，幕下复用张子房。

And Zhang Zifang has been restored to his position again.

Revered Mr. Zhang is like a wanderer all his life,

Nine feet tall, with black eyebrows and a beard.

It was not until his appointment in wartime that such a talented man met such a wise monarch.

Until the time he fought for the state were his brilliant strategies appreciated.

Rebels wearing blue gowns and riding white horses would not be seen,

And then our state would be as prosperous as the Han and Zhou Dynasties.

Regions of all size have all come to pay tribute.

Miraculous auspicious signs are seen far and wide.

No one knows from which place came the white ring

And in which mountain the silver jar was found again.

Hermits should live in recluse no longer;

Literary men should sing praise for the peaceful life.

Farmers are expecting rain to conquer the drought;

Cuckoos are urging people to plough and sow.

Soldiers should not delay their journey home,

As their worried wives are missing them in their dreams.

Where could we find soldiers mighty enough to call down heaven's water

To wash their weapons clean, never to be used again for many a long year.

　　According to content, the poem can be divided into four stanzas, with each stanza containing twelve lines. The first stanza described the current situation of the suppression of the rebellion. On the whole, the government troops were winning one victory after another while the rebels were on the verge of destruction, just waiting for Guo Ziyi, Governor of Shuofang, to mop of the remaining rebel troops. However, there were still worries, as there were Huihe troops, who had come to assist the Tang Empire in suppressing the rebellion, still stationed in the capital. He hoped that Emperor Suzong would remain vigilant in peace time and not forget the hardships of the past three years, when the emperor and his ministers fled from one place to another and when soldiers and civilians fought bitterly. The second stanza praised those well-known generals, including Guo Ziyi and Li Guangbi, for their achievements in

张公一生江海客，身长九尺须眉苍。

征起适遇风云会，扶颠始知筹策良。

青袍白马更何有，后汉今周喜再昌。

寸地尺天皆入贡，奇祥异瑞争来送。

不知何国致白环，复道诸山得银瓮。

隐士休歌紫芝曲，词人解撰河清颂。

田家望望惜雨干，布谷处处催春种。

淇上健儿归莫懒，城南思妇愁多梦。

安得壮士挽天河，净洗甲兵长不用。

诗歌按内容可分为四段，每段十二句。第一段写当前的平叛形势：总体上是官兵节节胜利，叛军亡在旦夕，只待朔方节度使郭子仪去收拾残局；但也有让人担忧的事，那就是帮助唐王朝平叛的回纥军队在京城驻扎。他希望肃宗安不忘危，勿忘三年来君臣播迁、军民苦战的艰难。第二段盛赞郭子仪、李光

长安皇宫（大明宫）复原图
The restored map of palace in Chang' an

bringing order to China. It showed Du Fu's great joy over the prosperity that followed the retaking of the capital. But it also mildly satirized the conflict between Emperor Suzong and his father Emperor Xuanzong, insinuating that Emperor Suzong should fulfill his duty as a son and show his filial respect to Emperor Xuanzong. The third stanza satirized the court's arbitrary conferring of titles of earls and princes, hoping that Emperor Suzong would trust and give important positions to talented ministers such as Fang Guan and Zhang Hao so as to complete the great cause of prosperity. The fourth stanza said that victory was in view, as auspicious signs appeared one after another, expressing the wish that war would disappear and that the world would be in peace.

When writing about the generals in the poem, Du Fu combined individual depiction with group portrayal and integrated heroic group portraits with sharp individual images. The poem also displayed a high degree of artistic generalization when writing about current affairs. For example, the poet used the two lines "Music of homesickness has been played by the pipes for three years / There every bush and tree looks like an enemy" to summarize the situation in the three years since the An Shi Rebellion. He also used the two lines "Where could we find soldiers mighty enough to call down heaven's water / To wash their weapons clean, never to be used again for many a long year" to show the people's hatred of war, as well as their earnest expectation and yearning for peace. Each twelve lines of the forty-eight line poem shared one rhyme, and the corresponding content also formed one stanza. The poem had a strongly accented rhythm with a smooth and sonorous tone. Due to its rich connotations and high degree of artistic technique, this poem has earned a great many favorable comments throughout history. When compiling the poems of Du Fu, Ouyang Xiu, Han Yu and Li Bai into one collection, Wang Anshi of the Song Dynasty listed this poem as the first and best one.

In June of the first year of the Qianyuan reign (758 A.D.), Emperor Suzong ordered that Fang Guan be convicted and demoted to be Governor of Binzhou. Those closely related to Fang Guan, such as Yan Wu, were also implicated, and even Du Fu was demoted to be Commissioner of Education in Huazhou (now Huaxian County in Shaanxi). With boundless love for the imperial city in his heart, Du Fu was forced to walk again through the Golden Light Gate, the same gate through which he had fled from Chang'an when he escaped from the rebels. He stopped his horse, gazing for a long time at Chang'an's thousands of gates and millions of houses. Perhaps he realized that his own political career was at an end. In fact, Du Fu would never return to the capital for the rest of his life.

The commissioner of education was a post whose duty was to assist local

弼等中兴名将整顿乾坤之功，为收京后初见的中兴气象而欣喜，但也委婉地讽刺了肃宗与其父玄宗之间的矛盾，表达了对肃宗克尽子道、孝敬玄宗的期望。第三段讽刺朝廷滥封爵王，望肃宗信任并重用房琯、张镐等有才能的大臣，完成中兴大业。第四段说胜利在望，祥瑞纷呈，企盼从此消弭战祸，天下太平。

这首诗在写中兴诸将时，将个体描写和群像描写结合起来，既有统一的英雄群像，又有鲜明的个体形象。在写时事方面，表现出高度的艺术概括力。例如，用"三年笛里关山月，万国兵前草木风"二句，就将安史之乱三年来的形势概括出来。又如用"安得壮士挽天河，净洗甲兵长不用"二句，表达了人民痛恨战争，渴望和平的热切期盼。全诗四十八句，每十二句一转韵，内容也自成一节，读来声调铿锵，节奏鲜明而语气流畅。由于它丰富的内涵和高度的艺术技巧，历来受到大量好评。宋代的王安石选杜甫、欧阳修、韩愈、李白四家诗，将这首诗列为压卷之作。

乾元元年（758）六月，肃宗下制数房琯罪，贬豳州刺史，与房琯关系密切的严武等人受到牵连，杜甫也被贬为华州（今陕西华县）司功参军。怀着对皇城的无限留恋，诗人被迫又一次穿过金光门——这也是当年他从叛军手里逃脱，逃出长安的城门。他勒住马久久地回望着皇城的千门万户，也许已经意识到自己的政治生涯将从此结束。而事实上，从此一别，杜甫一生再没有回到京城中来。

司功参军是协助地方长官管理当地祭祀、礼乐、学校、选

officials in managing local sacrifices, rites, schools, elections, social welfare and examinations. On behalf of Governor Guo, the senior official of Huazhou, Du Fu wrote an essay entitled "Analysis of Progress Made in Wiping out Enemy Remnants" and another article entitled "Five Strategies Presented by a Candidate Selected from the Exam Held in Huazhou in the First Year of the Qianyuan Reign," in which he insightfully put forward many ideas. Despite all this, Governor Guo treated him as nothing but a common document-writing official. It was July at the time, with severe heat and troublesome flies and scorpions. Looking at the documents piled up on the desk, Du Fu found it hard to tolerate.

But Du Fu's passion for poetry did not abate. During the one-year term as Commissioner of Education in Huazhou, he composed numerous poems on a broad range of themes. Since he was now closer to the common people after having left the capital, the poems he wrote were also closer to reality. In September of that year, Emperor Suzong ordered nine governors, including Guo Ziyi (Governor of Shuofang), Li Guangbi (Governor of Hedong) and Dong Ting (Governor of Forces of Pinglu), to lead one hundred thousand troops to encircle and suppress the rebel troops. As the troops of Li Siye, Governor of Zhenxi and Beiting, passed Huazhou, Du Fu watched the measured formation of the troops from four garrison posts including Guici, Yutian, Shule and Suiye and wrote the poems entitled "Two Poems on Watching Troops of Anxi Heading for Central Shaanxi to Wait for Orders." In the poems, he commented that "The four garrison posts were manned by elite troops / Who were matchless in humbling the enemy." He also thought that "They could conquer regions north of the Yellow River / And devote their own lives to the emperor."

At the end of that year, Du Fu returned to Luoyang and Yanshi to visit his hometown. At the beginning of the next year, Du Fu arrived at his old residence Luhun Village, which had changed beyond recognition, having been desolated at its capture by the rebels.

> Flowers have come into bud in the old garden;
> Birds have flown back in the spring days.
> As it has been deserted for such a long time,
> Little news is heard between the east and the west.
> ("Two Poems on Recalling My Younger Brothers")

One of his brothers was seeking refuge elsewhere, and his sister-in-law has also gone away from home. In addition, one of his cousins had perished in

举、医篓、考课等事的官职。杜甫为华州的长官郭使君代笔，写了一篇献给皇帝的《进灭残寇形势图状》，又写过一篇《乾元元年华州试进士策问五首》，都提出一些很有见地的主张。但是郭使君只把他当一般的笔吏任用。当时正逢七月酷暑，蝇蝎扰人，文书堆案，诗人觉得难以忍受。

但是他的诗兴却没有因此而减退，在任华州司功参军一年的时间里作诗颇多，题材也很丰富。由于离开京城，更加接近社会生活和人民群众，因而他笔下的诗歌也更加贴近现实。这年九月，唐肃宗令朔方节度使郭子仪、河东节度使李光弼等九位节度及平卢兵马使董庭等率数十万大军围剿叛军。当镇西北庭节度使李嗣业的军队经过华州时，杜甫观看了龟兹、于阗、疏勒、碎叶四镇大军的严整阵容，写下了《观安西兵过赴关中待命二首》，赞扬道："四镇富精锐，摧锋皆绝伦。"并觉得他们能够"谈笑无河北，心肝奉至尊"。

年底，杜甫曾回到洛阳、偃师探望家乡。第二年初，诗人到达旧居陆浑庄。这里经过叛军占领，已经人事全非，十分萧条：

　　故园花自发，春日鸟还飞。
　　断绝人烟久，东西消息稀。
　　　　——《忆弟二首》

他的一个弟弟逃难在外，弟媳也已辞家而去，还有一个从

Hejian Prefecture (now Hejian in Hebei) three years before. Du Fu was devastated, and even the dog he once raised was sad, nestling up against him. "The old dog understood my worry and hate / So it lowered its head to lean against my bed" ("Hearing the News about My Brothers"). He stayed at Yanshi for a short while and then returned to Luoyang in February.

At that moment, An Qingxu was strongly entrenched in Yecheng City (now Anyang in Henan), resisting the hundreds of thousands of government troops besieging the city. An Qingxu turned to Shi Siming for help, promising to give up the throne to him. As a result, Shi Siming betrayed the court again and announced himself to be "Saint King of the Great Yan" in Weizhou in February of the second year of the Qianyuan reign (759 A.D.). Later, he led his troops southward to the aid of Yecheng City. As there was no general who could command all the soldiers, the Tang troops encircling the city waited to attack for several months, thus losing their opportunity to win the battle. On the third of March, just at the moment when the two sides were fighting the decisive battle, a fierce gale suddenly sprang up, darkening the sky and obscuring everything so that troops of both sides fled in terror. The Tang troops suffered hundreds of thousands of losses. Guo Ziyi had to lead the troops of Shuofang to destroy Heyang Bridge so that they could buy time for their retreat to Luoyang, hoping to defend it with the help of troops from Wang Sili, Governor of Zelu. Because of the defeat, all the other troops retreated to their own provinces. The once relaxed situation became tense again. Du Fu, then staying at Luoyang, had to leave in a hurry at this moment of war. He traveled first to Xin'an (now Xin'an in Henan), then went to Shihao Village (now Shaan-xian in Henan) and returned to Huazhou through Tongguan Pass later. On his way, he met with people who were seeking refuge, witnessing the hardships suffered by the people as a result of the oppression of both the rebels and the government.

On the road to Xin'an, Du Fu was making his way in a hurry when he saw several minor officials fussing about and creating a total mess. He wondered if they were gathering and reviewing soldiers, so he went up to ask one official about it.

Seeing that Du Fu was his superior, the official answered, "We are recruiting soldiers to deal with the emergency. An order came last night that young boys and older men should all be recruited."

Du Fu asked, "What can boys of seventeen or eighteen do? Will they be able to hold the cities?"

"What can we do then? Our county is so small that only these boys are left

弟三年前已死在河间郡（今河北河间）。杜甫感到十分悲伤，连以前养过的那条狗也悲伤起来，和他相依相偎："旧犬知愁恨，垂头傍我床。"（《得舍弟消息》）他在偃师稍事停留，二月回到洛阳。

这时安庆绪固守邺城（今河南安阳），唐十节度数十万大军围困邺城后，安庆绪向史思明求救，许愿让位。于是史思明又一次叛变朝廷，于乾元二年（759）二月在魏州自称"大燕圣王"，然后引兵南下，救援邺城。唐军因为没有节制全军的统帅，围攻邺城已达数月而没有发动总攻，丧失了战机。三月三日，正当两军决战时，突然狂风大作，天昏地暗，两军惊走。唐军损失惨重，十万甲仗遗弃殆尽，郭子仪引朔方兵断河阳桥，与关内泽潞节度使王思礼退保洛阳，其他诸路兵马都溃归本镇。一度缓和的形势重新变得紧张起来。身在洛阳的杜甫值此战乱，只得匆忙离开。他先到新安（今河南新安），再到石壕村（今河南陕县），经潼关而后回到华州。他一路上都遇见了逃难的百姓，亲眼看见在叛军和官府的双重压迫下人民所遭受的苦难。

在新安道上，诗人匆匆赶路，远远看见一群村民中夹杂着几个小吏，吵吵闹闹，乱成一片。诗人心想：莫不是又在点兵？他走上前去向一个小吏询问。

小吏见杜甫是个官员，回答说："这是征兵咧，情况紧急得很，昨日夜里才来的命令，说中男以上的都得应征。"

"这十七八岁小孩能干啥？他们守得住城池？"诗人说道。

"那有啥办法？咱们这个县小，成年男子都选完了，就只

after the men were all recruited. If another order comes to recruit soldiers, I have no idea who is left to draft."

Thus, continued the war to suppress the rebellion. Some of the young boys who were to go to war were sent off by their mothers, while others stood alone by the roadside with nobody to bid farewell to. Seeing these miserable people and listening to their mournful sobbing, Du Fu felt as though a knife were piercing his heart; nevertheless, he could do nothing but try to control his own mood and manage to offer a few words of consolation and encouragement. Thus, came the poem entitled "Minor Officials of Xin'an."

> Traveling alone, I came to the road in Xin'an,
> Where I heard noisy mustering of soldiers for a roll call.
> I asked one minor official of Xin'an about the matter,
> And he said, "There are no more male adults, as the county is small.
> But an order came last night
> That younger boys are to be recruited as well."
> "As boys are too short and young,
> How are they to guard the cities?"
> Plump boys bid farewell to their mothers
> While lean boys said goodbye to nobody at all.
> They went like water flowing to the east with no return
> While their family were still crying against the green hill.
> "Don't dry your eyes from too much crying.
> Just stop weeping your flood of tears.
> Even if your eyes are blinded and your bones laid bare,
> Heaven and earth would still grant no mercy to you.
> Our troops had laid siege to Yecheng city;
> Day and night, we hoped it could be conquered soon.
> Who knew that the rebels were so tenacious
> That our troops retreated in defeat like scattered stars.
> They would eat near their old camps;
> They would have drill in the old capital.
> They would not dig the trenches too deep,
> And the work of herding horses wouldn't be too heavy.
> In the righteous war we are fighting,
> The soldiers are well-treated by their officers.
> Try not to shed tears of blood
> As the commander treats soldiers like fathers and brothers."

有这些小男孩咧！再来一次征兵，连我也不知道让谁去咧。"

　　形势已至如此，但平叛的战争是一定要进行下去的。看着将要赶赴战场的小男孩，他们中有的尚有母亲相送，有的竟然无人相送，孤零零地站在路旁。看着这些可怜的人们，听着他们凄惨的哭声，诗人心如刀绞，但只能控制住自己的情绪，勉强说了一番宽慰和勉励的话，这就是《新安吏》：

　　　客行新安道，喧呼闻点兵。
　　　借问新安吏，"县小更无丁。
　　　府帖昨夜下，次选中男行。"
　　　"中男绝短小，何以守王城？"
　　　肥男有母送，瘦男独伶俜。
　　　白水暮东流，青山犹哭声。
　　　"莫自使眼枯，收汝泪纵横。
　　　眼枯即见骨，天地终无情。
　　　我军取相州，日夕望其平。
　　　岂意贼难料，归军星散营。
　　　就粮近故垒，练卒依旧京。
　　　掘壕不到水，牧马役亦轻。
　　　况乃王师顺，抚养甚分明。
　　　送行勿泣血，仆射如父兄。"

Du Fu continued his way. One evening, he stayed at a family's house in Shihao Village. At midnight, there came a heavy bang on the door. Knowing that the government officials were coming to recruit men again, the old man of the family immediately climbed over the wall to escape, while the old woman went out to see what was happening. Du Fu heard the officials scolding the old woman loudly and angrily while she pled with them for mercy, weeping and sniffling. It turned out that two boys of the family had died on the battlefield while another son was still fighting at the frontier. One of the dead sons had been married with a baby, and since the baby had not yet been weaned, the daughter-in-law had not yet remarried. But as the family was too poor to even have a dress for her to wear, she couldn't come out to meet people at all. Finally, the old woman told the officials that she was willing to go to the frontier with them, old and feeble as she was. She urged them to take her away quickly so that she could be in time to cook breakfast for the soldiers the next day.

> I came to Shihao Village to stop over for the night,
> When I heard officials coming to recruit men.
> The old man climbed over the wall to flee
> While the old woman came out to watch.
> How angrily the officials shouted!
> How bitterly the woman cried out,
> Pleading them to listen to her miserable life:
> "My three sons all went to Yecheng battle.
> One of them just sent a letter home,
> Telling the news of the death of the other two.
> The alive could only drag out a miserable existence
> While the dead are long gone with the wind.
> There is no man to be found in my house
> Except for my grandson still in need of suckling.
> Because of this young grandson, his mother has not yet left,
> But she's unable to come out for lack of a dress.
> Though I am a feeble and old woman,
> I volunteer to go with you tonight
> So that I can get to Heyang Post as early as possible,
> In time to prepare breakfast for them."
> It became dead silent late at night,
> But the sound of weeping seemed to be heard.
> I set out on my journey at daybreak,

诗人继续赶路，一天晚上，投宿在石壕村的一户人家。半夜里，突然响起巨大的打门声，这家的老汉知道又是官吏来捉人，便赶紧翻过院墙逃跑了，老妇人就出门去察看。杜甫听到官吏们怒气冲冲地呵斥老妇人，老妇人则哭哭啼啼地求着情。原来他们家的两个男孩子已经战死，另一个儿子还在前线。阵亡的儿子中有一个已经结婚生子，因为孩子还在哺乳期，所以儿媳妇并没有改嫁，但是家里穷得连一件完整的裙子都没有，所以根本无法出门见人。最后那老妇人请求官吏：自己虽然年老体衰，但是情愿跟随官吏上前线去。她催促差役快点领着自己出发，这样还能赶上为士兵们做第二天的早餐：

暮投石壕村，有吏夜捉人。

老翁逾墙走，老妇出门看。

吏呼一何怒，妇啼一何苦！

听妇前致词："三男邺城戍。

一男附书至，二男新战死。

存者且偷生，死者长已矣。

室中更无人，惟有乳下孙。

有孙母未去，出入无完裙。

老妪力虽衰，请从吏夜归。

急应河阳役，犹得备晨炊。"

夜久语声绝，如闻泣幽咽。

Bidding farewell to the old man alone.
　　　("Minor Officials of Shihao")

The poem provided objective narration in plain words, with no subjective commentary at all, but the writing exuded the strong emotions of the poet. The line "When I heard officials coming to recruit men" expressed the poet's indignation that these officials did not recruit soldiers in the daytime but rather came stealthily under the cover of night. In addition, they did not select men by official records, but caught people arbitrarily, be they men or women, young or old. The old woman's painful account to the officials showed the poet's sympathy for the miserable fate of the family and his respect for the old woman's strong character and loyalty. The poem ended with the line "Bidding farewell to the old man alone," making readers lapse into deep thought, grief and indignation.

Du Fu went on with his journey and came to Tongguan Pass. Tongguan Pass was the east door of Chang'an, so when An Lushan seized it three years before, Emperor Xuanzong had to flee westward in a panic. Perhaps because the Tang court had learnt its lesson, or perhaps because it was under pressure after the defeat in Yecheng City, the present Tongguan Pass garrison had been made very sturdy. Du Fu asked an official supervising the building of the city about how the construction was going, and the officer boasted with great confidence to Du Fu about the sturdiness of the city. Hearing this, Du Fu persuaded them in all sincerity to exercise utmost caution to ensure that the tragedy of losing the capital due to the capture of Tongguan Pass three years before would never repeat itself.

How busy the soldiers were moving around,
Building the city walls of Tongguan Pass.
Giant city walls were more solid than iron
While small ones were thousands of meters tall.
To an official, I asked the following question:
"Are the walls built to defend against the Tartar rebels once again?"
Asking me to get off my horse,
He pointed at the distant mountains and said to me,
"The dense defensive stakes rise high up into the sky,
So that even birds have no way to fly over.
When the Tartar rebels come, the walls will surely be safe,
Leaving no worry as to the recapture of the Western Capital.
Please look at this strategic position, old sir.

天明登前途，独与老翁别。

——《石壕吏》

全诗只以朴素的笔墨做客观叙述，没有任何主观评论，但笔端却流露着诗人强烈的感情。"有吏夜捉人"表达出作者的愤怒：官吏不是在白天征兵，而是在夜幕的掩护下偷偷潜至。不是按帖选人，而是不分男女老幼地胡乱捉人。对老妇人向官吏痛苦陈词的叙述，渗透着诗人对这家人悲惨遭遇的同情，也流露出对那位老妪坚强品格和奉献精神的敬意。最后以"独与老翁别"作结，戛然而止，更让读者陷入无穷的沉思和悲愤中。

杜甫继续前行，来到潼关。潼关是长安东面的门户，三年前安禄山攻陷潼关，导致玄宗仓皇西奔。也许是接受了这次教训，也许是迫于邺城兵败之后的严峻形势，如今的潼关城修筑得十分坚固。杜甫向正在督促筑城的一个官吏打听筑城情况，那官吏就信心十足地向杜甫夸耀起城防之坚来。杜甫听了后，还是语重心长地劝告他们一定要慎之又慎，千万不要让三年前潼关失而京城陷的悲剧重演：

士卒何草草，筑城潼关道。

大城铁不如，小城万丈余。

借问潼关吏："修关还备胡？"

要我下马行，为我指山隅：

"连云列战格，飞鸟不能逾。

胡来但自守，岂复忧西都？

It is so narrow that only one cart can cross at a time.
When a soldier wields his long halberd with force,
He is mighty enough to guard the pass alone."
"What grief we feel for the battle in the Peach Orchard,
Where millions of soldiers turned into food for fish!
So please tell the generals who guard the pass
Not to learn from general Geshu any more."

("Minor Officials of Tongguan Pass")

When writing the "Three Poems on Minor Officials," Du Fu's feelings were mixed. He firmly advocated the war by the Tang court to suppress the rebellion and safeguard the unity of the nation. He had great sympathy for the people, many of whom had made the ultimate sacrifice to support the war. He harbored bitter hatred for people like An Lushan and Shi Siming who launched the rebellion. He also felt grieved because of those rulers who had caused the disaster by not caring about the well-being of the people. All these complex feelings of indignation, grief, irony, sorrow and consolation were juxtaposed in this collection of poems.

The poet also wrote a group of "Three Poems on Departure."

Departure on a Wedding Night

Like dodders climbing up short fleabanes and hemps,
Our marriage is doomed not to last long.
Marrying a recruited soldier like you,
I'd rather be abandoned at the side of road.
Though I have become your wife,
I can hardly get our bed warm before you have to leave.
I have to say goodbye to you at dawn.
Is there such a rush for you to depart?
Though you will not travel far,
Just going to Heyang to guard the frontier,
My place as your wife is not yet made clear.
How can I render service to your parents?
When my parents were raising me,
They always hid me inside home all day long.
A daughter will always marry a man,
Following him wherever he goes.
You are heading for the place of death soon,
Which grieves me deeply.
I wish to follow you to war,

丈人视要处，窄狭容单车。

艰难奋长戟，万古用一夫。"

"哀哉桃林战，百万化为鱼。

请嘱防关将，慎勿学哥舒。"

——《潼关吏》

在写"三吏"这组诗时，杜甫的心情非常矛盾。对于唐王朝平定叛乱、维护国家统一的战争，他坚决拥护。但百姓为支持这场战争作出了惨重的牺牲，他又是极为同情。对于发动叛乱的安史之流，他切齿痛恨，而对于酿成灾祸却不管人民死活的统治者，他也感到无比的愤慨。所以这组诗里，激愤、悲痛、讽刺、哀伤、抚慰等情感融合在一起，构成了诗人复杂的心态。

这期间，诗人还创作了"三别"一组诗。

新婚别

兔丝附蓬麻，引蔓故不长。

嫁女与征夫，不如弃路旁。

结发为妻子，席不暖君床。

暮婚晨告别，无乃太匆忙。

君行虽不远，守边赴河阳。

妾身未分明，何以拜姑嫜。

父母养我时，日夜令我藏。

生女有所归，鸡狗亦得将。

君今往死地，沈痛迫中肠。

But I'm afraid that I'll only bring trouble to you.

Please don't worry about me.

Work hard and do your best in the army.

If a woman stays with the army,

The morale of soldiers will be affected.

I feel so sorry to be born of a poor family

That it has taken me such a long time to get this wedding dress.

But I'm taking it off and will never wear it again,

And I'm washing the make-up off my face.

Looking up at the flying birds,

I see they fly in couples, be they big or small.

Though life is never easy,

I'll look forward to seeing you forever.

In the ancient times, new brides usually didn't meet their husbands until their wedding, so they always felt very shy and unwilling to speak. This holds true for the "I" depicted in this poem. Who could imagine that her husband would be forced to head for "the place of death," forcing her to part forever with her husband after her wedding night? Because of this she was not able to think about anything else, left only to pour out her feelings to her husband, telling him about her sadness and sense of loss. Nevertheless, she knew clearly what was right and proper and understood the necessity of the war against the rebels, so she also encouraged her husband to fight hard and asked him not to miss her. In her husband's presence, she took off the wedding dress that her family had sacrificed to buy and washed the new make-up off her face: This meant that she would never be attracted to any other man as "a woman applies make-up only for the man who loves her." With this resolute gesture, she showed her faithful love, hoping also to relieve her husband of his family worries so that he would have more courage to fight against the enemy. The poem began and ended with metaphors, mirroring the tone of a village woman. Her sweet tone became resolute and decisive as she encouraged her husband to set off and as she showed her own loyalty. The poem took the form of self-narration by the bride, but it vividly depicted a lively and moving image of a newly-married woman. The poet's sympathy and admiration for the people permeated through the whole piece.

Departure of an Old Man

As there is a constant ruckus all around,

I, an old man, can find no peace.

誓欲随君去，形势反苍黄。

勿为新婚念，努力事戎行。

妇人在军中，兵气恐不扬。

自嗟贫家女，久致罗襦裳。

罗襦不复施，对君洗红妆。

仰视百鸟飞，大小必双翔。

人事多错迕，与君永相望。

在古代，刚过门的新媳妇多半与丈夫没有见过面，要开口说话总是很羞涩，此诗中所写的"我"也是如此。可是谁料新婚才一夜就面临着生离死别，丈夫被迫前往"死地"，她也就顾不得许多了。她絮絮叨叨地向丈夫倾吐衷肠，诉说自己的伤心与失落。可是她又是一位深明大义的妇女，深知平叛战争的必要性，所以又鼓励丈夫努力作战，勿以新婚为念。她当着新婚丈夫的面脱下全家人费尽心血才置办起来的新嫁衣，洗去脸上新化的红妆——"女为悦己者容"，她从此不会再为别的异性而动心了。她以如此果决的行动表明了自己坚贞不渝的爱情，这也是为了消除丈夫的后顾之忧以增加他的杀敌勇气。全诗以比喻开头，以比喻作结，酷肖农村妇女的口吻。在鼓励丈夫前行、表白自己忠贞时，她的语气则从缠绵委婉变为斩钉截铁。全诗皆为新娘自述，却逼真、传神地塑造出了新嫁女子生动感人的形象，而且诗人对人民的同情、敬佩也充溢于字里行间。

垂老别

四郊未宁静，垂老不得安。

Since my children have all been killed in battle,
How can I live in the world alone?
Throwing away my walking stick, I leave home.
Even those who will travel together feel sad for me.
It is fortunate that my teeth are still in my mouth,
But my energy has long since left me.
Putting on armor and helm,
All I can do is to bow low to the officers.
My old wife is crouching on the roadside, crying.
She's still wearing thin clothes at the end of the year.
I understand we could be forever parted,
But I'm still worried that she will be too cold.
It is destined that I not return,
But my wife still asks me to eat more.
The city walls are solid and safe,
And it won't be easy to cross the Xingyuan Town.
The situation now is different than before,
So it will be a long time before I die.
Parting is inevitable in life.
How could we know whether it will come at young or old age?
Recalling the days when I was still young,
I linger about and heave a deep sigh.
The whole country is at war,
So that beacon fires cover all the hills.
Grass and trees give out smell of blood from numerous bodies.
Mountains and fields are covered with streams of blood.
Where can we find a paradise
That would make us linger on and not leave?
Giving up my old cottage forever,
My old heart is broken.

The poem is composed of the parting words of an old man drafted into the army. All his sons and grandsons had died in the war, and now he was to lay down his walking stick to head for the battlefield. Even those who were recruited at the same time grieved for his miserable experience. In the severe northern winter, his wife wore thin clothes, crouching on the roadside, shivering and crying in the cold wind. Though the old couple knew clearly that they would be parted in life or separated by death, the old wife still urged her husband to have more food at the moment of departure. Looking far and wide,

子孙阵亡尽，焉用身独完。
投杖出门去，同行为辛酸。
幸有牙齿存，所悲骨髓干。
男儿既介胄，长揖别上官。
老妻卧路啼，岁暮衣裳单。
孰知是死别，且复伤其寒。
此去必不归，还闻劝加餐。
土门壁甚坚，杏园度亦难。
势异邺城下，纵死时犹宽。
人生有离合，岂择衰盛端。
忆昔少壮日，迟回竟长叹。
万国尽征戍，烽火被冈峦。
积尸草木腥，流血川原丹。
何乡为乐土，安敢尚盘桓。
弃绝蓬室居，塌然摧肺肝。

一位垂暮老人被征入伍，全诗就由他临行时的话语组成。他的所有子孙都已在战争中阵亡了，现在他又要放下拐杖，前往战场，连同时被征召的人也为他如此辛酸的遭遇而叹息。在中国北方寒冷的隆冬季节，他的老妻还身穿单衣，这阵子正蜷缩在路边的寒风中战栗哭泣。尽管夫妻二人深知此番定是生离死别，但临行之际，老妻还是勉强劝丈夫要多吃点饭。放眼望

one could find battlefields with foul winds and blood like rain. The miserable fate of the old man was enough to break his heart. The emotions conveyed in this poem were deep and woeful; the thoughts expressed in it were complicated and subtle. Written in the words of the old man, the poem showed Du Fu's boundless sympathy and admiration.

Though the main characters of the last two poems met with great misfortune, they were still able to pour out their feelings to their family and friends. The hero in the poem entitled "Departure Alone" did not even have someone to bid farewell to, only able to grieve to himself after being recruited for the second time.

Departure Alone

I felt so lonely after the Tianbao reign;
My home was overgrown with wild grass.
There used to be about a hundred families,
Who fled in all directions at the outbreak of war.
Those alive were nowhere to be found
While those dead have turned to dirt and mud.
After the defeat at Yecheng battle,
I came back to find the old way.
Walking for a long time, I saw empty lanes
In dim light and desolation all around.
I finally found a couple of foxes
Growling angrily at me with their fur on end.
Where are all the old neighbors?
Only a couple of widowed old women are left home.
Even birds love their own branches.
How could I leave my home in its poverty?
I did the hoeing in spring
And watered the fields at dusk.
As the county officials knew my return,
They called me to practice beating drums.
Though I am to serve in the local place,
I have not even a family member to part with at home.
I'm lucky to serve in a place so close to home,
For who knows what would happen if I were sent far away.
Since my hometown no longer exists,
What's the difference between close and distant places?
I would forever grieve for my sick mother,

去，到处是腥风血雨的战场，此情此景，此种命运，让这垂暮老人心如刀割，肝肠寸断。诗中写情缱绻悱恻，心事曲折细微，毕肖老人口吻，其中倾注着诗人无限的同情和敬佩之情。

上面两首诗中的主人公虽然遭遇不幸，但总算还可以对自己的亲友倾诉一番，而《无家别》中的主人公则连告别的对象都没有，只好在第二次被征入伍时孤零零地喃喃自语：

无家别

寂寞天宝后，园庐但蒿藜。
我里百余家，世乱各东西。
存者无消息，死者为尘泥。
贱子因阵败，归来寻旧蹊。
久行见空巷，日瘦气惨凄。
但对狐与狸，竖毛怒我啼。
四邻何所有？一二老寡妻。
宿鸟恋本枝，安辞且穷栖。
方春独荷锄，日暮还灌畦。
县吏知我至，召令习鼓鞞。
虽从本州役，内顾无所携。
近行止一身，远去终转迷。
家乡既荡尽，远近理亦齐。
永痛长病母，五年委沟豁。

Who died five years ago with no coffin.
As her son, I could do nothing for her,
So both of us felt remorseful all our lives.
If a person has no family to part with,
How can he be asked to be human?

The man in the poem told of his own miserable experience, but as there was no one to listen, his tone appeared very smooth, revealing his grievous and resigned mood. In this extreme state of resignation, he even used patient words to comfort himself, but in the end, he still uttered words of sorrow and indignation. Weren't the ones he denounced those rulers of the Tang Dynasty who should have shouldered the most responsibility for bringing about this war?

This poem group of six well-structured poems reflected social life during the An Shi Rebellion. The poems revealed the great disaster that the rebellion had brought to the common folk, bitterly condemning the bloody crimes of the rebels and criticizing the Tang rulers who had caused the war by not caring about the well-being of the people. In the poems, Du Fu successfully portrayed the people at the bottom of society who, despite suffering extreme pain and heartache, were still strong-willed when faced with hardships, singing praise to the people's patriotism and heroic spirit. In terms of writing techniques, readers are offered both a general view of the whole society and vivid detailed description. In the "Three Poems on Minor Officials," the poet appeared on the scene himself, employing dialogues, which featured great narrative power, vivid scene creation and lifelike details. In the "Three Poems on Departure," the poet selected three typical plots, including wedding departure, departure of an old man and departure alone, employing the form of monologue by the central character to reveal their fate and the inner conflict in their mind. In this way, three typical personalities were depicted with strong emotions.

In contrast to "Feelings Expressed in Five Hundred Words after Traveling from the Capital to Fengxian County" and "Traveling to the North," the "Three Poems on Minor Officials" and the "Three Poems on Departure" covered a broader range of themes. The first two poems were about the court, the emperor and the poet himself, while these six poems were about lower society and the common people. These were also a group of *Yuefu* folk songs with new themes. Compared with the two groups of poems, entitled "Coming out to the Border Area," composed before and after, the content was more profound. The other two poems each described one soldier, while this group of poems wrote about six characters who were all well-rounded, vivid and lifelike. In terms of artistic approach, the "Three Poems on Minor Officials"

　　生我不得力，终身两酸嘶。

　　人生无家别，何以为蒸黎？

　　诗歌中的男子诉说着自己的悲惨遭遇，由于无人倾听，他的语气显得比较平缓，流露出沉痛的无奈情绪。在极端的无奈中，他甚至用近似旷达的话语来安慰自己，但是最后他还是发出了悲愤的诘责。这诘责的对象，不正是应该为造成这场战乱负最大责任的唐朝统治者吗？

　　这六首精心结构的大型组诗，是安史之乱中社会生活面貌的真实写照。诗歌真实地反映了安史之乱给广大人民所造成的惨重灾难，沉痛控诉了安史叛军的血腥罪恶，鞭挞了造成战乱而又不顾人民死活的唐王朝统治者。诗中成功地塑造了几个在战争中遭受了各种巨大的伤害而依然坚强面对苦难的底层老百姓的形象，热情歌颂了人民的爱国精神和英雄气概。写法上，既有对整个社会面貌的鸟瞰，又有生动的细节描写。在"三吏"中，诗人自己出场，采用对话的方式，叙事性较强，场景逼真，细节生动。在"三别"中，选取新婚别、垂老别、无家别三个典型的情节，采用抒情主人公独白的方式展现其命运，揭示其内心的矛盾和冲突，从而刻画了几个个性鲜明的典型人物形象，抒情性很浓。

　　与《自京赴奉先县咏怀五百字》和《北征》相比，"三吏""三别"题材更扩大了。那两首写的是朝廷、皇帝和诗人自己，这六首写的是下层社会和劳动人民。这又是一组新题乐府诗，与前、后《出塞》两组旧题乐府比起来，内容更深入了：那两组各写一个士兵，这一组则写了六个人物，而且个个形象丰满，有血有肉，栩栩如生。在艺术表现上，"三吏""三别"也取得

and the "Three Poems on Departure" also made new achievements. For example, when describing sceneries, the poems infused feelings into the landscape so that the feelings and the setting were successfully integrated; when narrating stories, the poems gave careful description to common plots so as to reflect a broader range of social life; when writing about people, the poems carried on the tradition of the *Yuefu* folk songs of the Han Dynasty, employing individualized language to depict the images of the characters. All in all, the "Three Poems on Minor Officials" and the "Three Poems on Departure" represent a high point in Du Fu's five-character ancient verses.

Altogether, Du Fu wrote over two hundred and sixty five-character ancient verses, bringing the development of this style of poetry to its high point. Among his representative works were single poems, including such masterpieces as "Feelings Expressed in Five Hundred Words after Traveling from the Capital to Fengxian County" and "Traveling to the North," as well as short-length ones such as "Driving My Sons to Pick Cockleburs" and "Dispelling Depression from a Perilous Experience." The representative group poems included the poems entitled "Coming out to the Border Area," "Three Poems Written at Qiangcun Village," the "Three Poems on Minor Officials" and the "Three Poems on Departure" and so on. In terms of art, his techniques of expression were rich and colorful, the structure was complex and meticulous, and the language was penetrating, epigrammatic and profound, representing the highest achievement in the Chinese poetic history of five-character ancient verse composition.

Laozi said, "Lean years follow a great war." At the beginning of the Qianyuan reign, the Central Shaanxi Region suffered from severe drought and famine. Du Fu wrote two poems, both starting from the drought and heat: "Sigh in Summer Days" and "Sigh in Summer Nights." He sympathized with the people in misery, saying, "Millions of people are still wandering about / So only wild grass could be seen when one looked about" ("Sigh in Summer Days"). He also had pity on the soldiers guarding the frontier: "Pity on the soldiers carrying weapons / Who have to guard the frontier all the year round / How can they find a way to take a hot bath? / They have no choice but to look at each other in the heat" ("Sigh in Summer Nights"). He suspected that it was the tyranny of the court that had brought about the wrath of Heaven and the anger of man, exclaiming, "There has been no thunder sent from heaven / Is it because something is wrong with heaven's order?" ("Sigh in Summer Days") This showed his growing disappointment with the politics of the court.

了新的成就，如：写景方面善于融情入景，做到情景交融；叙事方面，善于细致刻画典型的情节以展现广阔的社会生活；写人方面，继承并发扬了汉乐府的优秀传统，用个性化的人物语言来刻画人物形象。总之，"三吏""三别"是杜甫五古创作中的新高峰。

杜甫一共写了二百六十多首五言古诗，把这种诗歌体裁发展到了登峰造极的地步。其代表作，单篇的既有《自京赴奉先县咏怀五百字》《北征》这样的鸿篇巨制，也有《驱竖子摘苍耳》《遭遇》等较小的篇什，组诗有《前出塞》、《后出塞》、《羌村三首》、"三吏""三别"等。这些诗歌具有极强的现实意义。艺术上，表现手法丰富多彩，结构错综复杂而又严整缜密，语言精警深沉，代表了中国古代诗歌史上五言古诗创作的最高成就。

《老子》云："大军之后，必有凶年。"乾元初，关中地区一直旱得厉害，发生了大饥荒，杜甫以旱热起兴，作《夏日叹》和《夏夜叹》，他同情苦难的人民："万人尚流冗，举目唯蒿莱。"（《夏日叹》）又悲悯着戍边的士兵："念彼荷戈士，穷年守边疆。何由一洗濯，执热互相望。"（《夏夜叹》）他怀疑是朝廷的暴政引起天怒人怨："上天久无雷，无乃号令乖？"（《夏日叹》）可见他对朝廷政治是越来越失望了。

《垂老别》诗意画
Painting of *Departure of an Old Man*

四　流离陇蜀

Chapter Ⅳ　Drifting Through the Long and Shu Regions

Having experienced countless frustrations and political hazards in his official career, and having witnessed the miserable condition in the Central Shaanxi Region caused by political unrest, Du Fu finally saw through the nature of officialdom, and the idea of resignation, which he had revealed unintentionally during his time in office as Commissioner of the Left in Chang'an, grew ever stronger. Besides, the price of food was extremely high in the second year of the Qianyuan reign (759 A.D.) due to the severe drought in the Central Shaanxi Region, which strengthened his resolution to resign. In July of that year, he finally gave up his low position as Commissioner of Education in Huazhou. With deep resignation and disappointment, he took his family and left the war-torn Central Shaanxi Region. From then on, he left political life forever and started his wandering life, covering "tens of thousands of miles bustling about for food and clothing."

Du Fu's nephew Du Zuo lived in Qinzhou (now Tianshui in Gansu), eight hundred miles west of Chang'an, and his friend, Monk Zangong whom he had known in Chang'an, was also living in exile there. As Qinzhou had a good harvest that year, Du Fu took his family along to seek refuge there.

As the chill autumn wind sighed, the family took a treacherous road over the towering Longshan Mountain and arrived at Qinzhou. Du Fu wanted to buy a piece of land there and build a cottage on it to settle his family. He heard that there were dozens of families living in Dongke Valley, fifty *li* ❶ to the east of the city where Du Zuo lived. The valley was deep and quiet, its land suitable for growing millet, and its sunny slopes suitable for growing melons, so he investigated there but found no suitable place to settle in. Afterwards, he went to Xizhi Village to visit Zangong, who then accompanied him to the south hill to see another plot of land. He had intended to find a sunny place, but came back empty-handed. Later, he also heard that there were dense fir and lacquer trees to the west of Xizhi Village, where the climate was mild and the land fertile. He wanted to settle down there, but was again unable to find a suitable place. Such being the case, his life began to be difficult again. A new friend who was also living in seclusion, Ruan Fang, gave him thirty bundles of chives, which was not enough food to last for long. To make matters worse, he suffered a return of malaria that he had once caught in Chang'an. Stricken by hunger, cold and poverty, Du Fu had no choice but to resume his old profession of gathering and selling herbs to maintain his livelihood. Nevertheless, the poet did not feel dejected, a sentiment which can be seen in the following lines: "Cypress seeds are bitter, but they are still edible; / Shining rays of the sunlight are high, but they are just good as food" ("Empty

在经历了数次的仕途挫折和政治风险，目睹了关中乱离的惨状之后，杜甫终于看清了官场的本质。他在长安任左拾遗期间就流露出来的辞官念头这时更强烈了。加之乾元二年（759）关中大旱，粮价奇贵，这让杜甫更加坚定了去意。这年七月，他终于抛弃了华州司功参军的微职，怀着深深的无奈和失望，携带家小，离开了满目疮痍的关中地区，从此永远离开了政治中心，开始了"万里饥驱"的漂泊生活。

杜甫的侄儿杜佐住在长安以西八百里外的秦州（今甘肃天水），杜甫在长安认识的朋友赞公和尚也被放逐在那里，而这一年秦州的收成较好，所以杜甫便带着一家人投奔秦州而去。

秋风萧瑟的季节，一家人翻过高大陡峭、历来被视为畏途的陇山，到达秦州。杜甫想在秦州买一块地，盖一座草堂以安顿全家。他听说城东五十里❶处杜佐居住的东柯谷有十几户人家，山谷幽深寂静，土地可种小米，向阳坡上宜于种瓜，于是去那里察看，却没有找到合适的住处。他又去西枝村造访赞公，赞公陪他到南山看地址。他想找一个向阳的地方，可是没有如愿。后来又听说西枝村的西面有稠密的杉树、漆树，气候暖和，土地肥沃，他想在那里定居，还是没有成功。他的生活又发生了困难。新朋友阮昉是个隐士，他送给杜甫三十束韭菜，但显然解决不了问题。更糟的是在长安患过的疟疾又复发了。饥寒困顿中，杜甫只好又干起了采药、卖药的老本行来维持生计。但诗人并不颓唐："翠柏苦犹食，明霞高可餐。"（《空囊》）"囊

---

❶ 译者注：里，中国常用的长度单位。1里合500米。

❶ Translator's note: *li* - Chinese unit of length, equal to 500 metres.

Pockets"). " I'm afraid I'll be embarrassed if my pockets are empty / So I leave a coin in one pocket just in case" (ibid). It was through poetic expression that he kept his spirits high.

The family lived temporarily in Qinzhou City. As the surrounding landscape was full of beautiful scenry and as there were many places of historical interest nearby, Du Fu often went sightseeing when he had spare time. He visited Chongning Temple, north of Maiji Mountain, and Nanguo Temple, halfway up a hill in the south of the city, jotting down a series of poems. He also had great admiration for a household in the Red Valley seven miles to the west of the city, with pine trees and chrysanthemums highlighting each other's beauty, saying that it was just like the mysterious Land of Peach Blossoms depicted by Tao Yuanming of the Jin Dynasty.

In fact, Qinzhou was not a peaceful land either, for it contained a courier route to the Western Regions and was a strategic thoroughfare of the northwest. At that time, Qinzhou was threatened by the ever-stronger Tubo, making the situation extremely tense. Troops were stationed there, envoys came and went, and horns were often heard at dusk.

After experiencing the unique natural scenery and social customs of the border city of Qinzhou, Du Fu's poetry experienced a new change, creating a number of refreshing shorter poems. In these poems, Du Fu captured both the beautiful natural landscape as well as the distinctive border city atmosphere, thus organically integrating scenic poems with frontier poems. At the same time, due to the profound influence of the war, these poems also embodied Du Fu's consistent vigorous style, filled with concern for his country and his people.

These poems surpassed the scenic and pastoral poems which were prevelant at the height of the Tang Dynasty. Meng Haoran and Wang Wei, the representative poets of this style, both advocated reclusive living and freeing oneself from worldly cares; as such, they attempted to create a serene, beautiful, and idealized state in their scenic poems, which, either explicitly or implicitly, often revealed the concept of staying above worldly considerations contained in Buddhist doctrines and Taoist ideals. The images adopted in these poems often included lonely brushwood doors, empty woods beneath drizzling rain, fishermen or woodmen returning home at night, and so on. Because of their great number, such poems gradually became the norm of that time. But Du Fu did not follow this practice. Though he frequently mentioned living in seclusion, he did not want to transcend the worldly but just hope to find a quiet place to stay in. Since he was constantly concerned with real life, he kept depicting real scenes to express true emotions, without concentrating on

空恐羞涩，留得一钱看。"（同上）他就这样调节着自己的心情。

一家人暂时住在秦州城里，附近山水景致颇佳，且有很多名胜古迹，杜甫空闲时便去游览。他到过麦积山北面的崇宁寺，参观过城南半山腰的南郭寺，写下一系列的诗歌。他还对城西七里赤谷中一户松菊掩映的人家颇为羡慕，说这个地方就像晋代陶渊明笔下神秘的桃花源一样。

事实上，这里也不太平。秦州一直是西域驿道，也是西北军事要道，此时这座边城正受到日益强大的吐蕃的威胁，气氛也很紧张。军队驻防，使节过往，黄昏时常常听到号角之声。

感受着边城秦州独特的自然风光和社会风情，杜甫这一时期的诗歌创作产生了颇为鲜明的变化。一些短小、清新的诗歌产生了。这些诗里，既有山水风光，也有边塞特有的气氛，山水诗和边塞诗，在诗人的笔下十分有机地结合在了一起。同时，由于战乱背景的深刻影响，这些诗又保持着杜甫一贯的遒劲风格，满含着忧国忧民的情怀。

这些诗歌，超越了盛唐时代的山水田园诗。盛唐山水田园诗的代表作家孟浩然和王维在生活中都崇尚隐逸，追求超尘脱俗的境界，因而他们在山水诗中努力营造幽美、宁静的理想化境界，常常或明或暗地蕴涵着佛理、禅机和道家的出世思想。诗歌意象也多选取寂寞柴门、空林细雨、渔樵夜归等，作品既多，渐成模式。而杜甫则没有落入这一套路中。他虽然屡次说到卜居以隐，但他并不是要超尘脱俗，只是为了寻找一个安静的栖身之处。因为他时刻关心着现实人生，所以他坚持写实景

heightening the peaceful and unperturbed atmosphere. When he wrote about the peaceful scenery, he wouldn't merely describe it with reclusive themes, always maintaining his concern for the situation of suppressing the rebellion and for national affairs. In the poems he wrote in Qinzhou, he described the quiet countryside as shown in the following example: "Birds have returned, as it was too cold / So it was even more quiet when the moon rose" ("Staying up in the Clay House of Zangong after Trying to Choose a Site for My Cottage in Xizhi Village" No. Two). He depicted troop horns and signal beacons as shown in the following example: "Beacon fires are often burned to report urgent alarms / War proclamations are flying over frequently from all directions" ("Twenty Mixed Poems Written in Qinzhou" No. Eighteen). He also showed his concern for the war as shown in the following example: "I asked if there was war ahead while traveling to the west / But felt so sad that I had to stay here for long" ("Twenty Mixed Poems Written in Qinzhou" No. One). The above elements would often appear together within one poem, creating a unique and realistic scene.

> Thin clouds float to the top of the Kunlun Mountains.
> Intermittent rains fall along the borderland.
> The Qiang children are watching the Weihe River;
> The envoy is looking toward the river head.
> Cooking smoke curls up from the army camps;
> Herds of cattle and sheep roam in the mountain village.
> With the wicker door of my humble cottage closed,
> I'm watching the clean autumn grass outside my house.
>   ("Twenty Mixed Poems Written in Qinzhou" No. Ten)

These poems also surpassed the frontier poems written at the prosperous age of the Tang Dynasty. Gao Shi and Cen Shen were representative frontier poets, whose poems usually described battles at the frontier, expressing idealistic sentiments of accomplishing great feats, rich in imagination and full of romantic atmosphere. However, Du Fu's poems described truthful scenes and conveyed the feelings of a common man living in the border cities. Consider the following.

> Thin autumn clouds are floating in the sky;
> The wind is blowing from the west, covering thousands of miles.
> It's a brilliant day today with a fine view,
> But raining for a long time will do no harm to farming.
> Rows of willow trees dot the border with spots of green

以抒真情，没有着意渲染幽静、恬然的气氛，写到幽静的景色时也不会一味在其中融入隐逸主题，更没有失掉对平乱形势、国家大事的关心。在他的秦州诗中，既有乡村的宁静，如"天寒鸟以归，月出山更静"（《西枝村寻置草堂地夜宿赞公土室二首》其二），也有军队的鼓角和通报敌情的烽火，如"警急烽常报，传闻檄屡飞"（《秦州杂诗二十首》其十八），更有诗人对战乱的关切，如"西征问烽火，心折此淹留"（《秦州杂诗二十首》其一）。这些因素甚至常常出现在同一首诗中，构成一幅奇特而真实的景象：

> 云气接昆仑，涔涔塞雨繁。
> 羌童看渭水，使客向河源。
> 烟火军中幕，牛羊岭上村。
> 所居秋草净，正闭小蓬门。
> ——《秦州杂诗二十首》其十

这些诗歌，也超越了盛唐的边塞诗。高适、岑参是盛唐边塞诗人的代表，他们的边塞诗，多描写边疆战事，抒发建功立业的豪情，富于想象，充满浪漫气息。而杜甫的诗则是描绘实际风貌，传达了一个普通人在边城的真实感受。如：

> 天水秋云薄，从西万里风。
> 今朝好晴景，久雨不妨农。

> While sorb trees bear little red fruits.
> As reed pipes are played in the tower,
> A wild goose flies high into the sky.
> ("Stopping of the Rain")

This poem mentioned "willows at the frontier" and "reed pipes," mainly describing the local manners and customs of the frontier, which were all common themes of frontier poems. But the tone of the poem was very moderate, subtly conveying the poet's inner feelings while still maintaining its identity as a border poem by means of scenery description. Du Fu was in fact using the style of scenic poems to write about the manners and customs of the frontier.

Living a lonely life in Qinzhou, Du Fu deeply thought longingly of his family and friends, and of the old days. He worried about his brothers, whose lives were in danger, composing the following lines: "It is the day of White Dew today / But I believe the moon in my hometown is brighter" ("Recalling My Brothers on a Moonlight Night"); he missed his old friend Zheng Qian, who was banished to a lonely seaside city. Du Fu considered him as talented and free-spirited as Ruan Ji and Ji Kang of the Jin Dynasty, arousing the jealousy of the court of his time; he also missed Cen Shen and Gao Shi who was banished from the capital because of Li Fuguo's false accusations, declaring that their poems could match those of Shen Yue and Bao Zhao of the Southern Dynasty.

> Though Gao Shi and Cen Shen rose to fame late,
> Their achievements can match those of Shen Yue and Bao Zhao.
> Proper messages are woven together with inspiring force,
> And appeals still linger on even when their poems come to a close.
> ("A Thirty-Rhyme Poem to Gao Shi, Governor of Pengzhou, and
> Cen Shen, Adjutant of the Governor of Guozhou")

He even wrote poems for Jia Zhi, Yan Wu, Xue Ju, Bi Yao and Zhang Biao to express his respect for them. By reading between the lines, one can find that these poems were permeated with sincerity.

Of course, it was Li Bai that he missed most. Since they parted with each other at the Stone Gate in Yanzhou in the autumn of the fourth year of the Tianbao reign (745 A.D.), Li Bai had been traveling back and forth from Qi to Lu. From Liangyuan Garden, he had traveled southward to the Wu and Yue Regions and northward to the Yan and Zhao Regions. When the An Shi Rebellion broke out, he went to Shanzhong by way of Xuancheng City to

塞柳行疏翠，山梨结小红。

胡笳楼上发，一雁入高空。

——《雨晴》

诗中有"塞柳"、"胡笳"，主要描写边塞风情，都是边塞诗的题材。但全诗的基调很平和，通过写景，微妙地传达出诗人身处边城的内心感情。这是用山水诗的风格去写边塞风情。

秦州的生活十分寂寞，杜甫深切怀念着他的亲人和往日的朋友。他既惦念着生死未卜的兄弟："露从今夜白，月是故乡明"（《月夜忆舍弟》），又怀念贬谪在海畔孤城的老朋友郑虔，认为他像晋代的阮籍、嵇康一样才高疏放，因而遭时俗的嫉恨。他还怀念岑参和因遭李辅国忌恨而被贬出京城的高适，称赞他们的诗比得上南朝的沈约和鲍照：

高岑殊缓步，沈鲍得同行。

意惬关飞动，篇终接混茫。

——《寄彭州高三十五使君适、虢州岑二十七长史参三十韵》

他还给贾至、严武、薛据、毕曜以及隐士张彪等人写诗致意，拳拳之情充满字里行间。

他最不能忘怀的人则是李白。天宝四载（745）秋天，他们在兖州石门分手后，李白以梁园为中心，南游吴越，北涉燕赵，往来于齐鲁之间。安史乱起，他由宣城避乱剡中，不久又

escape the war and soon established himself on Lushan Mountain.

At the beginning, Emperor Xuanzong took Fang Guan's suggestions on the plan of escape. He divided the whole country into several major military regions in July of the fifteenth year of the Tianbao reign (755 A.D.) and ordered several of his sons to be the commanders of each region. The crown prince Li Heng acted as the commander-in-chief of all the military forces, responsible for recovering the Yellow River Valley, while Prince Li Lin was responsible for the Yangtze River Valley. But when he became emperor, Li Heng ordered Li Lin not to lead his troops to the eastern regions. When Li Lin refused to obey his order, he even thought that Li Lin was plotting a rebellion, causing him to send troops to fight against Li Lin. When Li Lin passed Xunyang (now Jiujiang in Jiangxi), he called on Li Bai three times to demonstrate his admiration for him, so Li Bai joined Li Lin's office. Soon after, Li Lin committed suicide after being defeated, and Li Bai was convicted of the crime of "serving the rebels" and was thus banished to Yelang (now the area around Zhijiang River in Hunan). He had been traveling for fifteen months when he was pardoned halfway through the second year of the Qianyuan reign (759 A.D.). He then took a boat to travel eastward, returning to the region south of the Yangtze River.

Du Fu stayed in Qinzhou, having no idea that Li Bai had been pardoned. There were rumors that Li Bai had died in the river. Hearing such news, he was so worried that he dreamed of Li Bai, but his dreams only caused more worry. He wrote "Two Poems on Seeing Li Bai in a Dream." One of them goes like this:

> Separation at death stops with sobbing,
> But parting in life often brings boundless grief.
> Diseases are prevalent in the areas south of the Yangtze River,
> Where my friend stays in exile, sending no news to me.
> But he came to me in a dream,
> Indicating how much I have been missing him.
> I was so afraid that his dead soul was visiting me,
> For I had no idea of his fate due to the great distance between us.
> His soul came from the maple woods at dusk
> And returned from the fortress in darkness.
> As he was trapped in the mesh,
> How could he lift his wings to fly here?
> I woke up to find the roof bathed in moonlight,
> But it seemed as if his face were before my eyes.
> As the water was deep with turbulent waves,

居于庐山。

当初，唐玄宗在逃亡途中，听从房琯的建议，于天宝十五载（755）七月将全国分为几个军事大区，并命令几个儿子分别担任这几个区域的统帅。其中太子李亨为天下兵马元帅，负责收复黄河流域，永王李璘负责经营长江流域。但是当了皇帝的李亨却下令李璘不得率军东下，当李璘拒不从命后便认为他是在谋反，于是派兵攻打李璘。李璘兵过浔阳（今江西九江）时，因慕李白之名，三次征召他，李白便加入了李璘的幕府。不久，李璘兵败自杀，李白被定为"附逆"之罪，流放夜郎（今湖南芷江附近），途中走了十五个月，乾元二年（759）三月，中途遇赦，他便放舟东下，返回江南。

杜甫在秦州，不知道李白已经遇赦，一些传闻说李白已经死于江中，他听了十分担心，因思而梦，因梦而思，便写了《梦李白二首》，其一曰：

死别已吞声，生别常恻恻。

江南瘴疠地，逐客无消息。

故人入我梦，明我长相忆。

恐非平生魂，路远不可测。

魂来枫林青，魂返关塞黑。

君今在罗网，何以有羽翼。

落月满屋梁，犹疑照颜色。

I wished his soul would stay away from flood dragons.

The beginning of the poem mentioned parting in life and separation by death without any reservation. One would only speak this way to one's bosom friend. Suddenly, his old friend, whom he had missed deeply and whom he hadn't heard from for a long time, visited as if specially to comfort Du Fu, whom he missed so much. But this made Du Fu feel even more uneasy instead. Not realizing that he was dreaming, he was worried that he was seeing his friend's ghost. Only towards someone whom he truly missed would he have such feelings. Where the two lines starting with "His soul came" contained unique and indelible images, leaving a deep impression, the two lines starting with "I woke up" were natural and meaningful, vividly conveying the poet's surprised and bewildered feeling because he just woke up from a dream and still could not tell dream from reality. The last two lines showed that the poet was still immersed in the atmosphere of his dream, even though he had woken up. Worried about the dangers facing his old friend, he urged his friend again and again to take care. What deep worries and what sincere friendship!

The second poem goes like this:

> Clouds drifted in the sky all day long.
> The wanderer hasn't returned for long.
> I have dreamt of him for days,
> Which shows his profound affection for me.
> But he always said goodbye in such a hurry
> And kept telling me of the hard journey he was about to take.
> As the waters were turbulent with stormy waves,
> He was afraid of shipwrecks and falling into the water.
> Coming out of the door, he kept scratching his head,
> As if he had failed to live up to his lifelong ambition.
> High dignitaries are seen all over the capital,
> While he's the only one who looks wan and sallow.
> Who says the ubiquitous net of justice closes all loopholes?
> Then why should he suffer punishment at such an old age?
> Though his fame lasts for thousands of generations,
> What is the point for him when he's dead and gone?

Perhaps because Li Bai hadn't answered Du Fu in the dream before, it made him even more worried. Then Li Bai entered his dreams for two nights in succession. In the dreams, Li Bai talked with Du Fu, pouring out his grievances to Du, while Du Fu listened to him quietly and looked at him in

　　水深波浪阔，无使蛟龙得。

开头即说生别死别，直言无隐，只有对真正的知己才会这样说。
突然，日思夜想、杳无音讯的老朋友竟来做客了，好像是专门
来慰藉杜甫对他的思念。但这反而引起了杜甫的不安，他不知
道是在梦里，担心站在面前的是老友的亡灵——也只有对真正
挂念的人才会产生这样的心理。如果说"魂来"两句，意象奇
警，给人以深刻印象的话，"落月"两句，则平实隽永，将大
梦初醒、似真似假、惊疑不定的心情，逼真地表达了出来。最
后两句，已经醒来的诗人却依然沉浸在梦境的气氛中，记挂着
老友路途中的险恶，叮嘱他要注意安全，这是何等深切的牵念，
又是何等深挚的友谊。

　　其二曰：

　　　　浮云终日行，游子久不至。
　　　　三夜频梦君，情亲见君意。
　　　　告归常局促，苦道来不易。
　　　　江湖多风波，舟楫恐失坠。
　　　　出门搔白首，若负平生志。
　　　　冠盖满京华，斯人独憔悴。
　　　　孰云网恢恢，将老身反累。
　　　　千秋万岁名，寂寞身后事。

或许由于前一次的梦境中李白没有回答杜甫的问话，让杜甫更
加挂怀，接下来李白竟连续两夜走进杜甫的梦境。梦中的李白
讲话了，他向杜甫诉苦，杜甫静静地倾听，默默地看着他。李

silence. Li Bai's clear words and countenance came vividly before Du Fu's eyes, and Du Fu especially could not forget the moment when Li Bai scratched his white hair while saying goodbye and walking out of the gate. That kind of bleak and indignant situation was engraved in Du Fu's heart. Under such dangerous circumstances where "the ruling class were all interested in killing," only Du Fu would speak in defense of such a man convicted with a serious crime, and only Du Fu knew that he would leave a name in history: "Though his fame lasts for thousands of generations / What is the point for him when he's dead and gone?"

As the autumn wind blew, Du Fu remembered Li Bai again.

> When the cold wind blows from the end of the sky,
> What is on your mind, my dear friend?
> Wild geese have yet to bring me your news
> Perhaps because the waters are flooded with autumn rain.
> Poems loathe men with prosperous fates
> While evil spirits love passing wanderers,
> So pour your heart to the wronged ghost
> By casting poems into the Miluo River.
> ("Missing Li Bai at the End of the Sky")

At this moment, it was still not clear whether Li Bai was alive or dead, so Du Fu's poem was filled with anxiety and worry for him.

While he was missing Li Bai by day and dreaming of him by night, Du Fu finally heard the news that Li Bai had been pardoned and returned to the east, bringing Du Fu great comfort. Therefore, he wrote a long poem with twenty rhymes in one breath entitled "A Poem Written to Li Bai with Twenty Rhymes," praising Li Bai's writing: "Wind and rain were both shocked when he put down his pen / Ghosts and gods all cried when his poem was completed." It also gave objective descriptions to Li Bai's experiences in an attempt to redress the wrongs done to him.

Suffering poverty, illness, hunger and cold and living in solitude, Du Fu could no longer go on after staying in Qinzhou for three months, so he determined to leave. However, "As all lands are mired in war / To where can I go?" ("Twenty Mixed Poems Written in Qinzhou" No. Four) Where could the poet settle himself in such a vast land?

Just when Du Fu had no place to turn, he received a letter from the magistrate of Tonggu County, inviting him to go there. Tonggu lay two hundred sixty *li* to the south of Qinzhou, with mild climate and rich farming; Du Fu made up his mind to go there. In October of the second year of the

白那清晰的语言和神态历历分明，尤其忘不了的是他告辞出门时抓挠满头白发的情形，那种苍凉悲愤的情状真是永远刻在了杜甫的心中。这样一个身负重罪的人，在"世人皆欲杀"的险恶处境中，只有杜甫替他辩解，只有杜甫知道他将名垂千古："千秋万岁名，寂寞身后事！"

秋风一起，杜甫又想起了李白：

　　凉风起天末，君子意如何。

　　鸿雁几时到，江湖秋水多。

　　文章憎命达，魑魅喜人过。

　　应共冤魂语，投诗赠汨罗。

　　　　——《天末怀李白》

此时李白依然生死不明，杜甫诗中依然充满了对李白的惦念和担忧。

魂牵梦绕中，终于听到了李白遇赦东归的消息，杜甫感到一丝安慰，一口气写下了一首二十韵的长诗《寄李十二白二十韵》，诗中高度评价李白的创作："笔落惊风雨，诗成泣鬼神。"并客观记叙李白的经历，为其伸冤。

贫病饥寒，离群索居，杜甫在秦州过了三个月，实在过不下去了，他决计要离开，可是"万方声一概，吾道竟何之！"（《秦州杂诗二十首》其四），天地茫茫，何处是诗人的安身之处呢？

正当杜甫走投无路时，接到同谷县县宰的来信，欢迎他前去同谷。同谷在秦州南面约二百六十里，气候较温暖，物产也丰富，于是诗人决计前往。乾元二年（759）十月，杜甫告别

Qianyuan reign (759 A.D.), Du Fu said good-bye to Monk Zangong and dragged a large hand cart with his family to set out southward just as "Numerous jumbled stars and the moon are high up in the sky / Amid the vast floating mist and clouds" ("Setting out from Qinzhou"). He was filled with hope for this journey as can be seen in the following lines: "This universe is so vast / There must be a long way for me to go at last" ("ibid"). Having covered seventy *li*, they entered Tietang Gorge, on both sides of which were cliffs with towering black stones. The road was covered with ice, and it was so cold that even their horses were freezing. The poet lamented:

> I've suffered a lot from endless wars in my life,
> And the bandits haven't yet been defeated.
> I've been leading a wandering life for three years.
> Looking back I feel restless and depressed.
>
> > ("Tietang Gorge")

Soon they came to the Cold Gorge and Du Fu thought, "The Cold Gorge cannot be crossed / For my clothes are so thin" ("The Cold Gorge").

Finding no families living near the Cold Gorge, they had to prepare a hasty meal by the river bank and then set off again. As they traveled on southward, the road grew harder and more dangerous. Passing Fajing Temple, they arrived at Qingyang Gorge, which was too perilous to cross.

> Precipitous rocks came pressing on us, blocking out the distant forest.
> The cliffs were so steep that the sky in front of us seemed so narrow.
> A giant stone hanging five *li* west of the path
> Seemed about to fall down on me in anger.
> Looking up, I was afraid that the sun chariot would overturn;
> Looking down, I was afraid that the earth would sink.
> Sinister wind whistled like cries from evil spirits;
> Frost and snow fell down, covering vast land with boundless white.
>
> > ("Qingyang Gorge")

Having come all this way, the poet was used to perilous gorges, and had taken great efforts to describe them. However, it seemed that nature intended to display its full power while Du Fu tried to tame it with his own powerful writing ability. In his writing, the whole Qingyang Gorge came to life. Its precipitous cliffs seemed to challenge him. A giant stone hanging on the cliff

了赞公和尚，在一个"磊落星月高，苍茫云雾浮"（《发秦州》）的时刻，全家人拉着大车，向南出发了。他对此行充满了希望："大哉乾坤内，吾道长悠悠。"（同上）走了七十里，进入铁堂峡，两边石壁上耸立着铁青色的石头，路上到处是冰，马骨都快要冻折了，诗人感叹道：

> 生涯抵弧矢，盗贼殊未灭。
>
> 飘蓬逾三年，回首肝肺热。
>
> ——《铁堂峡》

不久来到寒峡，诗人感觉到："寒峡不可度，我实衣裳单。"（《寒峡》）

因没有碰到人家，只好在河岸边草草吃了点东西就继续赶路。越往南行，道路越艰险，经过法境寺，进入青阳峡，这地方真是太险恶了：

> 林迥硖角来，天窄壁面削。
>
> 溪西五里石，奋怒向我落。
>
> 仰看日车侧，俯恐坤轴弱。
>
> 魑魅啸有风，霜霰浩漠漠。
>
> ——《青阳峡》

一路走来已见惯了险峻的山峡，诗人也极力地描写了它们，可是造物主仿佛诚心要显示其伟力，而诗人也用自己雄强的笔力与造物主一比高低。在诗人笔下，青阳峡的一切都变得生动起来，主动以它的险峻来迎接杜甫，尤其是悬挂在五里开外崖

over five *li* away seemed particularly daunting to passers-by, its angry stance seeming to say that it was about to fall at any time. This caused travelers to pass with fear in their hearts. At last, Du Fu wrote that he walked as fast as his feet could carry him to leave those precipitous cliffs far behind, but they "not only paraded their towering posture but also took advantage of him" by pressing hard upon him, to which he could do nothing but merely utter a sigh.

After trudging through continuous hardship, they arrived at the Dragon Gate Town, where they saw flags in the camps through the mist, and heard soldiers sobbing at night.

After crossing Jicao Mountain, they entered Tonggu County. Their journey became much harder as they climbed over Nigong Mountain: The family had to trudge through mud all day long, causing Du Fu to fear that he would sink into the blue mud. His white horse turned black from the mud, and his children's every step came laboriously, as they puffed and panted like old folks. Despite his own difficulties crossing the mountain, Du Fu didn't forget to tell those who would come after, "A word to those coming from the north: / Don't be in a hurry while climbing this mountain!" ("Nigong Mountain")

Finally, they found Tonggu County lying ahead of them. Having climbed atop the Phoenix Mountain seven *li* southeast of the county, Du Fu stopped to look up to the tall Phoenix Tower, losing himself in a stream of thoughts.

> I'm afraid there might be a motherless young phoenix there,
> Chirping all day long from hunger and cold.
> I would give it my heart blood,
> To ease its sadness with drink and food.
> Since my heart could be taken as bamboo fruit,
> My mind is at ease as there's no need to ask for help.
> My blood could be taken as sweet spring water,
> For it would be as good, if not better than that.
> Since the phoenix is a symbol of the monarch,
> I feel willing to give up my life for its sake.
>   ("On the Phoenix Tower")

He imagined there might be a young phoenix crying plaintively in hunger and cold on the tower having lost its mother. He expressed his willingness to turn his own heart and blood into bamboo fruit and sweet spring water to feed this divine, auspicious, peace-bringing bird. At the end of the poem, the poet poured out his heart, hoping that the Tang Dynasty would be prosperous.

Prosperity will be restored to our state again,

壁上的一块巨石，更以其愤怒欲落的姿态挑战着来人的心理极限。行人走在这里都会心惊胆战，杜甫最后也不得不说，我拼命向前赶路，要把这险峻的山崖抛在后面，可是它们"突兀犹趁人"，穷追不舍，实在让我无可奈何，徒然叹息。

经过艰苦跋涉，来到龙门镇，傍晚只见驻守的军营里旗影暗淡，还听见士兵在夜间哭泣。

走出积草岭，就进入了同谷县。翻越泥功山时，路途难行，一家人一整天都踩着泥泞，诗人生怕陷入青泥中。那匹白色的马全身沾满泥，变成了黑色；小孩子寸步难行，气喘吁吁，好像变成了老头。但诗人还不忘告诫后来人："寄语北来人，后来莫匆匆。"（《泥功山》）

马上就要到同谷县城了，在县城东南七里的凤凰山顶，诗人驻足仰望着高高的凤凰台，不禁思绪联翩：

> 恐有无母雏，饥寒日啾啾。
>
> 我能剖心血，饮啄慰孤愁。
>
> 心以当竹实，炯然无外求。
>
> 血以当醴泉，岂徒比清流。
>
> 所贵王者瑞，敢辞微命休。
>
> ——《凤凰台》

他想到台上可能有失去母亲的小凤凰正在饥寒交迫中哀鸣，他愿意把自己的心血化为竹实和甘泉，来喂养这能致太平的吉祥神鸟。诗末倾吐了自己希望唐朝中兴的衷肠：

> 再光中兴业，一洗苍生忧。

And worries of the commoners will be washed away.
This is my deepest wish.
How long could gangs of bandits maintain their lives then?

("On the Phoenix Tower")

During this journey, Du Fu passed the Red Valley, the Tietang Gorge, the Salt Well, the Cold Gorge, Fajing Temple and so on, coming all the way to the Phoenix Tower. About these experiences, he produced altogether a group of twelve lifelike documentary poems, not only describing the hardships on the journey but also expressing feelings in his heart.

The magistrate of Tonggu County was unable to provide much assistance to Du Fu, so Du Fu and his family stayed at Liting first, before moving to the Phoenix Village near Wanzhang Pond. There were many places of interest in Tonggu County, but Du Fu only traveled to Wanzhang Pond. Like Qinzhou, this was also a place with barren land, without much farm produce. Consequently, Du Fu's family felt trapped once again into a miserable life. It was already November at that time, so cold that the earth was already frozen, forcing the white-haired Du Fu to gather acorns and dig tubers in the mountains to allay his family's hunger. But how many tubers could he expect to find in such severe winter when all grass had withered and when the whole valley was covered with heavy snow? He returned empty-handed, so his family had nothing to do but lean against the wall, moaning in hunger. Thinking of his own miserable fate and recalling his brothers, sister and hometown, the poet was so distraught that tears streamed down his face. In a hoarse and tearful voice, he composed one mournful song after another, which came to be called together "Seven Poems Written in Tonggu County in the Qianyuan Reign."

I

I'm a man called Du Zimei,
With dishevelled white hair hanging over my ears.
I followed the man who raised monkeys to gather acorns
In the cold valley at dusk at the end of the year.
With no letter from my hometown, I could not go back.
My hands and feet are frostbitten.
Alas, while I sing the first song that is indeed morose,
The dismal wind blows from heaven for me.

II

The long trowel with a white wooden handle
Is what I depend on to survive.

深衷正为此，群盗何淹留。

——《凤凰台》

这一路经过赤谷、铁堂峡、盐井、寒峡、法境寺……直到凤凰台，杜甫留下了一组十二首生动纪实的诗篇，不仅描写了旅途的艰辛，也尽情抒发了内心的感慨。

同谷的县宰似乎并没有怎么帮助杜甫，杜甫一家先寓居于栗亭，不久又搬到万丈潭附近的凤凰村。同谷县内名胜很多，但是诗人只到过万丈潭。这里和秦州一样，土地贫瘠，物产不丰，一家人的生活更加悲惨了，简直陷入了绝境。此时已是十一月了，天寒地冻，白发蓬乱的诗人只好在山间拾一些橡栗，挖一些黄独的块茎来充饥。可是严冬草枯，山谷里覆盖着厚厚的积雪，哪里还能挖到多少黄独呢？他空着手回来，一家人饿得倚壁呻吟。诗人想起自己的悲惨身世，想起兄弟姐妹和故乡，不禁悲痛难耐，涕泗横流，用沙哑的喉咙，声泪俱下地唱出了一曲曲悲歌，即《乾元中寓居同谷县作歌七首》：

（一）

有客有客字子美，白头乱发垂过耳。

岁拾橡栗随狙公，天寒日暮山谷里。

中原无书归不得，手脚冻皴皮肉死。

呜呼一歌兮歌已哀，悲风为我从天来。

（二）

长镵长镵白木柄，我生托子以为命。

黄独无苗山雪盛，短衣数挽不掩胫。

Tuber plants are lost in the heavy snows on the mountains.

My clothes are too short to cover my legs no matter how I pull them down.

Emptyhanded, I have no choice but to return with my sons,

So my family moan in hunger against silent walls.

Alas, while I start to sing the second song,

My neighbors all turn grieved for me.

III

I have younger brothers in remote places,

The three of them are all thin, without exception.

We parted with each other as we all wandered here and there.

Since the Tartar rebels began plundering, the country has been in disarray.

The way to road to our reunion has become so long.

When I see many birds flying in the east,

How I wish they could carry me to my brothers' side!

Alas, I'm singing the third song now,

But where will you find my bones should you return.

IV

I have a younger sister living in Zhongli,

Whose dead husband left her a single son.

The waves of the Huaihe River are high and the wind strong,

Preventing her from seeing me for ten years.

I wanted to visit her by boat, but was held back by arrows.

In the distant south, flags and banners are seen everywhere.

Alas, while I sing the fourth song,

Apes in the forest cry for me in the somber day.

V

Wind blows without cease and streams flow swiftly in the mountains.

Withered leaves are wet in the cold rain while the wind whistles.

Wormwood grows in the ancient city under a cloudy sky;

White foxes jump while yellow ones stand.

Why should I be stuck in such a poor valley?

I sit up at midnight, all sorts of feelings welling up in my heart.

Alas, while I sing the fifth song,

My soul will not be called back, for it has returned to my hometown.

此时与子空归来，男呻女吟四壁静。
呜呼二歌兮歌始放，邻里为我色惆怅。

（三）

有弟有弟在远方，三人各瘦何人强。
生别展转不相见，胡尘暗天道路长。
前飞鴐鹅后鹙鸧，安得送我置汝旁。
呜呼三歌兮歌三发，汝归何处收兄骨。

（四）

有妹有妹在钟离，良人早殁诸孤痴。
长淮浪高蛟龙怒，十年不见来何时。
扁舟欲往箭满眼，杳杳南国多旌旗。
呜呼四歌兮歌四奏，林猿为我啼清昼。

（五）

四山多风溪水急，寒雨飒飒枯树湿。
黄蒿古城云不开，白狐跳梁黄狐立。
我生何为在穷谷，中夜起坐万感集。
呜呼五歌兮歌正长，魂招不来归故乡。

VI

There are dragons in the south mountain ponds.

Ancient trees grow high with their branches curling and drooping down.

When leaves turn yellow and fall down, the dragons are sleeping still

While pit vipers swim up from the east.

It feels so strange that they dare to come out,

So I pull out my sword to kill them but give it up at last.

Alas, while I sing the sixth song,

Brooks and hills take on the look of spring in my eyes.

VII

I have been old and not famous.

During the three years of famine, I roamed along wild mountain roads.

Why are many ministers and officials in Chang'an so young?

To obtain power and wealth, one should secure personal gain as early as possible.

Several Confucian scholars in the mountains are my old friends.

Talking with them about the past, I feel deeply grieved.

Alas, when I sing the seventh song as the end,

I look up the heaven, feeling days pass too fast.

The seven poems composed in Tonggu were written with tears and blood, and the deep grievance expressed in them is unparalleled among Du Fu's poems. These were a group of seven-character ancient verses. Over a hundred and forty such poems written by Du Fu have been preserved to this day. Building on the basis of the achievements of his predecessors, Du Fu extended the range of thematic contents of seven-character ancient verses, making significant contributions in such areas as structure, syntax, rhyme and so on; therefore, Shi Buhua of the Qing Dynasty considered his poems to be "the best of such poems since the birth of seven-character ancient verses," referring to them as "authentic" seven-character ancient verses ("A Common Man Commenting on Poetry at Xianshan Mountain").

Du Fu stayed in Tonggu for about a month and then moved with his family to Chengdu on the first of December, as the whole family could no longer maintain their livelihood in Tonggu. This was the hardest year in the poet's life: He returned from Luoyang to Huazhou in spring, traveling from

（六）

南有龙兮在山湫，古木巃嵸枝相樛。

木叶黄落龙正蛰，蝮蛇东来水上游。

我行怪此安敢出，拔剑欲斩且复休。

呜呼六歌兮歌思迟，溪壑为我回春姿。

（七）

男儿生不成名身已老，三年饥走荒山道。

长安卿相多少年，富贵应须致身早。

山中儒生旧相识，但话宿昔伤怀抱。

呜呼七歌兮悄终曲，仰视皇天白日速。

同谷七歌字字是血泪，感情之沉痛在杜诗中亦属极致。这是一组七言古诗。杜甫的七古，现存一百四十多首，在继承前人成就的基础上，拓展了七古的题材内容，在谋篇、用句、用韵等方面都有很多创造，被清代的施补华称为"自有七古以来之极盛"，为七古"正宗"（《岘佣说诗》）。

杜甫在同谷停留了一个月左右，全家的生活实在维持不下去了，到了十二月一日，杜甫一家又向成都转移。这一年是诗人一生中最辛苦的年头：春天从洛阳返回华州，秋天从华州至

Huazhou to Qinzhou in autumn, and then continuing to Tonggu from Qinzhou in winter, and was preparing to leave this hopeless land for Chengdu at this time. This cause him to lament, "I had no choice but to be worn out by earthly matters / So that I made four trips within a single year" ("Setting out from Tonggu County").

Though forced to trudge over tall mountains and raging rivers, Du Fu was not as frightened by his hardships as before. He wrote the poem "Setting out from Tonggu County," preparing to record the scenery on the way to Chengdu in poetry just as he had done on the way to Tonggu County.

On the way from Qinzhou to Tonggu, they mainly traveled through gorges and crossed high mountains, but on the way to Chengdu, they had to ford many rivers. They also passed by Mupi Mountain, which made the poet feel that "Beside the Five Sacred Mountains / There are still other mountains deserving respect" ("Mupi Mountain"). At first, they trekked across the White Sand Ferry of the Jialing River under a high cliff. Seeing clear water and white sand here, the poet's spirits improved, feeling that "It was so different that my worry and misery were washed away / And all illnesses vanished into thin air" ("The White Sand Ferry").

One night, Du Fu took a boat across Shuihui Ferry. It was a starry, moonless night. The river was so wide that its water melded into the starry sky, making it impossible to distinguish one from the other. This scene made such a deep impression on the poet that after crossing the river, he exclaimed "Looking back at places beyond the river waters / I came to know all stars were still dry, hanging up in the sky" ("Shuihui Ferry").

In the ancient times, people usually took plank roads built along cliffs to enter the Shu Region. Such roads were also called rack roads, built by fixing bridges into holes chiseled in cliffs. Du Fu walked over several sections of long and dangerous plank road on this journey and wrote four poems to record his traveling experience, including "The Flying God Rack Road," "Five Windings," "The Dragon Gate Rack Road" and "The Stone Cabinet Rack Road." The Dragon Gate rack road was the most dangerous of them, for the waves of the Jialing River under it rose so high in violent storms that one would feel dizzy when walking on it. Falling from it meant certain death. Du Fu thought, "Though I have gone through hardships all my life / It was here that I started to feel fear" ("The Dragon Gate Rack Road").

After crossing the Jubai Ferry, Du Fu came to the gateway to the Shu Region: the Sword Gate Pass. The precipice of the Great Sword Mountain cracked open in the middle, creating two cliffs facing each other, as if two

秦州，冬天自秦州来同谷，现在又要从"绝境"去成都，所以，他感叹道："奈何迫物累，一岁四行役。"(《发同谷县》)

这一路照样跋山涉水，诗人也照样没有被困难吓倒，并写下《发同谷县》一诗，准备着像来同谷县的路上一样，用诗笔记载下往成都去的沿途风景。

从秦州来同谷时，主要是穿越峡谷和翻越高山，这次去成都，虽然也有让诗人感到"始知五岳外，别有他山尊"(《木皮岭》)的木皮岭，但更多的则是要涉水。先是在一个傍晚，渡过悬崖下面嘉陵江上的白沙渡。这里水清沙白，诗人的心情也好起来，觉得："迥然洗愁辛，多病一疏散。"(《白沙渡》)

在一个夜晚，诗人又乘船渡过水会渡。是夜无月而繁星满天，江面宽阔，水面与星空连成一片，无法分辨，这给诗人留下深刻的影响，以至于渡过江后，诗人感觉："回眺积水外，始知众星干。"(《水会渡》)

古代人蜀多走栈道，栈道又叫阁道、栈阁，是在悬崖峭壁上凿孔架桥而成的道路。杜甫此行经过数段又长又险的阁道，并作诗四首以记录阁道之行，分别是：《飞仙阁》《五盘》《龙门阁》和《石柜阁》。龙门阁最险，阁道下的嘉陵江风急浪高，走在阁道上让人头晕目眩，一旦掉下去，将必死无疑。诗人觉得："终身历艰险，恐惧从此始。"(《龙门阁》)

过了桔柏渡，来到了蜀中的门户——剑门，这里大剑山的峭壁从中间断开，两崖相对，像立了两把笔直的剑；从穿过两崖间的通道上向前看，又仿佛开着一道狭窄的门，所以叫做剑

straight swords had been erected there. Standing on the pass between the two cliffs looking ahead, one would find that there seemed to be a narrow gate, called the Sword Gate. Upon arrival, Du Fu couldn't help exclaiming that "the Sword Gate was the grandest in the world," composing the poem "The Sword Gate," filled with powerful writing and bold spirit. This poem depicted the strategic position of the Sword Gate, where "If a single man guarded the pass in rage / Millions of soldiers would be unable to fight against him," but the main part of its content was made up of the comments of the poet, making it more like a political commentary written in verse. The poet pointed out in the poem that emperors of all dynasties established government offices in the Shu Region to collect tribute and extort money, arousing such great resentment from the people that some local strongmen seized the opportunity offered by its strategic location to establish renegade regimes against the central government. Such conditions existed up until Du Fu's time. The poet said in indignation, "Laying the blame on Nature / I intended to remove these rows of mountains." Here, "rows of mountains" referred both to physical mountains that blocked transportation, including the Sword Gate, as well as to all the forces that hindered national peace and reunification.

Traveling on to the southwest, the poet came to the Deer Head Mountain, where the rolling hills suddenly stopped. What lay before his eyes were thousands of *li* of open fields, making the whole land appear suddenly before his eyes. Having survived all kinds of hardships and dangers, Du Fu finally was able to become much more optimistic. In the poem "The Deer Head Mountain," he recalled the achievements of Liu Bei, the emperor of Shu in the Three Kingdoms Period; he recalled Yang Xiong and Sima Xiangru, the great literary men of Sichuan in the Western Han Dynasty; he also praised the present governor of Sichuan, Governor Pei Mian in charge of Chengdu and the western Sichuan.

Chengdu lay a hundred and fifty *li* south of the Deer Head Mountain. On a night of the twelfth month of the lunar year, in the second year of the Qianyuan reign (759 A.D.), Du Fu and his family walked into Chengdu at sunset. What they saw before their eyes were different looking people and tall city walls, within which gorgeous houses could be seen everywhere. With a noisy crowd and music played by different musical instruments, Chengdu was indeed a beautiful metropolis. Du Fu should have felt excited at having successfully arrived at Chengdu, but the feeling of being a stranger made him feel at a loss, so he began to miss his own hometown. Having traveled farther and farther away from his hometown, the poet could do nothing but comfort himself,

门。诗人来到此处，不禁发出"剑门天下壮"的感叹，并以雄肆的笔力和豪放的气概创作了《剑门》一诗。这首诗对剑门"一夫怒临关，百万未可傍"的险要地形作了描写，但更多的内容则是议论，就像一篇用诗体写成的政论。诗中指出，历代帝王在蜀地设官取贡，搜刮钱财，引起百姓不满，致使一些豪杰乘机凭借着险峻的地形割据叛乱，而这种状况至今还存在着。诗人发出愤言："吾将罪真宰，意欲铲叠嶂。"叠嶂，既是指包括剑门在内阻碍交通的重峦叠嶂，也是指妨碍国家和平与统一的一切力量。

继续向西南方向行进，来到鹿头山时，连绵的群山从中间断开，千里阔野平铺在眼前，呈现出一片豁然开朗的景色。险阻终于历尽，杜甫的心情也开朗多了。他在《鹿头山》一诗里回顾了三国时蜀国皇帝刘备的业绩，回顾了西汉时四川的大文学家杨雄和司马相如，末尾还赞扬了一下现任四川行政长官——成都尹充剑南西川节度使裴冕。

自鹿头山南行一百五十里，就是成都。那是乾元二年（759）腊月末的一个傍晚，杜甫一家披着夕阳的余晖，走进成都府。眼前所见的是别具风貌的人民，高大的城墙内填满了华丽的房屋，人声喧闹，笙箫错杂，真是一个美丽的都会。来到这里，本应欣喜，但初来乍到的陌生感却让杜甫觉得无所适从，开始怀念起自己的故乡来。离故乡越来越远的诗人只能宽慰自

saying: "As it's been a common practice to live away from one's native land / Why should I feel so grieved?" ("Chengdu City")

After leaving Qinzhou in October, Du Fu stayed in Tonggu for a short period of time and arrived at Chengdu at last, covering over a thousand *li* and composing two groups of poems. Each of these two groups included twelve poems, most of which were named after the places he visited, except for the first poem of each group, "Setting out from Qinzhou" and "Setting out from Tonggu," giving people a sense of order and chronology.

己："自古有羁旅，我何苦哀伤。"(《成都府》)

　从十月离开秦州以来，经过同谷的短暂停留，最后到达成都，杜甫行程超过一千多里，分别作了两组纪行诗。这两组诗各十二首，除了每组第一首的《发秦州》和《发同谷县》外，其余的诗都以所历地名为题，井然有序，历历可考。

进入四川（蜀）的 道路——栈道
Road alongside cliffs to Sichuai

后人重修的杜甫草堂一景
The repaired cottage once Du Fu lived

五　成都草堂里的野老

Chapter V　Cottage Life in Chengdu

Located in the southwest of China, Chengdu Basin has always been called "Nature's Storehouse" for its plentiful produce. The Minjiang River flows right through the basin, while Chengdu City is situated in the center of the basin. It has always been the political, economic, cultural and military center of the southwest region since the Western Han Dynasty, and was quite prosperous in the Tang Dynasty. It was composed of the Major City and the Minor City, inhabited by some thirty or forty thousand households, with a population of over a hundred thousand people. Since Emperor Xuanzong fled to Chengdu in the fifteenth year of the Tianbao reign (755 A.D.), its name was temporarily changed to the Southern Capital. As far as Du Fu was concerned, he only hoped for a haven where he could be free from cold and hunger.

The family first established a temporary residence in a cottage temple in the western suburbs of the city for three months, living on grain given by old friends and vegetables from neighbors. But it was not feasible to live permanently in the temple, so Du Fu started building his own house the next spring. He found a piece of empty land by the Huanhua Stream three *li* away from the cottage temple. With the help of relatives and friends, he there built a thatched hut. Facing the Qingjiang River and located in an expanse of bamboo forest, its surroundings were both serene and beautiful, so Du Fu affectionately called it his "thatched hall." He asked his friends for some peach trees, bamboo trees, alder trees, pine trees and young fruit plants, and carefully planted them around his cottage. It was in late spring that the cottage was finally completed, and then the fifty-year-old poet had a place to live at last, so he happily wrote the poem "The Completion of My Cottage" to celebrate the occasion.

> My cottage is built at the back of the city with cogon covering its roof.
> Situated along the river, it looks down over green open countryside.
> Alder trees blot out the sun with their leaves singing with the wind;
> Bamboo woods are enveloped in mist with dew dripping from their tips.
> Crows fly over with their young for a short stay
> While twittering swallows come frequently to settle down.
> Others mistakenly compare my cottage to Yang Xiong's house,
> But I'm too lazy to follow his example to write an essay to explain it away.

"Wandering in Shu for five years and staying in Zizhou for another year"

　　中国西南部的成都盆地物产丰富，历来被称为"天府之国"。岷江从盆地中间穿过，成都府就处在盆地的中心。自西汉以来成都一直是西南地区的政治、经济、文化和军事中心。唐时的成都已经很繁荣了，分为大城、少城，约有三四万户，十多万人。由于唐玄宗于天宝十五载（755）逃到这里，因而又被改称为南京。不过对于杜甫来说，他所希望的仅仅是一个能免于饥寒的安身之所而已。

　　一家人先在城西郊的草堂寺里寄居了三个月，有老朋友分给他一些米粮，邻居也常送些菜蔬给他。但久居寺庙显然不可，次年春天，杜甫便开始自己筑室了。他在距离草堂寺三里远的浣花溪边觅得一块荒地，在亲友的帮助下，修筑了茅屋。茅屋前临清江，坐落在一片竹木林中，环境幽美，杜甫喜爱地称它"草堂"。他又向朋友们要了一些桃树、绵竹、桤木、松树和果树的幼苗，精心地栽种在周围。到了暮春时节，草堂落成了，五十岁的诗人终于有了一个安身之地，于是高兴地写了《堂成》一诗以纪之：

　　　　背郭堂成荫白茅，缘江路熟俯青郊。

　　　　桤林碍日吟风叶，笼竹和烟滴露梢。

　　　　暂止飞乌将数子，频来语燕定新巢。

　　　　旁人错比扬雄宅，懒惰无心作《解嘲》。

　　"五载客蜀郡，一年居梓州"（《去蜀》），自上元元年（760）

("Leaving Shu"), Du Fu spent most of his time in the cottage during the five years from the spring of the first year of the Shangyuan reign (760 A.D.) to the early summer of the first year of Emperor Daizong's Yongtai reign (765 A.D.). He fled to Zizhou (now Santai in Sichuan) and Langzhou (now Langzhong in Sichuan) in the autumn of Emperor Daizong's Baoying reign (762 A.D.) to escape war, staying there until the second year of the Guangde reign (764 A.D.). The serene and beautiful natural scenery of Huanhua Village and the comparatively stable life there gave Du Fu some comfort, so he wrote with great interest about his own life as well as the grass and trees around the cottage. He wrote four hundred and thirty poems (including a hundred and seventy poems written in Zizhou and Langzhou) during the five years of life here, accounting for nearly one third of the total number of poems, a period of prolific writing during Du Fu's career.

Though the cottage was shabby and small, Du Fu did not feel lonely there, because eight or nine families lived nearby. Mr. Jinli, a neighbor living to the south of the cottage, was also an official in recluse. Du Fu went rowing with him in autumn in a small boat, enjoying himself so much that he was not willing to go back home, even when the moon was high up in the sky. The neighbor living north of the cottage was a county magistrate, who resigned from his office before his term was over. He was fond of drinking, and was good at composing poems, so he often came through the wormwood plants to visit the poet. Another neighbor was named Hu Sirong. He was good at writing monumental inscriptions and was Du Fu's drinking companion. Another neighbor was named Huang Siniang, in whose courtyard grew plots of flowers and trees. Du Fu once walked along Huanhua Stream to her home to enjoy the flowers. The rest of his neighbors were all kind-hearted peasants, with whom Du Fu had close contact. They often sent him some vegetables, and he often sent them the herbs he grew. From the poem "Cold Food Festival," it can be inferred that Du Fu had a close relationship with peasants.

> On the road of the riverside village during Cold Food Festival,
> Fallen flowers danced up and down in the wild wind.
> Thin smoke was wisped up slowly along the riverside.
> The sunlight filtering through the bamboo trees was bright.
> I would go no matter which peasant may invite me;
> I would take any gift my neighbors make.
> As it's a remote small village, we know each other so well
> That even chickens and dogs would forget to return home.

春至代宗永泰元年（765）初夏的五年里，杜甫除了代宗宝应（762）秋避乱至梓州（今四川三台）、阆州（今四川阆中），居留至广德二年（764）之外，其余时间都是在草堂度过的。浣花村幽美宁静的自然风光和相对安定的生活抚慰了诗人的心，他便饶有兴趣地把自己的生活和草堂周围的一草一木写进诗歌。诗人在这五年里写出四百三十首诗（其中作于梓州、阆州的有一百七十首），几乎占杜甫全集中诗歌总数的三分之一，是杜甫创作过程中的又一个丰收时期。

草堂虽陋，却不孤寂，周围散居着八九户人家。南面的邻居锦里先生是位隐士，杜甫与他乘着小船在秋水中泛舟，流连忘返，直到月亮升起还不肯回家。北面的邻居原是一位县令，任期未满就辞了官职，好饮酒，善赋诗，常常穿过蓬蒿来看望诗人。另一位邻居叫斛斯融，善写碑文，是杜甫的酒友。还有一位黄四娘，院子里种着成畦的花木，杜甫曾沿着浣花溪漫步至她家赏花。剩下的几户人家都是心地善良的农民，杜甫与他们的交往很密切。农家时常送他一些菜蔬，他也常把自己种的草药赠给他们。从《寒食》这首诗可以看出他与农民的亲睦：

> 寒食江村路，风花高下飞。
>
> 汀烟轻冉冉，竹日静晖晖。
>
> 田父要皆去，邻家问不违。
>
> 地偏相识尽，鸡犬亦忘归。

Here the word "*Yao*" means inviting, and the word "*Wen*" means presenting a gift. He was sure to go if there was an invitation from the peasants, and he was sure to accept presents if they made to him, showing that he had become one with the peasants. Once, when the poet was taking a walk in the village, he was pulled aside by an old peasant to his home to taste some newly brewed spring wine.

> In straw shoes, I walked in the spring wind,
> Watching flowers and willows in every village.
> An old peasant was about to offer the spring sacrifice,
> So he invited me to have a taste of the spring wine.
> Having drunk his fill, he began to praise the new governor,
> Whom he regarded as a good official not often seen.
> He then turned back and pointed at his eldest son,
> Telling me that he was an archer,
> Who was registered in the cavalry,
> And thus hadn't been farming for long.
> This son was given leave the day before yesterday
> To work in the field to save his feeble father.
> He claimed that he'd pay service and taxes unless he were dead,
> And that he would never move away with his family.
> The family was about to hold a grand sacrifice this year,
> So he wondered if I could stay for a while.
> He shouted and asked his wife to open a big bottle
> And get wine from the basin for me.
> I was so moved by his high spirit and will
> Then understanding the priority of men's education.
> Though he talked a lot with no clear structure,
> He kept praising the new governor.
> I took a casual walk in the morning,
> But kept drinking until it became dark.
> I have come to cherish human relations more the longer I wander.
> How could I decline this neighbor's earnest request?
> When he shouted to his wife for fruit and food,
> I was about to stand up but was pulled back by him.
> Though his actions showed no good manners,
> I didn't feel he was improper in any way.
> When the moon rose, still he retained me,
> Asking if I could still drink another cup.

　　这里"要"同邀，即邀约的意思；"问"是馈赠的意思。有邀必赴，有赠必收，真是已和农民打成一片。一次诗人在村里漫步，被一个老农夫拉到家里去尝新酿的春酒：

步屧随着风，村村自花柳。
田翁逼社日，邀我尝春酒。
酒酣夸新尹，畜眼未见有。
回头指大男，渠是弓弩手。
名在飞骑籍，长番岁时久。
前日放营农，辛苦救衰朽。
差科死则已，誓不举家走。
今年大作社，拾遗能住否。
叫妇开大瓶，盆中为吾取。
感此气扬扬，须知风化首。
语多虽杂乱，说尹终在口。
朝来偶然出，自卯将及酉。
久客惜人情，如何拒邻叟。
高声索果栗，欲起时被肘。
指挥过无礼，未觉村野丑。
月出遮我留，仍嗔问升斗。

("Drinking with an Old Peasant at His Earnest Request Who Highly Praised Governor Yan Wu")

Though the two drank wine from morning till night, the old peasant wouldn't let Du Fu go when the moon had risen. The old peasant was overjoyed, for his eldest son had come back on leave from the army to help with the family farming. He praised Yan Wu, the new governor of Chengdu, for his concern for the people. The straightforward peasant got himself drunk first, and then kept directing his wife to get wine and fruit to entertain Du Fu. Though he talked loudly and unintelligibly, ordering his wife about rather rudely, Du Fu didn't consider him ill-mannered. On the contrary, he felt the warmth of human emotion from this simple peasant. Du Fu's poem was vivid and plain, showing deep affection and feelings. From this, it can be inferred that Du Fu had a close relationship with peasants.

In contrast to most of the ancient poets, Du Fu willingly performed manual labor while living in Chengdu and later in Kuizhou.

> Since the vegetables I grew on my own were still so sparse,
> I picked just a few for my friends.
>
> ("A Guest Coming for a Visit")
> I often walk on the path around my quiet cottage,
> Carrying a small ax in my hand.
>
> ("Evil Trees")
> With a hoe on my shoulder, I walked before the children,
> Searching for nettle leaves until the sun set.
>
> ("Removing Weeds")
> When dates became ripe, I allowed people to pick them;
> When weeds appeared among vegetables, I would hoe them up myself.
>
> ("Five Poems on the Autumn Field")
> When matters arose in court, they would certainly go to the governors,
> So I was quite delighted to learn farming in the village.
>
> ("Getting Late")

He was also concerned with agricultural production, so excessive rain and drought were both common themes in his poems. He wrote the poem "The Stopping of the Rain" in Qinzhou and then wrote "A Timely Rain on a Spring Night" when arriving at Chengdu.

——《遭田父泥饮美严中丞》

这酒竟从早晨一直尝到晚上，直到月亮出来，老农还不肯让杜甫走。因为当兵的大儿子放假回家帮助农活，老农心情十分舒畅，一个劲地夸新来的成都尹严武体贴民心。豪爽的老农自己先喝醉了，又不停地指挥老伴拿酒和果品招待杜甫。虽然他语多杂乱，指挥无礼，但杜甫并不以为村野之丑，反而感到人情的温暖。这首诗写得生动朴实、情深意长。可以看出杜甫和农民关系的亲密。

与古代绝大多数诗人不同的是，杜甫在成都和后来在夔州，都乐于亲自参加一些体力劳动：

自锄稀菜甲，小摘为情亲。（《有客》）

独绕虚斋里，常持小斧柯。（《恶树》）

荷锄先童稚，日入仍讨求。（《除草》）

熟枣从人打，葵荒欲自锄。（《秋野五首》）

朝廷问府主，耕稼学山村。（《晚》）

他还关心农业生产，雨涝天旱，都是他反复吟咏的题材。在秦州他写过《雨晴》，到成都则写了《春夜喜雨》：

The heaven-sent rain knew the time,
Arriving just as the grass and trees started growing.
Coming after the wind at night,
The rain provided moisture for all living creatures in silence.
The field paths were dark under heavy clouds
While on the river boats burned lonely lights.
Looking at the red marshes in the morning,
I saw brighter flowers decorating up the city.

The *Book on Literature* of *The Old Book of Tang* mocked Du Fu, saying that he "idled with old farmers and peasants too familiarly, without behaving himself with reserve and caution," providing evidence of the great gap between scholar-officials and farmers at the time. It was commendable of Du Fu that he could break through the *de facto* barriers around scholar-officials and made contact with the laboring people. Examining the poetic circles of all ages, how many poets could actually take such a step? Undoubtedly, it was due to his hard life that Du Fu was able to relate so personally to laboring people at the bottom of society, but it also had a lot to do with his sincere and honest nature. "Staying in the Eastern Capital for two years / I have been fed up with speculation and tricks" ("To Li Bai")."As they are brazen and without shame / How could I remain among princes and dukes" ("On a Parting Trip"). "I hate to work in government / For I am afraid that officials loathe my sincerity / When I returned to my thatched cottage / My neighbors were never angry with me" ("Walking in the Garden at Leisure Time to Ease My Illness, Plant Autumn Vegetables, Supervise the Farm Cattle and Write down What I See). These lines show that he indeed had the sincere and honest nature of farmers and peasants. This made Du Fu's friendship with farmers and peasants very natural.

Living in his quiet cottage among such plain and honest people and watching the beautiful scenery along the Huanhua Stream, Du Fu gradually regained his strength and health. He grew accustomed to taking walks along the Huanhua Stream with his clothes draped over his shoulders, drinking at will, reading aimlessly and "Looking up to steal a glance at birds at random / So that I often reply to wrong persons when turning back" ("Two Poems Written at Random" No. Two).

The beautiful and quiet rural scenery became an important element of Du Fu's poetry during this period.

My farmhouse lies on a bend in the Qingjiang River;

好雨知时节，当春乃发生。

随风潜入夜，润物细无声。

野径云俱黑，江船火独明。

晓看红湿处，花重锦官城。

《旧唐书·文苑传》讥笑杜甫"与田父野老相狎荡，无拘检"，说明封建士大夫与农民之间的隔膜是何等厚重，冲破这种隔膜又是何等不易。杜甫能冲破士大夫的精神营垒，与劳动人民接触，这正是他的可贵之处、可爱之处和伟大之处。检视千古诗坛，能跨出这一步的又有几个？杜甫与下层劳动人民的交往，固然是由于艰苦生活的推动，但也与他朴实的秉性大有关系。"二年客东都，所历厌机巧。"（《赠李白》）"野人旷荡无颜，岂可久在王侯间。"（《去矣行》）"不爱入州府，畏人嫌我真。及乎归茅宇，旁舍未曾嗔。"（《暇日小园散病，将种秋菜，督勒耕牛，兼书触目》）这说明他确实具有朴实的秉性，而这种朴实也正是农民的特点。所以杜甫与农民交往，是情理中的事。

生活在这幽静的草堂和朴实的人民中间，欣赏着浣花溪畔美丽的景色，杜甫的心情舒畅起来，久病的身体也好了很多。他习惯于随意地披着衣服漫步于浣花溪边，随意地喝点酒，随意地读点书，随意地"仰头贪看鸟，回头错应人。"（《漫成二首》其二）

幽美宁静的田园风光，成为这一时期杜甫诗歌的重要内容：

田舍清江曲，柴门古道旁。

My brushwood door opens onto an ancient road.
The grass grows so tall that shops and streets cannot be seen;
The place is so isolated that I don't feel like dressing myself neatly.
Each branch of the beech trees is so soft;
Each loquat tree smells so fragrantly.
Standing on the beam of a fishing boat,
Cormorants spread their wings in the setting sun.

("The Farmhouse")

Quiet farmhouses and simple customs, together with flowers, trees, fish and birds, all brimming with vigor and vitality, combined to make up this peaceful river village, giving us a glimpse into the tranquil heart of the poet. This kind of peace had never appeared in Du Fu's writings before. The last couplet of this poem was rare beautiful lines of pastoral poetry. Cormorant is a kind of water bird, which the people of Shu raised and trained to catch fish. At the moment, they stood on the weir, spreading their wings to air out their plumes in the setting sun. The villagers had finished the whole day's labor by then. As there were not many people around, the water birds could afford to relax somewhat. Only Du Fu, who had always emphasized realistic writing and had personally experienced the daily life of a river village, could depict such vivid and lifelike scenery with personal feelings. If he wrote poems from a recluse's point of view like Wang Wei, Meng Haoran and other pastoral poets, he would not have been able to attain such high achievements.

Chengdu was a famous cultural city with a long history, and there were also places of interest in its neighboring Xinjin County (now Xinjin in Sichuan) and Qingcheng County (now the west of Guanxi County in Sichuan), so Du Fu often traveled throughout the region in his leisure time. Sima Xiangru of the Han Dynasty had once played his zither in Linqiong (now Qionglai in Sichuan), using music to seduce Zhuo Wenjun, the newly widowed daughter of a wealthy man, to elope with him one night. After that, the couple operated a tavern to make a living. When Du Fu visited the zither tower of Sima Xiangru, he thought wistfully about this romantic love story. He also paid a special visit to the Wuhou Memorial Temple of Zhuge Liang, the brilliant statesman and military strategist in the Three Kingdoms Period, writing the following lines known throughout all ages: "You died before winning any battle / Which often reduced men to tears" ("Prime Minister of Shu").

Besides scenery, Du Fu often depicted daily life in his poems. In poems such as "Traveling to the North" written several years before and "To the Recluse Ruan for Sending Me Thirty Bundles of Shallots in Autumn" written

> 草深迷市井，地僻懒衣裳。
>
> 榉柳枝枝弱，枇杷树树香。
>
> 鸬鹚西日照，晒翅满鱼梁。
>
> ——《田舍》

幽静的农舍，古朴的风俗，生机盎然而又富有地方特征的花木鱼鸟，组成一幅恬静、和谐的江村晚景图，从中我们感受到诗人那颗宁静的心。这是以前杜甫笔下未曾出现过的。这首诗的尾联更是田园诗中少有的佳句：鸬鹚是一种水鸟，蜀人常驯养用来捕鱼，此时它们正站在鱼梁上展开双翅，在夕阳下晾晒羽毛，可见这时村民一天的劳动已经结束，村头人迹稀少，所以水鸟能够如此悠然自得。只有注重写实并且亲身体验了江村日常生活的杜甫才能描绘出这种真实生动而带有生活气息和地方特色的景象。如果像王维、孟浩然等山水田园诗人一样，以隐士的心态观景作诗，是不会达到这一高度的。

成都是一个著名的文化古城，附近的新津县（今四川新津）、青城县（今四川灌溪县西）也有游览胜地，杜甫闲暇时便四处走走。汉代的司马相如曾在临邛（今四川邛崃）弹琴，新寡的富家千金卓文君被琴声吸引，随他夜奔，夫妻二人开一酒店维持生活。杜甫游览司马相如的琴台时，对这一浪漫的爱情故事遐想不已。他还专程前往拜谒三国时代杰出的政治家、军事家诸葛亮的武侯祠，写下千古名句：“出师未捷身先死，常使英雄泪满襟。”（《蜀相》）

在写景的同时，平凡的日常生活情景也常被杜甫大量地写进了诗歌。在几年前写的《北征》和在秦州时写的《秋日阮隐

in Qinzhou, Du Fu included descriptions of some odd trivial matters. After Du Fu moved to the cottage in Chengdu, these seemingly trivial matters became a more important part of Du Fu's poetry. This was an obvious change of subject matter in the poems he composed; it was also an important turning point in Chinese poetic history.

Chinese poetry in the ancient times had always tended to be solemn and elegant, so the choice of subject matter usually followed certain set patterns. In general, most poetry told of visiting historical sites and musing over the past or missing one's family and friends. Only poems written by order of the emperor would give colorful accounts of royal rites, sacrificial ceremonies and court life. Tao Yuanming of the Eastern Jin Dynasty had once attempted to include daily life in his poems, often describing his poor life as well as such everyday actions as moving, begging, harvesting and drinking. But Tao Yuanming's poems were not great in number and the actions depicted were rather monotonous. It was not until Du Fu's time and especially in his time in Chengdu that daily life became a viable poetic subject matter. Du Fu produced a good number of poems reflecting daily life, among which there were the ones describing pleasure of secluded life and his feelings about living in peace and comfort, such as "The River Village" and "Rowing a Small Boat." Let's first look at "The River Village."

> A clean river runs around the village,
> Where everything is so quiet during the long summer.
> Swallows come and go, flying in the courtroom;
> Gulls gather together, living in love and harmony.
> My old wife makes a chessboard by drawing on paper;
> My little son gets a hook by curving an awl.
> I only need herbs as I'm often down with illness.
> What else do I need for such a humble body as mine?

The poem was written in a very natural and free-flowing style, a new phase in Du Fu's poetry.

There were also poems about life's vexations: For example, in the poem "Collection of Hundreds of Worries," the poet recalled his boyhood when he was strong and free of worries, sighing regretfully about his present conditions:

> Having turned fifty in the blink of an eye,
> I sat and lay much longer than I stood.
> I tried to look happy to please the hosts
> But was sad to find hundreds of worries around me.

居致薤三十束》等诗中，就有一些零星的生活琐事，而住在成都草堂后，这类题材则成了杜诗的主要内容之一。这是杜甫诗歌创作中主题的一个明显变化，也是中国诗歌史上的一个重要转折。

中国古代诗歌一向比较严肃高雅，题材选择有着一定的传统。大体来说，除了应制诗会夸张地渲染皇家的典礼、祭祀和宫廷生活外，一般的诗歌题材不外乎感时吊古、思亲怀友等。而人们的日常生活内容、生活情景则很少在诗中得以表现。东晋陶渊明有过这方面的尝试，他的诗中时常描写自己窘困的生活情景、平常的生活内容，比如移居、乞食、获稻、饮酒等等，但陶诗数量不多，所咏的生活内容也比较单一。直到杜甫，尤其是杜甫到成都后，日常生活的内容才在诗国中得到大力开拓。杜甫留下了大量反映日常生活的诗篇，其中有反映幽居乐事和安适情怀的，如《江村》、《进艇》等，让我们看《江村》：

清江一曲抱村流，长夏江村事事幽。

自去自来堂上燕，相亲相近水中鸥。

老妻画纸为棋局，稚子敲针作钓钩。

多病所须唯药物，微躯此外更何求？

全诗写得潇洒飘逸，在杜诗中是一种新的面目。

也有写烦心事的，如《百忧集行》中回忆起自己身体强健、无忧无虑的少年时代，并慨叹现在的情况则是：

即今倏忽已五十，坐卧只多少行立。

强将笑语供主人，悲见生涯百忧集。

> Inside my cottage, I still had nothing but bare walls.
> My old wife also looked as worried as I did.
> My silly sons had no idea of proper ethics between father and son,
> So they angrily asked me to get food at the east gate.

Du Fu did not have much income, but there were seven or eight members in his family, including his wife Yang, his younger brother Du Zhan, his sons Zongwen and Zongwu, two to three daughters and maybe some servants. Therefore, he had to shoulder considerable family burden, often landing them in difficult circumstances. The poem "Collection of Hundreds of Worries" vividly reflected the utterly destitute condition of the family. The scene in which the children "angrily asked me to get food" was especially lifelike.

The vicissitudes of life were sometimes caused by the weather. The old tree near his cottage, which Du Fu liked a lot, was uprooted in a storm, making him very sad. On one evening of the August in the second year of the Shangyuan reign (761 A.D.), the howling autumn wind blew the straw off his cottage, for which Du Fu wrote the poem "The Song of My Cottage Destroyed by Autumn Wind."

> One autumn in August, the sky was high with a howling wind,
> Blowing three layers of straw off my cottage roof.
> The straw flew over the river and scattered on the riverbank.
> Some hung high on the treetops; others floated down in the pond.
> Groups of children of the southern village took advantage of my old
> age,
> Stealing my straw in my presence,
> And openly carrying my straw to the bamboo woods.
> But I was too thirsty to shout out to stop them,
> So I could do nothing but come back and sigh, leaning on my stick.
> The wind stopped, the clouds became dark in a moment,
> And the sky became misty and then gradually turned dark.
> Our worn quilts felt as cold as iron, having been used for years.
> My son kept kicking in sleep, splitting the quilts from the inside.
> The beds were all wet since the cottage was leaking,
> But the rain kept dripping without cease.
> I have not slept since the breakout of the war.
> How could I endure the long nights when all was wet.
> Where could I find millions of buildings,
> Which would shelter all the poor people in the world and make

入门依旧四壁空，老妻睹我颜色同。

痴儿未知父子礼，叫怒索饭啼门东。

由于没有什么收入，而全家有七八口人，妻子杨氏、小弟杜占、儿子宗文和宗武、两三个女儿，可能还有仆人，家庭负担并不轻松，所以生活仍不免陷入窘境之中。《百忧集行》就生动地反映了家徒四壁的境况，小孩子"叫怒索饭"、气咻咻地喊着要饭吃的镜头尤其传神。

烦心事有时候是由天气造成的。草堂附近杜甫非常喜爱的那棵古楠树在一次暴风雨中被连根拔起，使杜甫十分悲伤。上元二年（761）八月的一天傍晚，秋风怒号，把草堂上的茅草也卷走了，杜甫为此写了《茅屋为秋风所破歌》：

八月秋高风怒号，卷我屋上三重茅。

茅飞渡江洒江郊，高者挂胃长林梢，下者飘转沉塘坳。

南村群童欺我老无力，忍能对面为盗贼，公然抱茅入竹去。

唇焦口燥呼不得，归来倚杖自叹息。

俄顷风定云墨色，秋天漠漠向昏黑。

布衾多年冷似铁，骄儿恶卧踏里裂。

床头屋漏无干处，雨脚如麻未断绝。

自经丧乱少睡眠，长夜沾湿何由彻。

them happy

And which would be as sturdy as mountains regardless of wind or rain.

Alas, when would such buildings appear before my eyes?

To make that dream come true, I would be willing to die from cold in this broken cottage.

This poem depicted extremely realistic details to reveal the plight of the poet. What was most important was that the poet did not just worry about his own hardships and difficulties, but put himself in others' positions, taking thought for all the poor people in the world who were suffering the same adversity. He was even willing to exchange his own life to allow all of them to live in peace and comfort, showing the benevolence and universal fraternity in his heart.

Du Fu had made contacts with some officials in Chengdu, as well as some local officials in the surrounding counties. They sometimes visited Du Fu, who entertained them in his cottage and composed poems such as "The Arrival of Guests" and "A Guest Coming for a Visit" for such occasions. Du Fu was also able to obtain their help. When building his cottage, he asked several county magistrates around for various young saplings. When he ran out of food and fuel, he wrote poems to Gao Shi, the regional governor of Pengzhou, for help. Gao Shi had written poems to ask about Du Fu when he arrived in Chengdu. When Du Fu sought help from him, he willingly agreed. Soon after, when Gao Shi was appointed to Shuzhou as regional governor, he took wine to Du Fu's cottage to visit him. The poet felt ashamed that there weren't delicious dishes to serve him, so he could do nothing but persuade him to drink more.

It was Yan Wu who offered the most help to Du Fu. In December of the first year of the Shangyuan reign (761 A.D.), the court appointed Yan Wu as governor of Chengdu, chief executive of Chengdu, grand minister of public works, as well as governor of Jiannan, Eastern Sichuan and Western Sichuan. Politically, Yan Wu and Fang Guan had a lot in common. Yan Wu, like Du Fu, had been banished from the court in the first year of the Qianyuan reign (758 A.D.) due to his involvement in the Fang Guan case, and the two of them had been in close contact with each other ever since. So when Yan Wu accepted the post of governor of Chengdu, Du Fu was overjoyed. Yan Wu often took care of Du Fu's daily life. Soon after he arrived at Chengdu, Yan Wu sent a poem to Du Fu, persuading him to join the government but received a polite letter of refusal from the poet. After that, Yan Wu would often take a small group of attendants, going to the suburbs to admire flowers and willow trees, and then continuing on to Huanhua Village to visit Du Fu. Sometimes, Yan Wu would

安得广厦千万间，大庇天下寒士俱欢颜，风雨不动安如山。

呜呼！何时眼前突兀见此屋，吾庐独破受冻死亦足。

全诗用一些极为真实的细节反映了生活的窘况。可贵的是，诗人忧心的不仅仅是一己的困苦，而是推己及人，想到了遭受同样痛苦的天下寒士，并且愿意以自己被冻死来换取天下寒士的安居，可见杜甫的仁厚博爱之心。

杜甫和成都府的一些官吏以及附近县邑的一些地方官颇有交往，他们有时会来看望杜甫，杜甫就在草堂接待客人，并写过《客至》、《有客》等诗。杜甫还得到过他们的一些帮助。营建草堂时，他向附近的几个县令要了各种树苗。在断炊的日子里，他给高适写诗求援，高适当时在距成都九十里的彭州任刺史，在杜甫刚到达成都时他就写诗来问候过。杜甫求援时，他又给了杜甫及时的帮助。高适不久改任蜀州刺史，曾带着酒到草堂拜会杜甫，诗人惭愧无肴招待，只好劝他多喝酒。

给杜甫帮助最大的人是严武。上元元年（761）十二月，朝廷派严武任成都的行政长官成都尹，充御史大夫，兼剑南东西川节度使。严武在政治上和房琯比较接近，曾和杜甫一起在乾元元年（758）受房琯牵连而遭贬谪，两人的来往一直比较密切，所以严武出任成都尹，诗人非常高兴。严武常在生活上照顾杜甫，来到成都不久，他就寄诗给杜甫，劝他出来做官，但被诗人婉言谢绝。其后严武曾不止一次地带着小队人马，走出郊外，赏花看柳，到浣花村看望杜甫。有时严武还会带来酒

bring some food and drink, and they would set a table near the bamboo woods, enjoying the landscape, drinking, and composing poems. The relation between Yan Wu and Du Fu also influenced other people. For example, Zhang Li, Governor of Zizhou and subordinate to Yan Wu, also gave Du Fu a lot of help while he stayed in Zizhou. Therefore, during his five year stay in the Shu Region, Du Fu could still have enough food and clothing most of the time, even as he fled the ravages of war.

"Those I met were merely strange people / Having no idea when to return to my hometown / The grand river flowed to the east as it always did / But the days of wandering men always seem so long" ("Chengdu City"). This was Du Fu's initial feeling when he first arrived at Chengdu. Of course, longing for his home and family was always in the back of his mind. As time went on, this feeling grew even more intense. His hometown was thousands of miles away and was suffering from war; his younger brothers and sister were out of contact with him as he grew older and feebler with each passing day. Du Fu's heart became entangled by all kinds of feelings, such as longing for home and family, sadness at his old age and illness, nostalgia for his country, and weariness of war. This was Du Fu's other dominant mood as he lived in his cottage. He was worried that he couldn't return to his hometown because of his old age and poor health, and that he would not be able to see his brothers and sister who were scattered all over.

> As the war is still going without end in sight,
> I've no idea where my younger brothers and sister have gone.
> My clothes are stained with blood as I wipe away my tears;
> My hair is completely white as I comb it.
> The wilderness looks so vast as it lies below;
> The river flows slowly when it grows dark.
> Old and feeble, how long can I stay alive in the world?
> I'm afraid I cannot wait until the day we would meet again.
>
> ("Pouring out My Heart")

In March of the second year of the Qianyuan reign (759 A.D.), Shi Siming helped An Qingxu lift the siege of Yecheng City, killing An Qingxu in the very same month, after which he announced himself Emperor of the Great Yan. The Tang government let Li Guangbi take the place of Guo Ziyi as Governor of Shuofang and commander-in-chief of the military. From then on, the government troops and the rebel troops fought each other around the Eastern Capital and Heyang (now Mengxian County in Henan). On the whole, the

水菜肴，大家就在竹林边摆起案子，陈列酒食，观赏景物，饮酒赋诗。严武与杜甫的关系还影响到其他人，如梓州刺使章彝作为严武的僚属，在杜甫避乱梓州期间也给杜甫不少照顾。所以，杜甫在蜀五年，尽管有时也有避乱奔走、衣食不周之苦，但多数时候尚能温饱。

"但逢新人民，未卜见故乡。大江东流去，游子日月长"（《成都府》），这是杜甫刚刚踏上成都后产生的第一感受。可见，思乡念亲之情无时无刻不萦绕在杜甫心头。随着岁月的流逝，这种感情越发强烈。故乡远在几千里外，且又正处于兵戈之中。弟弟和妹妹音信阻隔，而自己却一天天老去，身体一天天衰弱。思乡、念亲、叹老、嗟病、怀国、厌战，这种种的心理纠缠在一起，困扰着杜甫。这是他在草堂中的另一种情绪。他担心自己年老体病，不能再回到故乡，见不到分散在各处的兄弟姐妹：

干戈犹未定，弟妹各何之。

拭泪沾襟血，梳头满面丝。

地卑荒野大，天远暮江迟。

衰疾那能久，应无见汝时。

——《遣兴》

乾元二年（759）三月，史思明帮安庆绪解了邺城之围后，当月便杀了安庆绪，并于四月自称大燕皇帝。唐政府以李光弼代郭子仪为朔方节度使、兵马元帅。此后官军和叛军一直在东京和河阳（今河南孟县）一带争夺，总体上，官军取胜较多。

government troops won more victories. However, Li Guangbi gave up the Eastern Capital out of strategic considerations and was not able to recover it even in the first year of the Shangyuan reign (760 A.D.). Du Fu felt grieved in Chengdu, composing the following lines: "There came no news of the government troops' capture of areas east of Chang'an / So the horn of Chengdu City sounded mournfully in autumn" ("An Old Village Man").

In April of the first year of the Shangyuan reign (760 A.D.), Li Guangbi defeated Shi Siming in Xizhu of Heyang, killing over fifteen hundred rebels. Hearing this, Du Fu hoped that the government troops could pursue the rebel troops and drive straight on to their den in Hebei, a sentiment which can be inferred from the following lines: "Hearing of the victory of the battle in Heyang / How I wish the general would drive straight on to defeat the rebels" ("Hating to Part").

In March, Shi Siming was murdered by his son Shi Chaoyi, who ascended to the throne after that. The rebels started to fight against each other then, and the end of the An Shi Rebellion was in sight. The poet grieved that he was old and feeble in Huanhua village, unable to devote himself to the court: "As I'm too old and sick with so many diseases / I can contribute nothing to the state" ("A Wild View").

Chengdu was no peaceful paradise. The Shu Region was close to the remote border districts and had always been under serious threat from Tubo. In addition, rebellions by warlords great and small rose one after another. In April of the second year of the Shangyuan reign (761 A.D.), Duan Zizhang, Governor of Zizhou, launched a rebellion, proclaiming himself King of Liang. In May, Cui Guangyuan, Governor of Chengdu and Western Sichuan, captured Mianzhou with his subordinate Hua Jingding and killed Duan Zizhang. Nevertheless, Hua Jingding allowed his troops to rob the people, committing all kinds of outrages. He even "used rites and music that only Son of Heaven deserved." Therefore, Du Fu wrote the poem "To Mr. Hua" to mock him.

> Music played in the city day after day,
> Half its sound traveling to the river and half to the clouds.
> Such music should only be heard in heaven.
> How often will people hear it on the earth?

In April of the first year of the Baoying reign (762 A.D.), Emperor Xuanzong and Suzong passed away one after another, and the crown prince Li Yu ascended to the throne, becoming Emperor Daizong. The court ordered Yan Wu to return to the capital and appointed him to the post of governor of the

然而九月，李光弼出于战略考虑，放弃东京，到上元元年（760）也一直没有收回。杜甫在成都为此悲哀，写道"王师未报收东郡，城阙秋生画角哀。"（《野老》）

上元元年（760）四月，李光弼破史思明于河阳西渚，斩首千五百余级。杜甫听到消息，希望官军乘胜前进，直捣叛军在河北的老巢："闻道河阳近乘胜，司徒急为破幽燕。"（《恨别》）

三月，史思明被其子史朝义所杀，史朝义即皇帝位，叛军内部自相残杀，安史之乱进入尾声。诗人感叹自己老病在浣花村，不能为朝廷出力了："惟将迟暮供多病，未有涓埃答圣朝。"（《野望》）

成都也并非世外桃源。蜀中地近边鄙，吐蕃人的威胁始终都很严重，地方上大小军阀的叛乱此起彼伏。上元二年（761）四月，梓州（今四川三台）刺史段子璋反，称梁王。五月，成都尹、西川节度使崔光远率牙将花敬定攻破绵州，消灭了段。花敬定又纵兵大肆抢掠，并胡作非为，"僭用天子礼乐"。杜甫作了《赠花卿》来讽刺他：

> 锦城丝管日纷纷，半入江风半入云。
>
> 此曲只应天上有，人间能得几回闻。

宝应元年（762）四月，玄宗、肃宗相继去世，太子李豫即位，是为代宗。朝廷命严武回京任京兆尹兼山陵桥道使，监

capital with the additional responsibility of building two royal tombs. In July, as Yan Wu left Chengdu, Du Fu also decided to return to Chang'an, which can be inferred from the following lines: "How can I spend the rest of my life in Shu? / I'm determined to return to Chang'an as long as I can breathe" ("A Ten-Rhyme Poem to Revered Mr. Yan Who was about to Go to the Court"). Du Fu sent Yan Wu off to Mianzhou and wrote a poem for him in the posthouse of Fengji, encouraging him to serve the country wholeheartedly after returning to the court, and even to sacrifice his life for the country if need be: "If you are made prime minister / Don't cherish your own life in the face of danger" (ibid).

修两个皇陵。七月，严武离开成都，杜甫也动了回长安的念头：
"此身那老蜀，不死会归秦。"（《奉送严公入朝十韵》）杜甫送
严武到绵州，在奉济驿作诗送别，他勉励严武回朝后要一心报
国，甚至不惜为国捐躯："公若登台辅，临危莫爱身。"（同上）

漂泊中的杜甫
Wandering Du Fu

六　流寓梓阆及重回草堂

Chapter VI　Wandering Through Zizhou and Langzhou
Before Returning to "Thatched Hall"

Soon after Yan Wu left, Xu Zhidao, assistant governor of Chengdu and military chief of Jiannan, staged a revolt, sending troops to seize Jiange and cutting communication between the south and the north. In August, he was defeated by Gao Shi, Governor of Chengdu, then killed by his own follower Li Zhonghou. Li allowed his troops to commit all kinds of atrocities in Chengdu, killing a lot of people. Due to this event, Du Fu couldn't return to Chengdu, so he headed for Zizhou to escape the war after he heard the news that his old acquaintance, Duke of Hanzhong Li Yu, was in Zizhou (now Santai in Sichuan).

While in Zizhou, Du Fu lived in extreme poverty: "Lacking food and clothing as I possess no working skill / I have to rely on friends to maintain my livelihood" ("Spending a Night in a Strange Land"). He was fortunate that Zhang Li, the newly appointed Governor of Zizhou and Eastern Sichuan, treated him well. Then, in the autumn of that year, he left his cottage to the care of his younger brother Du Zhan and took his wife and children to Zizhou as well.

Shehong County (now Shehong in Sichuan) was near Zizhou, and was also the hometown of Chen Zi'ang. Chen Zi'ang was a poetic reformer at the beginning of the Tang Dynasty. He accused the poetic style of Qi and Liang of only paying attention to artistic form while neglecting thought and content, putting forward the idea of carrying on "the tradition of conveying one's aspirations through the techniques of *Bi* and *Xing*" and "literary styles in Han and Wei." His goal was to compose bold poetry full of rhythm, emotional beauty, splendor and conciseness. Later some powerful and treacherous officials exacted revenge on him by having him locked away in the county prison of Shehong. Du Fu had great sympathy for Chen Zi'ang's fate, so when seeing off Governor Li in Mianzhou, who was to take office in Zizhou, he said the following words:

> Revered Cheng Zi'ang died from a false accusation
> Causing the people of Shu to sympathize with him even today.
> When you visit Shehong County someday,
> Please shed a tear for him for my sake.
> ("Seeing off Governor Li Who was to Take Office in Zizhou")

In the winter of that same year, he paid a special visit to Shehong to visit the places where Chen Zi'ang studied and lived and wrote poems to praise Chen's essays on morality.

In October, government troops allied with Huihe troops to suppress Shi

严武一走，成都少尹兼剑南兵马使徐知道叛乱，派兵占据剑阁，断绝南北交通。八月，被成都尹高适击破，徐被部将李忠厚杀死。李在成都纵兵胡作非为，杀戮人民。因此事件，杜甫不能回成都。他得知以前认识的汉中王李瑀在梓州（今四川三台），于是前往梓州避乱。

他在梓州，"计拙无衣食，途穷仗友生"（《客夜》），生活比较艰苦。后来，新任梓州刺史兼东川留后章彝优待他。于是，这年秋天，他留下弟弟杜占看守草堂，把妻子儿女也接到梓州来了。

梓州附近的射洪县（今四川射洪），是陈子昂的故乡。陈是初唐时期的诗文革新者，他指责齐梁诗风徒重艺术形式而忽视了思想内容，提出要继承"风雅兴寄"、"汉魏风骨"的传统，创作出"骨气端翔、音情顿挫、光英朗练"的作品。他后来遭到权奸打击，冤死在射洪县狱中。杜甫对陈子昂的遭遇十分同情，他在绵州送李使君去梓州赴任时曾说：

遇害陈公殒，于今蜀道怜。

君行射洪县，为我一潸然。

——《送梓州李使君之任》

这年冬天，他专程到射洪，参观了陈子昂的读书处和故居，写诗对陈子昂的道德文章给予了极高的评价。

这年十月，官军联合回纥兵讨伐史朝义，收复洛阳、怀州

Chaoyi. They soon recaptured Luoyang, Huaizhou (now Qinyang in Henan), Bianzhou (now Kaifeng in Henan) and other places. As a result, rebel officers surrendered one after another, and the collapse of the rebellion was within sight. In the first lunar month of the first year of the Guangde reign (763 A.D.), Shi Chaoyi had no choice but to commit suicide. The An Shi Rebellion that had lasted for eight years was finally all but over.

Hearing in Zizhou that Shi Chaoyi had killed himself, Du Fu was so overjoyed that he gave way to a flood of tears and composed the poem "Hearing the News That Government Troops had Recaptured Henan and Hebei."

> News suddenly came from beyond the Sword Gate that Jibei was captured.
> When I first heard it, I soaked my clothes with tears.
> Looking back at my wife and children, where could I find their worry?
> Flipping through my books of poetry at random, I was wild with joy.
> It's better to have some drink while singing a hearty song;
> It's such a joy to return home during such a fine spring.
> I wish to set out from Ba Gorge at once and travel through Wu Gorge,
> Arriving soon at Xiangyang and journeying to Luoyang from there.

During the An Shi Rebellion, the poet suffered a lot fleeing from place to place to escape war, so most of the poems he composed during this period contained sentiments of worry, anger and grief, forming "a gloomy staccato style." Now that the rebellion was put down, the poet finally felt an irresistible impulse to sing "the first delightful poem of his life."

Du Fu settled his family in Zizhou, while he himself traveled between Langzhou, Yanting, Mianzhou, Hanzhou, Fucheng and other regions. This was his way of not overstaying his welcome. He wandered in and around Zizhou and Langzhou for one year and nine months, during which time he wrote a hundred and sixty or seventy poems.

Though the An Shi Rebellion had been suppressed, the whole court was still a mess, with Eunuch Li Fuguo, Cheng Yuanzhen, and Yu Chao'en successively monopolizing power and bringing disorder to state affairs. While the country suffered from internal strife, foreign nations seized the opportunity to launch border raids; as a result, the situation grew ever more serious. In July of the first year of the Guangde reign (763 A.D.), Tubo launched a general

（今河南沁阳）、汴州（今河南开封）等，叛军将领纷纷投降，叛军已成溃势。广德元年（763）正月，史朝义被迫自缢。至此，历时八年的安史之乱基本结束。

杜甫在梓州听到史朝义自尽，欣喜若狂，老泪纵横，写下了《闻官军收河南河北》：

> 剑外忽传收蓟北，初闻涕泪满衣裳。
>
> 却看妻子愁何在，漫卷诗书喜欲狂。
>
> 白日放歌须纵酒，青春作伴好还乡。
>
> 即从巴峡穿巫峡，便下襄阳向洛阳。

诗人在安史之乱中，饱受战乱流离之苦，所写的作品多为忧愤悲伤的情调，表现出"沉郁顿挫"的风格。而今战乱平定，诗人终于情不自禁地吟出"生平第一首快诗"。

杜甫把家安置在梓州，自己则穿梭于阆州、盐亭、绵州、汉州、涪城等地。这也是寄人篱下的处境中，为了避免主人厌烦而不得已采取的办法。他在梓、阆一带，共流寓了一年零九个月，写了一百六七十首诗。

安史之乱虽然平息了，而朝廷上下，仍是一片混乱，宦官李辅国、程元振、鱼朝恩相继专权乱政，国家政治已无清明可言。国家内部动乱，外族更是借机侵扰，形势比以前更加严重。广德元年（763）七月，吐蕃发起进攻，几乎侵占了包括河西、

offensive against the Tang, capturing nearly all the northwestern land covering from the west of the Yellow River to the west of Longshan Mountain; however, because Cheng Yuanzhen did not report the news, the court took no action whatsoever. In October, Tubo seized Fengtian, forcing Emperor Daizong to flee to Shanzhou. However, no local governors dared send troops to rescue the emperor, for fear of arousing the jealousy of Eunuch Cheng Yuanzhen and thus suffering his persecution. Du Fu wrote poems to express the indignation in his heart: "The emperor flees in panic at a time of social uncertainties / Where have all the ministers and officers gone?" ("Bashan Mountain")

After entering Chang'an, the Tubo troops burnt and looted with abandon. They were later defeated by Guo Ziyi, and Chang'an was restored. But the vicious Cheng Yuanzhen was merely removed from his office and sent back to his hometown. Hearing this news in Langzhou, Du Fu was extremely resentful: "When the arch criminal is not given the punishment he deserves / How will it be possible to settle the crisis?" ("Five Songs Lamenting the Passing of Spring")

In December, Tubo captured Songzhou (now Songpan in Sichuan), Weizhou (now north of Lixian County in Sichuan) and Baozhou (now southwest of Lixian County in Sichuan). This prompted Du Fu to write the poem "The End of the Year" to express his concern for the safety of his country.

> I lived a wandering life in a remote place at the end of the year.
> War broke out again along the border between Tubo and Shu.
> And the rebel troops have been pressing on the snow-capped mountain;
> Drums and horns have been heard in the river city.
> There are people bleeding in the country every day;
> Which official of the court will volunteer for battle?
> I don't care about my own life at such a critical moment.
> I can only cherish my lofty aspirations in loneliness.

After the An Shi Rebellion, the power of local separatist regimes began to grow. In order to end the rebellion as soon as possible, the Tang government did not prosecute the surrendered rebel leaders, but rather let them keep their own strongholds. As a result, many rebel leaders rapidly made themselves governors in the Tang court, taking control of vast territories, and gradually establishing new separatist regimes. "Surrendered generals are still without check though their rebellion has been suppressed / Generals stationed in Hebei have great fear that they will lose power if their troops are reduced" ("Five

陇右在内的西北所有土地，程元振却不报军情，朝廷没有采取任何措施。十月，吐蕃攻陷奉天，代宗出奔陕州，各节度使畏于宦官程元振的嫉害，不敢出兵救援。杜甫曾写诗抒发满腔的愤慨："狼狈风尘里，群臣安在哉！"（《巴山》）

吐蕃攻入长安，大肆焚掠，后被郭子仪击退，长安恢复。但是罪臣程元振却只是削爵放归，杜甫在阆州听到此消息，非常不满："不成诛执法，焉得变危机？"（《伤春五首》）

十二月，吐蕃攻陷松州（今四川松潘）、维州（今四川理县北）、保州（今理县西南），诗人又写《岁暮》，表达对国家安危的关切：

岁暮远为客，边隅还用兵。

烟尘犯雪岭，鼓角动江城。

天地日流血，朝廷谁请缨。

济时敢爱死，寂寞壮心惊。

安史之乱后，地方割据势力开始膨胀起来。唐政府为了尽快平定叛乱，对投降的叛军将领不予追究，并让他们各守本镇。于是许多叛将摇身一变，成为唐朝的节度使，坐拥一方，形成藩镇割据的局面："胡灭人还乱，兵残将自疑。"（《有感五首》）

Poems Written When All Sorts of Feelings Welled up"). Du Fu had high hopes in Emperor Daizong, hoping that he would be able to stabilize the country and reassure the people.

The An Shi Rebellion brought about unprecedented catastrophe to the lives and property of the people. After the rebellion, the national population was reduced to less than a third of what it had been. The regions around the Central Plain suffered a great deal from the war, with all regions falling into economic depression, while the south suffered from famines due to heavy taxes and forced labor combined with flood and drought. In August of the first year of the Baoying reign (762 A.D.), a minor official named Yuan Chao led a peasant uprising in eastern Zhejiang because he was resentful of the exorbitant demands made on peasants by the government. In March of the next year, the uprising was put down by government troops and Yuan Chao was captured and sent to Chang'an to be killed. Du Fu expressed his view on this in his poem "Seasonable Rain."

> Due to the spring drought, it was dark all around,
> With the sun burning as red as blood.
> All farm work had to be stopped,
> The situation was aggravated by war.
> The people of Shu were hard pressed for military supplies,
> So they wailed in the burning heat of the earth in drought.
> As a timely rain arrived at the river in the night,
> Nature's sin of the long-lasting drought was washed away.
> The roots of crops could relax for a time,
> But the effects of the disaster did not yet disappear.
> How can we live in peace and tranquility,
> So that the worries pent up in my mind can be relieved.
> Clouds that have built up as high as mountains
> Met and piled upon others, stretching far and wide.
> How is it possible to whip the Thunder God
> So that heavy rain can wash clean the regions of Wu and Yue.

The poet added a note to this poem, saying that "he heard there were many robbers in eastern Zhejiang." He hated all kinds of war, including peasant uprisings and rebellions, condemning the destruction of agricultural production caused by war. But he sincerely sympathized with the people, felt concern for their sufferings, and could understand the truth that official exploitation drove the people to rebellion, commenting, "If the court could exercise thrift and love

杜甫寄希望于唐代宗，希望他能安定社稷、安抚百姓。

安史之乱使人民生命财产遭到空前的浩劫。乱后，全国户口减为不到原来的三分之一。中原一带饱受战乱，千里萧条，南方则因赋役繁重，加上水旱等灾，时生饥馑。宝应元年（762）八月，一个叫袁晁的小官吏因不满官府对农民敲骨吸髓般的诛求，愤而领导农民在浙东起义，次年三月被官军镇压，袁晁被俘往长安杀害。杜甫在《喜雨》一诗中表达了对这件事的看法：

春旱天地昏，日色赤如血。

农事都已休，兵戈况骚屑。

巴人困军须，恸哭厚土热。

沧江夜来雨，真宰罪一雪。

谷根小苏息，沴气终不灭。

何由见宁岁，解我忧思结。

峥嵘群山云，交会未断绝。

安得鞭雷公，滂沱洗吴越。

作者原注："时闻浙右多盗贼。"他痛恨包括农民起义和军阀叛乱在内的一切战争，控诉战争对农业生产的破坏。但他能真诚地同情人民，关心人民疾苦，而且还能多少认识到官逼民

to its people / Bandits and robbers would naturally be its subjects as before"
("Three Poems Written When All Sorts of Feelings Welled up" No. Three).

He demanded that bureaucrats not take bribes or strain the law. He further
put forward his idea that everyone should be equal in paying taxes and
performing yearly labor, saying, "All officials should be honest and clean /
While taxes and yearly labor should be borne equally by all" ("A Poem to
Governor of Lingzhou Who was about to Take Office").

Du Fu wrote these poems on current affairs and politics while traveling
around in Jiannan. Du Fu did never give up his concern for the country's
current situation.

In March of the second year of the Guangde reign (764 A.D.), Du Fu was
overjoyed to hear that in Langzhou, Yan Wu had been reappointed as Governor
of Western Sichuan and Jiannan, so Du Fu sent his fourth younger brother Du
Zhan, who often traveled between Chengdu, Zizhou and Langzhou, to return to
Chengdu first to make preparations for him to move there. Soon after, he took
his wife and children and returned to Chengdu.

On the road from Langzhou to Chengdu, Du Fu wrote five poems to Yan
Wu. He summarized his wandering life in Jiannan, saying, "I have been
wandering for three years like an empty body / Believing that life was hard in
the human world" ("Five Poems to Revered Mr. Yan Written before Setting
out to Chengdu").

Du Fu returned to Chengdu in the late spring to find his cottage in
disrepair: Wild mice were running about, the water gutter was tilting, and the
flower bed was destroyed. Nevertheless, he was still very excited to be home.

> I was delighted to see that the four pines trees still stood as I
> entered the yard
> And that I could walk through the sparse bamboo woods in
> wooden-soled shoes once again.
> Being pleased that I was back, my old dog lingered under the hem
> of my clothes.
> Being pleased that I was back, my neighbors bought wine with
> wine calabashes.
> Being pleased that I was back, officials sent their men on horses to
> ask what I needed.
> Being pleased that I was back, visitors crowded the narrow market
> in the city walls.
>
> ("Thatched Hall")

反的道理："不过行俭德，盗贼本王臣。"(《有感三首》其三）

他要求官僚不要贪赃枉法，还进一步提出一切赋税徭役都要人人平等："众僚宜洁白，万役但平均。"(《送陵州路使君之任》）

以上这些，都是杜甫在剑南流寓期间所写的时事诗和政治诗。诗人的心真是一刻也没有停止过对国家和时局的关心和思考。

广德二年（764）三月，杜甫在阆州听说严武重任剑南东西川节度使，真是喜出望外，于是打发经常往来于成都、梓州和阆州之间的四弟杜占，先回成都料理。不久，他就带领妻子儿女返回成都了。

杜甫从阆州返回成都的途中，寄了五首诗给严武。他总结流寓剑南的生活，说是："三年奔走空皮骨，信有人间行路难。"(《将赴成都寄严公五首》）

暮春时节，杜甫回到成都。草堂是一片荒凉景象，屋里野鼠乱窜，水槛倾斜，药栏破坏，但他却很兴奋：

入门四松在，步屟万竹疏。

旧犬喜我归，低徊入衣裾。

邻舍喜我归，酤酒携胡芦。

大官喜我来，遣骑问所须。

城郭喜我来，宾客隘村墟。

——《草堂》

He repaired his cottage, dug a well under the palm trees, and built a canal by the bamboo woods, bringing life back to Huanhua Village. The four young pine trees had grown to the height of a man. The five peach trees in his yard bore peaches every year, which he allowed poor people to pick. Spring was very much in the air in Huanhua Village again.

> The rivers and mountains are so beautiful in the spring days
> When the wind carries the fragrance of flowers and grass.
> Swallows are busy gathering soft mud to build nests
> While mandarin ducks sleep in the warm sand.
>
> ("Two Quatrains," No. One)

He paid a visit to the water pavilion of his southern neighbor Zhu Shanren and went before the gate of his northern neighbor Hu Sirong to mourn for him as he had passed away while Du Fu was gone. He called on old Zhu to taste plums, invited the young Ruan to watch the pine trees and visited places of interest in Chengdu with the recluse Wang Qi, who had once been a censor.

However, Du Fu's concern and worry for the state and the people never diminished. One day in late spring, he climbed on top of a tall tower and saw the memorial temple of Liu Shan, the emperor of Shu in the Three Kingdoms Period whose fatuity caused the destruction of his kingdom. Then, thinking of the numerous misfortunes pressing down upon the people of China, he couldn't help but chant Zhuge Liang's poem "The Song of Liangfu Mountain," afterwards composing a poem of his own:

> I am grieved to see flowers growing near the gate tower
> At a time when trouble arises throughout the country.
> Spring has returned to this side of the Jinjiang River.
> The clouds near Yulei Mountain have come and gone since the
> ancient times.
> Like the North Star, the court is constant through all,
> So bandits in the Western Mountain are better off not invading it.
> It's a pity that the last king of Shu still has a temple for people to
> worship him.
> I think of "The Song of Liangfu," as the sky turns dark.
>
> ("Climbing onto the City Gate Tower")

Yan Wu was not pleased that Du Fu continued to live in a small village, so he soon had Du Fu appointed to a position in his office. In June of the second

他把草堂修葺一新，棕树下面凿井，竹林旁边开渠，浣花村又恢复了往日的生机。他门前的四棵小松，已有一人高。他庭院里有五棵桃树，每年结出的桃子他都让贫苦人家前来采摘。浣花村又是春意盎然：

迟日江山丽，春风花草香。

泥融飞燕子，沙暖睡鸳鸯。

——《绝句二首》其一

他去南邻朱山人的水亭作客，北邻的斛斯融已经死去，他也去门前悼念一番。他招呼朱老来品尝梅子，又邀请阮生来看小松树，还与做过侍御的隐士王契同游成都名胜。

然而，杜甫的忧国忧民之情毫无衰减。暮春的一天，他登上高楼，看到三国时昏庸失国的蜀国后主刘禅的祠庙，想到万方多难的国家形势，情不自禁地吟咏起诸葛亮的《梁甫吟》，并写下一首诗：

花近高楼伤客心，万方多难此登临。

锦江春色来天地，玉垒浮云变古今。

北极朝廷终不改，西山寇盗莫相侵。

可怜后主还祠庙，日暮聊为梁甫吟。

——《登楼》

严武不赞成杜甫村居，不久就拉他到幕府任职。广德二年

year of the Guangde reign (764 A.D.), the court appointed Du Fu as governor's office consultant and vice director of the Ministry of Public Works granting him a scarlet gown and a bag covered with fish patterns, a symbol of an official position over the fifth rank. This was the highest position Du Fu would ever obtain.

It was after Tubo seized Songzhou, Weizhou and Baozhou that Yan Wu was ordered to defend Shu, and his immediate responsibility was to recover the lost land. So he reorganized the troops and stepped up combat readiness. In June, he held a banquet in his official residence and practiced horsemanship and archery, making preparations to dispatch troops. Du Fu was invited to watch the drilling, and he wrote an essay "On Eastern and Western Sichuan" to analyze the situation for Yan Wu's reference. He keenly pointed out, "If three cities are captured, officers in charge are responsible; soldiers are not to be blamed, for the failure is caused by shortage of food." He also remarked condemningly that officers of all ranks pocketed a portion of the soldiers' pay. To prevent confusion caused by language barriers in the militias of various nationalities, he suggested that commanders be appointed as soon as possible to give unified directions to militias of diverse nationalities. He also put forward the suggestion that the government "divide the land equally and collect fewer taxes" so as to "supply the emperor while comforting the tired people at the bottom."

In July, Yan Wu led troops west, arriving in person at the frontier. He then wrote the poem "Early Autumn in a Military Town," which resonated profoundly with Du Fu, who thereafter composed the poem "A Reply to Revered Yan's Poem 'Early Autumn in a Military Town.' "

> Flags and banners wave in the autumn wind.
> Bows are prepared in generals' tents to shoot at enemy camps.
> Dibo, the garrison shrouded in cloudy mist, has been captured;
> Pengpo, the city outside the snowy mountain, will be seized as well.

In September, Yan Wu defeated seventy thousand Tubo soldiers and recaptured Danggou City (now southeast of Lixian County in Sichuan) and Yanchuan City (now west of Zhangxian County in Gansu), all of which were great victories.

Returning in triumph, Yan Wu often invited Du Fu to enjoy scenery and recite poems with him. Yan Wu was around forty years old, more than ten years younger than Du Fu, but he was very respectful towards Du Fu, arousing considerable jealousy from some of his young subordinates, with whom Du Fu

（764）六月，朝廷任命杜甫为节度使署中参谋、检校工部员外郎，赐给他象征五品以上官阶的绯鱼袋。这是杜甫一生所任的最高官职。

严武是在吐蕃攻陷松州、维州、保州后镇蜀的，首要的职责是收复失地。他整顿军队，加强战备。六月，他在节度府中设宴，并演习骑射，准备出师。杜甫也受邀观摩了这次演习，并写了《东西两川说》分析形势，以资参谋。他尖锐地指出："顷三城失手，罪在职司，非兵之过也，粮不足故也。"批判了各级官吏层层克扣军饷的罪行。针对当地各族民兵号令不一的问题，他建议尽快设立指挥官，统一指挥各民族子弟兵。并提出"均亩薄敛"，"以此上供王命，下安疲人"的建议。

七月，严武率兵西征，亲临前线，写了《军城早秋》一诗。杜甫产生了共鸣，也写了《奉和严郑公军城早秋》：

秋风袅袅动高旌，玉帐分弓射虏营。

已收滴博云间戍，更夺蓬婆雪外城。

九月，严武打败吐蕃兵马七万，克复了当狗城（今四川理县东南），收复了盐川城（今甘肃漳县西），取得了胜利。

严武凯旋归来后，时常邀请杜甫同享观赏吟咏之乐。严武当时不过四十来岁，比杜甫小十多岁，他对杜甫很敬重，但是这却引起他手下一班年轻幕僚的嫉妒，让一向耿直的杜甫觉得

found it very difficult to socialize.

As I grow old, I trust my goodwill to young people,
Who appear to be sincere in my presence but laugh behind my
back.
I just want to inform these young people
That they needn't be suspicious, as I don't meant to compete with
them.

("A Song on Casting no Doubt")

There were strict rules and regulations in the offices of commanding
generals during the Tang Dynasty: Officials had to go to work early and come
back very late. Du Fu lived in the western suburbs rather far from his office, so
he often had to stay in the office alone. One night when he was on duty,
listening to the horn at midnight and watching the moon in the sky, Du Fu
wrote a sad and dismal poem entitled "Spending a Night in the Office."

The parasol trees by the well in the office seem so cold in the clear
autumn air
While I stay alone in the river city with candles that have burnt
down,
Listening to the horn blowing its lonely tune in the long night.
With whom could I enjoy such beautiful moonlight?
As the war never ends, I haven't heard from my friends and
relatives for long;
As the road has become treacherous, I'm unable to return to my
hometown.
I have already put up with this wandering life for ten years,
But now I have to move again, like a bird choosing another branch
on which to perch.

Working in the commanding general's office, Du Fu was still concerned
about the state and the people. In October of the second year of the Guangde
reign (764 A.D.), Pugu Huai'en conspired with Huihe and Tubo, leading a
hundred thousand soldiers in an advance on Fengtian, which shocked the
whole capital. In November, leading the remnants of his troops, Guo Ziyi
defeated the rebels, but civil strife and border troubles continued to plague the
land. With these thoughts in mind, Du Fu was filled with anxiety.

The star of the Tartars has fallen on the land of Yan,
But officers and men still fight on.

很难周旋：

　　　晚将末契托年少，当面输心背面笑。

　　　寄谢悠悠世上儿，不争好恶莫相疑。

　　　　　　　　　　——《莫相疑行》

　　唐朝的幕府有严格的制度，清早入府办公，夜晚才能出来。杜甫家住西郊，离幕府比较远，只好一个人住在幕府里。有一天他值夜，耳听着夜半的号角，眼看着当空的月亮，写了一首情绪悲凉的《宿府》：

　　　清秋幕府井梧寒，独宿江城蜡炬残。

　　　永夜角声悲自语，中天月色好谁看。

　　　风尘荏苒音书绝，关塞萧条行路难。

　　　已忍伶俜十年事，强移栖息一枝安。

　　身处幕府，杜甫仍然关心着国家和人民。广德二年（764）十月，仆固怀恩勾结回纥、吐蕃，引兵十万，进逼奉天，京师震动。十一月由郭子仪率残兵击退，而内乱和边患仍很严重，杜甫忧心忡忡：

　　　胡星坠燕地，汉将仍横戈。

The whole country has become so depressed
That wolves and tigers have outnumbered men.
Go not to places where few people live,
But feel free to walk in places where tigers prowl,
For hungry men exchange sons for food
While beasts are still afraid of hunting nets.
("Seeing off Tang Jie with a Poem to be Sent to Jia, the Deputy Minister of Rites")

Du Fu became acquainted with Wei Feng, an office clerk in Langzhou, and wrote him a farewell poem entitled "To Wei Feng, the Office Clerk of Langzhou." The poem explained that the war was not over and that the officials were endlessly making exorbitant demands on the people.

The whole nation is still trapped in hardship,
And the war continues without end.
Everywhere are people moaning,
For they have been providing military supplies for ten years.
The officials only concentrate on suppressing the people,
Sparing no time to worry about the revolts caused by oppression.
How many kinds of taxes do they collect from the people!
They should have understood that wise men rule by benevolence.

Then, Du Fu encouraged Wei Feng to be as upright as the strings of a harp in his duties, appealing forcefully, "To cure sore and wound in the world / You should eradicate all the pests." Du Fu compared corrupt officials who secure their belongings by force or trickery to field pests, thereby demonstrating his strong feelings and clear-cut stand.

In the second year of the Guangde reign (764 A.D.), plagues of locusts and numerous floods struck the Central Shaanxi region, causing the people there to suffer from a serious shortage of food. Su Yuanming, the deputy head of the archival bureau, died of starvation, and Zheng Qian, who was banished to Taizhou, also died of illness. Du Fu mourned for them, saying, "Who pitied me indeed among my old friends? / Zheng and Su valued me most in my whole life" ("Mourning the Death of Zheng Qian and Su Yuanming").

Of the famous poets of the time, Wang Wei died in the second year of the Shangyuan reign (761 A.D.), and Li Bai died in the first year of the Baoying reign (762 A.D.). Du Fu lamented, "Where are the men of real talent now? / Writings of genuine worth have all been swept away" (ibid).

Before long, in the first month of the first year of the Yongtai reign (765

萧条四海内，人少豺虎多。

少人慎莫投，多虎信所过。

饥有易子食，兽犹畏虞罗。

——《别唐十五诫，因寄礼部贾侍郎》

杜甫结识了阆州录事参军韦讽，为他写过一首优秀的送别诗《送韦讽上阆州录事参军》。诗歌先描写了战乱未息、官吏诛求不止的严峻现实：

国步犹艰难，兵革未衰息。

万方哀嗷嗷，十载供军食。

庶官务割剥，不暇忧反侧。

诛求何多门，贤者贵为德。

接着勉励韦讽赴任要像琴弦一样正直，并大声疾呼："必若救疮痍，先应去蟊贼。"诗人把那些巧取豪夺的贪官污吏比作田间的害虫，可以看出他的感情多么强烈，爱憎多么鲜明。

广德二年（764），关中发生蝗灾、水灾，粮食奇缺，秘书少监苏源明在长安饿死了。贬谪台州的郑虔，也因病去世了。诗人哀悼他们："故旧谁怜我？平生郑与苏。"（《哭台州郑司户苏少监》）

当代文坛，王维已于上元二年（761）去世，李白也在宝应元年（762）去世，杜甫悲痛地哀叹："豪俊何人在？文章扫地无。"（同上）

没过多久，永泰元年（765）正月，散骑常侍高适也逝世

A.D.), Gao Shi, Caliver Attendant-in-ordinary, also passed away, causing Du Fu to exclaim sentimentally, "Your unrivalled poems are still left in the world / Which only make your old friends grieve all the more" ("Hearing the News of Gao Shi's Death").

With the exception of Du Zhan, Du Fu's other younger brothers all lived apart from each other. One day, his second younger brother, Du Ying, paid an unexpected visit to Du Fu from Qizhou, which brought him a lot of comfort, but Du Ying had to return before long.

Du Fu always felt uncomfortable working in the commanding general's office, revealing his desire to return to his cottage on numerous occasions. In his youth, he had caught malaria and pneumonia, and as he grew older, his joints became arthritic. As a result, his limbs would become numb if he sat for too long. The strict, dull office life and subtleties of human relations wearied Du Fu, making him even more homesick. He could do nothing but write poems to "express his dreams and kill time," but this often made him feel even more lonely, writing, "I write poems to kill time when feeling too depressed / But I grow even more morose after completing the poems" ("After the Winter Solstice").

He worked in the commanding general's office for half a year. On the third day of the first lunar month of the first year of the Yongtai reign (765 A.D.), he finally resigned from his office and returned to his cottage. He was not satisfied with this period in his life, commenting, "Joining the commanding general's office when my hair turned grey / I felt deeply that I had wasted my own life" ("A Poem Written on the Third Day of the First Lunar Month after Returning to Huanhua Stream").

After returning to his cottage, Du Fu and his children replanted and weeded the garden, prompting Du Fu to say, "It is necessary to remove weeds / For we should hate evils like an enemy" ("Removing Weeds"). He had employed this technique of conveying messages through parables in expressing the importance of eradicating the evil and helping the good: "The newly planted pine trees grow as tall as a thousand feet / While a million evil bamboos must be cut" ("Five Poems to Revered Mr. Yan Written before Setting out to Chengdu"). These poetic lines contained political messages. He compared removing weeds to getting rid of the wicked, showing that he had a strong hatred of such evils as "treacherous court officials," "gangs of hoodlums," "Tartar traitors," "officials who secured their belongings by force," "worldly belongings" and "rich men feeding on delicacies."

了，诗人感伤地说："独步诗名在，只令故旧伤。"（《闻高常侍亡》）

除了杜占以外，杜甫的其他几个弟弟长期离散各地。一天，二弟杜颖却突然从齐州来成都看望杜甫，这给他带来很大安慰，不过杜颖不久就回去了。

杜甫在幕府，心情始终不太舒畅，一再流露出想返回草堂的意思。他早年患有疟疾和肺病，如今年纪衰老，又患"风痹"，坐得久了，便觉肢体麻木。严格而枯燥的幕府生活，复杂微妙的人事关系，使得年老体病的杜甫深感无趣，更加思念家乡。他只好写诗来"遣兴"，但结果往往反而更觉凄凉："愁极本凭诗遣兴，诗成吟咏转凄凉。"（《至后》）

他在幕府任职半年。永泰元年（765）正月三日，终于辞职回到草堂。对于这一段幕府生活，他的评价是不满意的："白头趋幕府，深觉负平生。"（《正月三日归溪上有作》）

他回到草堂，带领儿女修整园林，铲除恶草："芟夷不可缺，疾恶信如仇。"（《除草》）此前他也曾在诗歌中用托物寓意的手法表达过除恶扶善的内容："新松恨不高千尺，恶竹应须斩万竿。"（《将赴成都寄严公五首》）这些诗句，含有政治寓意，他是借除草喻除奸，对于"奸臣"、"群凶"、"逆胡"、"豪夺吏"、"俗物"、"膏粱客"等等，他确实是疾恶如仇的。

Life in the cottage began to take on the poetic charm it once had.

> Two orioles sing in green willow leaves
> While a row of egrets fly into the sky.
> The mountain where snow never melts can be seen from my
> window;
> The boats anchored outside my gate can travel as far as Eastern Wu.
>
> ("Four Quatrains" No. Three)

Whether he was conscious or not, Du Fu paid close attention to the boats that sailed eastward along the river.

Soon Yan Wu died of a sudden illness in April, causing Du Fu to lose his support in Chengdu, so he determined to take a boat eastward.

草堂的生活又呈现出诗情画意：

　　两个黄鹂鸣翠柳，一行白鹭上青天。

　　窗含西岭千秋雪，门泊东吴万里船。

　　　　　——《绝句四首》其三

他有意无意地关注起沿江东下的船只。

不久，四月里，严武暴病而亡，杜甫在成都失去生活依靠，就决意乘舟东下了。

杜甫诗意画——即从巴峡穿巫峡

Painting according to Du Fu's poem "I wish to set out from Ba Gorge at once
and travel through Wu Gorge"

七　白帝城头忆平生

Chapter Ⅶ　Recalling His Life While in Baidi City

In the early summer of the first year of the Yongtai reign (765 A.D.), Du Fu left Du Zhan his cottage in Chengdu and traveled eastward by boat with his wife and children. As he set off on his journey, he wrote a poem entitled "Leaving Shu," to express the sense of desolation brought about by his wandering life.

> I have wandered in Shu for five years
> And stayed in Zizhou for another year.
> How was I to know that my way would be blocked by perilous forts,
> Forcing me to turn around and travel along the Xiao and Xiang rivers.
> Since I'm too old for all the things in the world,
> I have to follow white gulls for the rest of my life.
> As there have been ministers fighting for the safety of the state,
> I do not need to shed endless tears.

The last two lines of the poem were ironic in tone; on one level, he expressed that he should not have shed endless tears for state affairs, because ministers and generals were responsible for the national security. However, how could a person like Du Fu, who was often concerned for the safety of the state, behave like this?

The family traveled eastward along the Minjiang River both day and night.

> By the river bank where thin grass waved in the breeze,
> A boat with a tall mast was anchored alone at night.
> The field was so vast that clusters of stars hung on the distant ground.
> The moonlight on the water flowed with the turbulent waves.
> How can one obtain fame through writing poems?
> Being old and ill, I will not stay in office much longer.
> What do I resemble, constantly wandering here and there as I do?
> A shorebird flying lonely between heaven and earth.
>
> > ("Pouring out My Heart on a Traveling Night")

Intermittedly walking and stopping during his journey, Du Fu also visited several old friends, climbed and toured places of interest such as Yu Temple in Zhongzhou, and wrote many poems describing natural scenery or meditating on the past. He arrived at Yun'an in autumn, and had to stay there to recuperate from the pneumonia and arthritis brought on by the journey. The family lived

永泰元年（765）初夏，杜甫把成都草堂留给杜占，自己乘船携带妻子儿女东下。他动身时写下一首《去蜀》，表达辗转漂泊的凄凉之感：

> 五载客蜀郡，一年居梓州。
> 如何关塞阻，转作潇湘游。
> 世事已黄发，残生随白鸥。
> 安危大臣在，不必泪长流。

最后两句实是反语，字面上说有文武大臣负责国家安全，自己不必担心国事以致眼泪长流，可是对于常常将国家安危装在心里的杜甫来说，怎么可能做到这一点呢？

一家人沿岷江东下，昼夜兼程：

> 细草微风岸，危樯独夜舟。
> 星垂平野阔，月涌大江流。
> 名岂文章著，官应老病休。
> 飘飘何所似，天地一沙鸥。
> ——《旅夜述怀》

一路上走走停停，也拜访过几位故旧，登览过忠州的禹庙等名胜，写了许多写景和怀古的诗歌。秋天到达云安，由于旅途劳顿，诗人肺病和风痹发作，只好留滞养病。一家人暂住在

for a time in the waterside pavilion of county magistrate Yan for about half a
year. The pavilion lay at the foot of a mountain and beside a river, where one
could often hear cuckoos crying in the woods. It was said that cuckoos were
incarnations of Du Yu, the ancient king of Shu, which caused Du Fu to feel
deep reverence whenever he heard the cries of cuckoos. Now that he was "too
ill to make obeisance," he could do nothing but "let tears flow down his face"
("Cuckoos").

Meanwhile, Shu fell into chaos due to the loss of such a good officer as
Yan Wu, its communications blocked and traveling merchants halting business.
Du Fu was often concerned about the situation in Shu, and he missed his
cottage in Huanhua Village. He also wanted to accomplish some important
deed during the remainder of his life.

At the end of the spring in the first year of the Dali reign (766 A.D.), with
the help of the judge of Yun'an, Du Fu and his family boarded a boat bound for
the east, arriving at Kuizhou in early summer. Kuizhou lay on the slope of
Baidi Mountain on the north bank of the mouth of Qutang Gorge of the
Yangtze River. Since it was built on the foundation of Baidi City established by
Gongsun Shu, a warlord of the Han Dynasty, and was later expanded to the
northwestern slope, the Tang people usually referred to Kuizhou as Baidi City.
Du Fu stayed there for one year and eight months, before leaving in the third
year of the Dali reign (768 A.D.). He first lived in the guest house on the slope
before moving to the western pavilion inside the city in autumn. At the
beginning of the next year, he moved to the Red Cliff Mountain, taking
residence in a cottage in Rangxi in March. Finally in autumn, he moved to the
East Village. Altogether, he moved five times and wrote over four hundred and
fifty poems on more than three hundred and thirty themes in Kuizhou: To
accomplish this feat, he wrote one poem almost every two days. Because of
this, his time in Kuizhou was another productive period in his writing career.

It was impossible to dig wells in Kuizhou, so drinking water was a big
problem. The local people all used bamboo pipes, which wound through the
mountains, to draw spring water for drinking. As soon as Du Fu settled down,
he also ordered his servant Aduan to draw water in this way. Because the
bamboo pipes which were already erected were broken, he asked Xinhang to
examine and repair them. Xinhang climbed up the valley, walking forty *li* in
all, and returning with the setting sun. Du Fu was sorry to have inconvenienced
him, so Du Fu brought melons and cakes to him to express gratitude. Since
there was a vacant lot below the cottage, Du Fu asked his servants to cultivate
it to grow lettuce. Since he heard that black-boned chickens could cure

严县令的水阁，约有半年之久。水阁依山傍水，树林间常传来杜鹃的啼叫。传说杜鹃是古代蜀王杜宇的化身，杜甫每听到杜鹃叫便肃然起敬，现在因为"身病不能拜"，就只好"泪下如迸泉"（《杜鹃》）了。

这时的蜀中，因失去了严武那样的良将而陷入大乱，交通阻塞，商旅断绝。杜甫经常关心蜀中局势，怀念浣花草堂。他还想以衰病之躯，有所作为。

大历元年（766）春末，在云安王判官的帮助下，杜甫一家又把行李搬上船，继续东下，夏初到达夔州。夔州在长江瞿塘峡口北岸的白帝山山腰上，是在汉代军阀公孙述所建的白帝城基础上向西北面山坡扩展而成的，所以唐人往往把夔州城直接称为白帝城。杜甫在这里住了一年零八个月，直到大历三年（768）离开。他先住在山腰上的客堂，秋天移居到城内的西阁，次年年初又搬到赤甲山，三月迁入瀼西草堂，秋天又移居东屯，一共搬了五处。他在夔州写诗三百三十余题，四百五十余首，平均不到两天就写一首，这是他一生创作的一个旺盛时期。

夔州不能凿井，饮水困难。当地人都是用盘绕山间的竹筒，引来泉水饮用。杜甫住下后，也吩咐獠奴阿段引水。后来架设的竹筒坏了，又叫信行去检修。信行爬上崖谷，来回走了四十里，太阳落山才回来。诗人心里很过意不去，拿出瓜和饼来慰劳他。堂下有一块空地，他叫仆人开垦出来栽种莴苣。因为听

arthritis, he also raised a hundred such chickens.

Owing to the good treatment of Bai Maolin, Governor of Kuizhou, Du Fu led a comfrotable life there. He bought a forty *mu* ❶ orchard in Rangxi and was in charge of a public field of a hundred *qing* ❷ in the East Village. He employed many servants including Aduan, Boyi, Xinxiu, Xinhang and a maid called Aji.

As it guarded Qutang Gorge in the middle reaches of the Yangtze River, Kuizhou was an important mountain pass in the Yangtze Gorges area, famous for its unique and beautiful scenery. With his powerful writing style, Du Fu depicted the majestic and perilous scenery in Kuizhou.

> Thousands of streams flow from the southwest into the Yangtze River.
> The two cliffs at the mouth of Qutang Gorge face each other like powerful rivals.
> The earth and the towering mountain crack open together,
> So that the river seems to flow from a cave on the moon to the west.
> > ("Meditating on the Past at Qutang Gorge")

He also recorded the local customs and practices in Kuizhou.

> Maidens of Kuizhou have half white hair,
> Unable to marry until forty or fifty.
> Living in wartime makes it more difficult to marry,
> Leaving them to sigh and lament for the rest of their lives.
> Men sit while women stand according to the customs;
> Men are in charge of the housework while women go out to work.
> Most of them come back with firewood on their back,
> Which they then sell to get money for the whole family.
> Their double hair buns hunging down to their old necks,
> Wild flowers and leaves are woven into their hair with silver hairpins.
> They gather all their strength and climb up to go to market.
> To make a greater profit, they risk their lives to sell salt.
> Their make-up and ornaments mix with tear stains.
> In thin clothes, they are trapped in crevasses at the foot of mountains.
> If one thinks the women of the Wushan Mountain are ugly and rough,
> > Why is there the village of Zhaojun in this place?
> > ("A Song on Women Carrying Firewood on Their Backs")

说乌鸡能治风痹，他还养了一百只乌鸡。

由于夔州都督柏茂琳的优待，杜甫在夔州的生活比较宽裕，他在瀼西买下果园四十亩❶，又主管东屯公田一百顷❷。有过仆人獠奴阿段、隶人伯夷、辛秀、信行、女奴阿稽等。

夔州雄镇瞿塘峡，地处长江中游，是以风景奇丽著称的长江三峡风景带上的关隘要地。杜甫用他如椽的诗笔，描绘出这里雄壮而惊险的景色：

西南万壑注，勃欱两崖开。

地与山根裂，江从月窟来。

——《瞿塘怀古》

他也记录下这里的风土人情：

夔州处女发半华，四十五十无夫家。

更遭丧乱嫁不售，一生抱恨堪咨嗟。

土风坐男使女立，男当门户女出入。

十犹八九负薪归，卖薪得钱应供给。

至老双鬟只垂颈，野花山叶银钗并。

筋力登危集市门，死生射利兼盐井。

面妆首饰杂啼痕，地褊衣寒困石根。

若道巫山女粗丑，何得此有昭君村。

——《负薪行》

---

❶ 译者注：亩，中国常用的土地面积单位，1亩合667平方米或1/15公顷。
❷ 译者注：顷，中国土地面积单位，1顷约合6.6667公顷。

---

❶ Translator's note: *mu* - Chinese unit of area, approximately equal to 667 sq. kms or 1/15 of a hectare.
❷ Translator's note: *qing* - Chinese unit of area, approximately equal to 6.6667 hectares.

It was because of war that year after year women outnumbered men, and that older women could not marry. Du Fu vividly recorded the local customs and practices around the Three Gorges after the An Shi Rebellion.

Living in a lonely city, Du Fu was almost secluded from the real world. His previous illnesses would disappear one moment only to return the next, forcing him to stay in bed a good deal of time. He often had time to let himself get lost in memories of his past life, writing several autobiographical works.

"Grand Tour" was a long poem, containing a hundred and twelve lines and five hundred and sixty characters. It was a complete autobiography, starting from his childhood when he began to learn writing poems at seven, and continuing to cover the important events of his life, including his boyhood journeys, his southern journey to Wu and Yue, his northern journey to Qi, Zhao, and Chang'an, sending *Fu* prose as gifts to the emperor, waiting for his position in Jixian Academy, the An Shi Rebellion, rescuing Fang Guan, and his temporary residence in Bashu. The poet integrated his own fate with the constant changing of the times. While "writing his own autobiography," he reflected the historical journey of the waning Tang Empire at large, revealing his profound sense of history.

The two poems "Traveling in the Past" and "Giving Vent to My Feelings" discussed his early traveling with Li Bai and Gao Shi.

The poet concentrated on writing poems after coming to Qinzhou. Whether he was living temporarily in a residence or traveling, he would try his best to record his own experiences and feelings. His writing reached an even more prosperous period after coming to Shu. The poems he wrote in Shu and Kuizhou accounted for one third of the total poems he composed throughout his life. These poems systematically recorded his whole life.

He also lamented the ceaseless war, composing the poem "Grievance over Eight Men" to commemorate eight people whom he respected or had close contact with. The first was Wang Sili, Minister of Public Works. As he had performed well in suppressing the An Shi Rebellion, he was depicted in Du Fu's writing as a resourceful and brave general. The second was Li Guangbi, Minister of the Interior. He was a man with many notable exploits, but Du Fu felt that his great leadership abilities were not allowed to fully blossom. The third was Yan Wu, Duke of Zheng and one of the heads of the executive bureau, whose achievements were praised by comparing him to Wen Weng, the able and virtuous official of the Western Han Dynasty, and Zhuge Liang, the brilliant statesman and military strategist in the Three Kingdoms Period. The fourth was Li Jin, Prince of Ruyang and junior tutor of the crown prince, and

正是由于连年的战祸，才出现女多男少，老女不嫁的怪现象。杜甫形象地记录下了安史之乱后三峡一带的风土民情。

身处孤城，几乎与外面的世界隔绝。多年来患有的多种疾病时好时坏，使杜甫时常卧床。在这种状态下他便常常陷入对过去生活的回忆中，写了几首自传性的作品。

《壮游》是一首一百一十二句、五百六十字的长诗。从自己七岁学诗写起，写了少年交游、南游吴越、北游齐赵、长安之游、献赋及待制集贤院、安史之乱、营救房琯，一直写到客居巴蜀，是一篇完整的自传。诗人将自己的遭遇与时代的风云变幻融为一体，在"自为列传"的同时，映带出唐王朝由盛转衰的历史过程，具有深沉的历史感。

两首《昔游》诗和《遣怀》诗，叙述了他早年同李白、高适的漫游。

诗人自入秦州后，就集中精力作诗，不论是暂居还是行路，他都努力地记下自己的见闻和感受。特别是入蜀以后，创作更加旺盛。蜀中和夔州的诗占他全部作品的三分之一。这些诗系统而完整地记录了他的一生，构成了主人公自己的生活史。

他还伤叹战乱不息的时局，写了《八哀诗》，纪念八个他敬重或交好的人物。第一位是司空王思礼，他在安史之乱中立有平叛的战功，杜甫笔下的他是一个剽悍的战将。第二位是司徒李光弼，他的功勋更为卓著，杜甫认为他的大将之才未能尽用。第三位是左仆射、郑国公严武，杜甫把他与西汉贤能的官吏文翁和三国时杰出的政治家及军事家诸葛亮相提并论，赞扬他治理蜀地的功绩。第四位是太子少师、汝阳王李琎，第五

the fifth was Li Yong, head of the archival bureau. Both of them had given Du Fu a lot of help in the past, so Du Fu wrote about them with great gratitude. The sixth was Su Yuanming, the deputy head of the archival bureau, and the seventh was Zheng Qian, who was originally a low level official at the archival bureau before being banished to Taizhou as an official in charge of household registration. The two were both good friends of Du Fu, for whom he grieved enormously. The eighth was Zhang Jiuling, one of the heads of the executive bureau and the prime minister, who was also the last virtuous prime minister during Emperor Xuanzong's reign. After he was banished, first Li Linfu then Yang Guozhong became prime minister, and from then on the Tang Empire was corrupted beyond repair. Writing about him showed Du Fu's yearning for the golden days of the Kaiyuan era. Among these eight people, Du Fu had no direct contact with Wang Sili, Li Guangbi and Zhang Jiuling, so he wrote about them to show his yearning for virtuous leaders. The other five men all had personal contact with Du Fu, so the descriptions of them showed his nostalgic affection for old friends. None of the eight people were able to fully utilize their talents, and thus were not able to fulfill their own aspirations before death. These individual tragedies which took place in the process of the national transition from prosperity to decline resonated powerfully with Du Fu, so "Grievance over Eight Men" was also a lament for the fate of the state as well as the poet himself.

As he experienced national hardships and personal sufferings, Du Fu's thoughts on state affairs became more and more comprehensive and profound. In a group of seven-character regular verses entitled "Five Poems on Generals," he commented on the political abuses of the country from five aspects, to remind the authorities to make all efforts to correct them. We will examine two lines from each of the poems to summarize their poetic implications.

The first poem concerned Tubo's invasion of the country, blaming the generals for their inability to resist the enemy.

> The imperial tombs of Han lie on the far side of the Zhongnan Mountain.
> The Tartar rebels invaded Xiao Pass again after a thousand years.

The second poem was about Huihe's invasion, blaming the generals for their inability to concern themselves with the troubles of the state.

> The generals only make the emperor worried about the state,
> But how can they return the favor while enjoying a peaceful life?

位是秘书监李邕，他们过去给诗人很多帮助，杜甫是怀着感激之情来写的。第六位是秘书少监苏源明，第七位是著作郎贬台州司户郑虔。这两人是杜甫的好朋友，诗人对他们表示无限的哀悼之情。第八位是右仆射、相国张九龄，他是唐玄宗统治期间的最后一位贤相。他被贬斥后，李林甫、杨国忠相继为相，唐王朝从此就腐朽不可救药了。杜甫写他，也就是对开元盛世的怀念。这八个人中，王思礼、李光弼和张九龄与杜甫没有直接来往，写他们，属于怀贤。其余的五个人都与杜甫有交往，属于怀旧。但是八个人物生前都有才能未得施展、抱负不能实现的悲哀。在国家由盛转衰过程中的这些个人悲剧，在诗人心中产生了强烈的共鸣，所以《八哀诗》也是对国家和诗人自身命运的哀叹。

历经国家和自身的苦难，诗人对国事有了越来越全面而深刻的思考，在七律组诗《诸将五首》中，他从五个方面评论国家政治的弊端，提醒当权者们努力改进。现分别从每首中择出两句来概括其诗意。

第一首为吐蕃内侵，责诸将不能御敌：

汉朝陵墓对南山，胡虏千秋尚入关。

第二首写回纥入侵，责诸将不能为朝廷分忧：

独使至尊忧社稷，诸将何以答升平？

The third poem commented on the hardships of the people after the war, blaming the generals for their inability to deploy troops to plow land to supply food for themselves.

Though there are many officials holding double posts,
The governors of the world should not subtract taxes for their own
sake.

The fourth poem was about the failure to renew tribute taxes on neighboring vassal states, blaming the generals for their inability to appease the people in the remote areas.

There has been no news about jade from Yueshang.
Pearls from the Southern Sea have been lonely for a long time.

The fifth poem was about appointing the wrong person to defend Shu, revealing thoughts on Yan Wu's competence in military leadership.

As the Shu Region occupies the most strategic position in the world,
We could only count on talented men to appear.

It was apparent that the old poet, though living in the remote Kuizhou, had a deep understanding of the political conditions of his country. This group of poems took the whole situation into account, advancing profound ideas. Only through long observation and calm thinking can one obtain such exceptional political capability and judgement. The feelings expressed in the poems were heavy, showing the aged poet's deep concern and worry for the fate of his country.

Du Fu also wrote a series of poems recalling past events during the social unrest, including eight well-planned five-character regular verses, such as the poem "The Innerest Room." All the eight poems recollected Chang'an's past in an ironic tone, meant as a warning to the present emperor and ministers. Each of the poems took the first two characters of the text as its title, continuing the tradition of naming poems passed down from *The Book of Poetry*.

There were many places of historical interest in Kuizhou, such as Baidi City where Gongsun Shu of the Han Dynasty jumped onto his horse to ascend to the throne and Yong'an Palace where Liu Bei, the first emperor of Shu in the Three Kingdoms Period, passed away; the System of Eight Battle Formations that was said to be arranged by Zhuge Liang, as well as Xianzhu Temple honoring Liu Bei and Wuhou Temple honoring Zhuge Liang; the former residence of Qu Yuan, the great patriotic poet in the Warring States

第三首写乱后民困，责诸将不能屯垦农田以自供军粮：

　　朝廷衮职虽多预，天下军储不自供。

第四首写周边属国给朝廷的贡赋不修，责诸将不能搞好怀远：

　　越裳翡翠无消息，南海明珠久寂寥。

第五首写镇蜀失人，而思严武的将略：

　　西蜀地形天下险，安危须仗出群才。

可以看出，僻居夔州的老诗人，对国家的政治现状并不隔膜。这组诗放眼全局而见解深刻，只有经过长时间的观察和冷静的思考，才能具有如此不凡的政治器识。诗歌感情沉痛迫切，表现出一个身患多病、垂垂老矣的诗人对国家命运的深切关怀和担忧。

　　杜甫还写了一系列回忆社会动乱往事的诗，有计划地写了《洞房》等八首五律。八首诗都追忆长安往事，语兼讽刺，以警醒当时的君臣。每首诗都以正文的最先两个字为题，是继承了《诗经》的命题传统。

　　夔州多名胜古迹。这里有汉代公孙述跃马称帝的白帝城，有三国蜀主刘备驾崩的宫殿永安宫，有传说中诸葛亮布阵御敌的八阵图，有祭祀刘备的先主庙和祭祀诸葛亮的武侯祠，有战国时代伟大的爱国诗人屈原的故居，有东汉远嫁匈奴的美丽宫

Period and Zhaojun Village, the hometown of Wang Zhaojun, the beautiful palace maid in the Eastern Han Dynasty who was married to a Xiongnu king; Kuizhou also contained the former residence of Song Yu, Qu Yuan's student and a famous literary man. Du Fu reflected on the ancient events associated with these places as he visited them, his thoughts turning back the pages of thousands of years of history. As a result, he recorded all the people related to the places of historical interest in his poems, among which a group of seven-character regular verses entitled "Five Poems on Feelings of Places of Historical Interest" were most typical.

Du Fu mentioned over three hundred and thirty historical figures in his poems, among whom Zhuge Liang figured prominently, appearing more than seven times. Du Fu thought highly of Zhuge Liang's strategic talent as well as for his great loyalty and utter devotion. He was a model for Du Fu's life as well as the incarnation of Du Fu's political ideals. However, his tragic fate, having "died before winning a single victory" also struck a sympathetic chord in Du Fu. In the poems concerning the past, Du Fu was able to not only make correct evaluations of historical figures, but also use the past to allude to the present, making the poems especially realistic. At the same time, these poems also conveyed strong feelings, which made them extremely appealing to readers.

"As I grew old, I became more and more at home with poetic meter and inflection." Du Fu was constantly exploring the art of poetry, paying special attention to seven-character regular verses, and developing these poems to a point that his predecessors had never reached before. His greatest achievements came after entering Shu, not only writing a series of often-quoted poems, but also composing groups of seven-character regular verses. Besides "Five Poems on Generals" and "Five Poems on Feelings of Places of Historical Interest" mentioned above, the most representative of these was "Eight Poems on Autumn Sentiments."

The first poem reads:

> As the white drops fall, the maple woods start to wither.
> The Wushan Mountain and Wu Gorge become gloomy and bleak.
> Surging river waves go up into the sky;
> Rolling clouds over the stronghold darken the hills.
> Clusters of chrysanthemums have bloomed twice while I've shed
> my tears.
> Though sitting on a lonely boat, my heart flies to my old home.

女王昭君的故乡昭君村，还有屈原的学生、著名文学家宋玉的故宅。诗人览物怀古、思接千载，把这些古迹和相关的人物一一写下来，最为集中的是七律组诗《咏怀古迹五首》。

杜甫诗歌中提到的历史人物有三百三十多个，其中直接吟咏最多的是诸葛亮，达七次之多。杜甫给了他极高的评价。他那运筹帷幄的政治谋略、鞠躬尽瘁的赤胆忠心，是杜甫心目中的光辉典范，也是杜甫政治理想的化身。而他"出师未捷身先死"的悲剧命运也引起杜甫心中强烈的共鸣。杜甫的咏史之作，不但能对历史人物做出正确评价，还能够借古喻今，具有很强的现实性，同时包含感情，具有强烈的感染力。

"晚节渐于诗律细"。杜甫在诗歌艺术方面不断探索，特别重视七律。杜甫将七律的艺术推进至炉火纯青的境界，达到前无古人的地步。入蜀以后，成就最高。不但写了一系列脍炙人口的名篇，还精心创作了七律组诗。除了前述《诸将五首》、《咏怀古迹五首》之外，最有代表性的是《秋兴八首》。

第一首：

玉露凋伤枫树林，巫山巫峡气萧森。

江间波浪兼天涌，塞上风云接地阴。

丛菊两开他日泪，孤舟一系故园心。

寒衣处处催刀尺，白帝城高急暮砧。

Every family is busy making winter clothes for the wanderers,

And sounds of beating clothes are often heard from the high places of Baidi City.

The "autumn sentiments" referred to thoughts and feelings aroused by autumn; therefore, the poems first concentrated on describing the autumn scenery in Kuizhou. The Wushan Mountain was situated in Sichuan, consisting of twelve towering peaks between which ran numerous rivers. Wu Gorge was formed by a stretch of the river that extended a hundred and sixty *li*. Since Du Fu left Chengdu through the gorges in May of the first year of the Yongtai reign (765 A.D.) to travel eastward, he had seen this autumn scene twice, so he said that "clusters of chrysanthemums have bloomed twice." The poem heightened the bleak and gloomy atmosphere, which was a symbol of the unstable national situation and Du Fu's personal fate, expressing the poet's homesickness for his hometown and his worry about the present situation. This set a tragic and heroic tone for the emotions to be expressed in the whole group of poems. The rythmic sound of beating clothes described at the end of the poem was not only a traditional image used to express the deep longing for home that one felt when staying in a foreign place, but also the sound the poet heard with his own ears.

The second poem reads:

After the sun set in lonely Kuizhou city,

I'd look toward the capital by the Big Dipper every night.

I shed tears when I heard the cries of apes nearby.

How I regretted I hadn't joined the governor in the boat in August?

My illness contrasted with the incense burners in the Department of Paintings.

The dismal sound of reed pipes was hidden among the gate towers.

Standing at length in meditation, I didn't notice that the moonlight had shifted

From wisterias growing on the rocks to the reed flowers in front of the islet in the river.

The poet looked up to the Big Dipper and started to miss Chang'an. As there were many apes on both sides of the Three Gorges, an ancient folksong told that "the longest among the Three Gorges in eastern Sichuan is Wu Gorge, where one could wet his clothes with tears upon hearing the three cries of the apes there." The poet was more likely to shed tears of grief when he heard the

所谓"秋兴"就是秋天生发的感触，所以先着意描绘夔州秋景。巫山在四川，有十二峰，夹江耸立，其间峡江绵延一百六十里，即是巫峡。杜甫自永泰元年（765）五月离开成都，出峡东去，已两见秋景，故曰"丛菊两开"。诗歌渲染出萧瑟阴森的气氛，这种气氛也是动荡时局和个人身世的象征，烘托出诗人去国怀乡、忧时伤感的情怀，为整组诗的感情定下了悲壮的基调。末尾所写的急促的捣衣声，不只是用传统意象烘托羁旅愁思，也是诗人的亲耳所闻。

第二首：

夔府孤城落日斜，每依北斗望京华。

听猿实下三声泪，奉使虚随八月槎。

画省香炉违伏枕，山楼粉堞隐悲笳。

请看石上藤萝月，已映洲前芦荻花。

诗人遥望北斗而思念长安。三峡两岸多猿，古代就有"巴东三峡巫峡长，猿鸣三声泪沾裳"的民歌，诗人在夕阳下听到

sad and shrill cries of apes in the sunset. The line "How I regretted I hadn't joined the governor in the boat in August" employed two allusions. According to what Zhang Hua of the Jin Dynasty recorded in *Records of a Myriad Things*, a man living by the seaside could see a raft drifting by every August. He was very curious, wanting to figure out the destination of the raft. Then one year, when the raft drifted by again, he got on board and after drifting for over ten months, came to a city where he met a man leading a bull and a woman weaving cloth. By consulting Yan Junping, an astronomer of Sichuan after coming back, he found out that the place he had been to was actually the Milky Way, and that the people he had met were the legendary Herd-boy and Weaving-girl. Later, a book named *Seasonal Records of Jin and Chu* associated this story with Zhang Qian of the Han Dynasty who was sent to the Western Regions on a diplomatic mission. In this poem, Du Fu compared Zhang Qian to Yan Wu. He had intended to follow Yan Wu to return to the court, but this hope could never be realized as Yan Wu had passed away. Because of this, he exclaimed, "How I regretted I hadn't joined the governor in the boat in August!" "Department of Paintings" referred to the Department of State Affairs, and the "incense burner" was an item used in this department. Du Fu was an official of the Ministry of Public Works in name, but he was bedridden by now, unable to take office in the Department of State Affairs in the capital. Because of this, he could do nothing but yearn for Chang'an stupidly. Suddenly, the dismal sound of reed pipes awoke Du Fu, for the moon had climbed into the sky, signaling the falling of late night.

The third poem reads:

Thousands of houses in the mountain city sleep in the morning sunlight.
I sit on the river tower surrounded by blue mountains every day.
Fishermen are sailing on the river day after day
While autumn swallows fly to and fro.
I had hoped to submit memorials like Kuang Heng, but failed in the end.
I had wanted to teach classics like Liu Xiang, but was not able to.
My former classmates have all become rich with fortune and fame,
Living luxurious lives in rich quarters around the Five Imperial Tombs.

Day after day, the poet would sit at length on the tower by the river. The coming of the new day would find him still sitting, watching fishermen come

猿猴凄厉的鸣叫更易伤心落泪。"奉使虚随八月槎"，化用了两个典故，晋代张华《博物志》中记载：一个住在海边的人，每年八月都能看见一个木筏漂过这里。这个人很好奇，想弄明白木筏的去处，于是有一年，当木筏重新漂过时，他便搭上它，经过十个多月的漂浮，最后来到一座城市，见到了一个牵牛的汉子和一个织布的女子。回来后通过请教四川的天文学家严君平，才知道自己到达的地方原来是天河，见到的人是传说中的牛郎和织女。后来有一本《荆楚岁时记》的书，把这个故事附会于汉代出使西域的张骞身上。杜甫这里以张骞比严武，自己本来想随严武回朝的，但严武去世，回朝的愿望再也无法实现了，所以是"奉使虚随八月槎"。"画省"是尚书省，"香炉"是尚书省中的用具，诗人名义上是检校工部员外郎，但现在卧病异乡，不能到京师的尚书省任职，只有痴痴地怀念着长安。突然城头悲凉的笳声惊醒了杜甫，原来已是月上沙洲，深夜来临了。

第三首：

千家山郭静朝晖，日日江楼坐翠微。

信宿渔人还泛泛，清秋燕子故飞飞。

匡衡抗疏功名薄，刘向传经心事违。

同学少年多不贱，五陵衣马自轻肥。

日复一日，诗人久久地坐在江楼上。又迎来了新的一天，

and go freely on the river and swallows flying endlessly in the sky. He had hoped to admonish the emperor like Kuang Heng of the Han Dynasty, but was banished; he had hoped to teach classical works like Liu Xiang of the Han Dynasty, but couldn't fulfill this ideal. On the other hand, his former classmates had now become rich with both fame and fortune. However, all they cared for was a luxurious life, something he considered unworthy of his attention.

The fourth poem reads:

> It grieves me that the situation of Chang'an is like playing chess.
> I mourn that I have experienced so many hardships in my life.
> Mansions of princes, lords and senior officials have found new owners,
> And attires of ministers and generals are different from the past.
> Wars and rebellions have broken out in fortresses and mountains to the north;
> War chariots and horses rush and feather dispatches fly to the west.
> Fish and dragons both hibernate when the autumn river is cold.
> Memories of all the past experiences in Chang'an float in my mind.

Here, Du Fu wrote directly about Chang'an, lamenting the inconstancy of the political situation. In the hundred years from the golden days of the Zhenguan era to the Kaiyuan era, then to the unstable times after the An Shi Rebellion, politics had grown darker day by day, with princes and dukes changing faster than a running horse lantern, causing great grief to the people. In addition, tensions never ceased along the border, and even areas around the capital were not free from the flames of war. At the same time, Tubo in the west kept invading the country. At this time of year when both good and evil people hibernated and when the autumn river was cold and lonely, memories of all the past experiences in Chang'an came back to Du Fu's mind. Du Fu opened the gate of his memories, causing them to flood into his consciousness. The following four poems were memories of his past experiences in Chang'an.

The fifth poem reads:

> Penglai Palace is situated on the far side of the Zhongnan Mountains.
> The golden dew-holding stem of the palace is erected high up into the sky.

看着江面上自由来去的渔人和空中不停翻飞的燕子，诗人想到自己本来想像汉代的匡衡那样劝谏皇帝，却遭到贬斥，想像汉代的刘向一样传讲经书，也无法实现。反过来他想起往日的同学少年如今都富贵发迹，不过他们追求裘马轻肥，又何足道哉！

第四首：

> 闻道长安似弈棋，百年世事不胜悲。
> 王侯第宅皆新主，文武衣冠异昔时。
> 直北关山金鼓振，征西车马羽书驰。
> 鱼龙寂寞秋江冷，故国平居有所思。

这首诗正面写长安，感叹政局多变。从太宗贞观之治到玄宗开元盛世，再到安史之乱后动荡不安的时代，百年之间，政治日趋黑暗，王侯如走马灯似的变换，而情形总让人悲伤。况且此时边境多事，连京师地区都烽火不断，西方的吐蕃又不断侵扰。在这鱼龙蛰伏、秋江冷寂之时，过去在长安时的种种经历浮上心头。诗人打开记忆的闸门，往事历历涌上心头，以下四首便对昔日在长安的所见所闻进行回忆。

第五首：

> 蓬莱高阙对南山，承露金茎霄汉间。

Looking west, one sees Queen Mother falling down from the Jasper Lake;

Looking east, one sees purple smoke enveloping Hangu Pass.

The pheasant-tail fans move apart like floating clouds.

I've seen the emperor in a gown embroidered with shining dragon strips.

But I'm now far away from the court, old and sick in a bed on the river.

In fact, I've been working in court, passing the palace gate many times.

The Penglai Palace was built in Chang'an during the Tang Dynasty. Emperor Wu of Han had once cast a giant statue out of bronze, whose giant palms would hold dew for the emperor to drink, so it was called the golden dew-holding stem. The first couplet was about the Tang capital Chang'an, using Han as a metaphor for Tang, giving a detailed account of the solemn and magnificent royal palace. The second couplet described the imposing manner of the royal palace, which looked into the distant Jasper Lake in the west and Hangu Pass in the east. Seeing blue birds gathering before the palace, Dongfang Shuo of the Han Dynasty knew that the Queen Mother of the West was to arrive; seeing purple smoke floating from the east, the governor of Hangu Pass knew that Laozi was to come from the pass. The poem used these two allusions to satirize Emperor Xuanzong's superstitious belief in celestial beings and Taoism. The third couplet used descriptions of the pheasant-tail fans in the emperor's procession and the embroidered dragon patterns on the emperor's dress to express his pride in having seen Emperor Suzong in person. The last couplet contrasted his present illness in bed with his past visits to court, revealing such complicated feelings of the poet as disappointment and indignation.

The sixth poem reads:

From the mouth of Qutang Gorge to the source of the Qujiang River,

Ten thousand *li* of wind and mist blended into the bleak autumn.

The tower of flowers and calyxes in the pass gave forth an imperial odor.

From the Lotus Garden came the news that war had broken out along the border.

Swans were surrounded by pearl curtains and carved pillars.

西望瑶池降王母，东来紫气满函关。

云移雉尾开宫扇，日绕龙鳞识圣颜。

一卧沧江惊岁晚，几回青琐点朝班。

唐代在长安筑有蓬莱宫，汉武帝曾在长安铸过巨大铜人，巨人用双掌承接露水以供皇帝饮服，叫承露金茎。首联实写唐都长安并借汉拟唐，铺叙皇宫的巍峨壮丽。颔联写皇宫的气势：西眺瑶池，东瞰函关。汉代的东方朔见到青鸟集于宫殿前而知道西王母要降临，春秋时的函谷关尹看到有紫气从东边飘来便知道圣人老子要出关。诗歌连用这两个典故，对唐玄宗迷信仙道的行为进行了讽刺。颈联通过对皇帝仪仗中雉尾扇和皇帝礼服上龙纹绣的描写，说自己曾见过肃宗，引以为荣。尾联在病卧沧江和应卯上朝的今昔对比中，流露出失意不平的复杂心理。

第六首：

瞿塘峡口曲江头，万里风烟接素秋。

花萼夹城通御气，芙蓉小苑入边愁。

朱帘绣柱围黄鹄，锦缆牙樯起白鸥。

With ropes of brocade and masts of elephant teeth, the boats startled white gulls.

I recalled the pitiable places of singing and dancing in the past.

Built in Central Shaanxi, it used to be home of ancient emperors.

The beginning of the poem associated Kuizhou with Chang'an by comparing the image of a cold and lifeless autumn of billowing vapor and smoke, in response to the line "I'd look toward the capital by the Big Dipper every night." Emperor Xuanzong often called his brothers to sleep, feast and play jokes together in "the tower where flowers and calyxes set off each other's radiance." He also often took his favorite concubines to go sightseeing through a secret pass along the Qujiang River and the Lotus Garden. The poet used "giving forth an imperial odor" and "the coming of the news that war had broken out along the border," to emphasize the contrast between happiness and unhappiness. This showed that it was Emperor Xuanzong's pursuit of comfort and pleasure and his sluggishness later in life that had brought about the captureof the capital and the endless war, turning the opulent entertainment and luxurious pleasure-boats in the "emperor's home" into fleeting clouds.

The seventh poem reads:

Kunming Pond was built thanks to the efforts of the Han Dynasty.

The banners and flags of Emperor Wu seemed to flap before my eyes.

The loom and thread of the Weaving-girl lay vainly in the moonlight;

The stone whale looked alive with its scales shining in the autumn wind.

On the river floated lush water rice that looked like dark clouds;

Pink petals covered with dew fell down from the lotus pods in the cold autumn air.

The roads in the fortress rose so high up into the sky that only birds could fly over.

Like a fisherman, I have drifted to and fro over rivers and lakes.

The Han Emperor Wu constructed Kunming Pond in the southwest area of Chang'an, where Emperor Xuanzong had once arranged warships to train soldiers. The poem wrote about Tang using description of Han, implying the strong national power of the Tang Dynasty during the Kaiyuan and Tianbao reigns. At that time, on the bank of Kunming Pond was a jade statue of the Weaving-girl, bathed in clear moonlight, and a stone whale whose scales

回首可怜歌舞地，秦中自古帝王州。

开篇用万里风烟的茫茫秋气把夔府和长安连接起来，回应"每依北斗望京华"。唐玄宗常常召集兄弟们在"花萼相辉之楼"同榻宴谑，以示友爱，又常常带着宠妃们穿过秘密的夹城去曲江边和芙蓉园游玩。诗人用"通御气"和"入边愁"这对乐与哀的对比，表明正是玄宗后期的安逸懈怠，导致都城沦陷，战乱不息，使得"帝王州"中的舞榭歌台、豪华游船变成过眼烟云。

第七首：

昆明池水汉时功，武帝旌旗在眼中。

织女机丝虚月夜，石鲸鳞甲动秋风。

波漂菰米沈云黑，露冷莲房坠粉红。

关塞极天唯鸟道，江湖满地一渔翁。

汉武帝在长安西南开凿了昆明池，唐玄宗曾在池中设置战船以练兵。诗歌以汉写唐，意味着开元、天宝年间唐朝国力的强盛。那时候昆明池边用玉石雕刻的织女沐浴着月亮的清辉，

seemed to be floating in the autumn wind; on the bank was lush water rice and in the water were red lotus flowers covered with dew. But as Du Fu was now stranded in Kuizhou, separated from the outside world by treacherous mountain passses, all these had turned into memories. Over the course of ten years, he wandered from one place to another. The sharp contrast between the past and present revealed his boundless melancholy and misery.

The eight poem reads:

> Walking on the winding mountain paths in Kunwu and Yusu,
> I arrived at Zige Peak and finally entered Meipo.
> I saw fragrant rice grains left after the parrots had pecked at them
> And old green phoenix trees still inhabited by phoenixes.
> Beautiful women picked flowers as gifts for each other
> While fellow travelers took tour boats at night.
> I wrote poems full of power and grandeur in my youth,
> But I often chant poems and long for Chang'an painfully in my old
> age, hanging my head and allowing my tears to stream down.

The last poem recalled the poet's past travel in Meipo, revealing his frustration at his old age and his wandering life. The first couplet described the topographical features of the beautiful scenery of the mountains around Meipo. The second couplet employed an inverted sentence structure to describe Meipo's rich products. The third couplet described a scene of noble ladies in Chang'an going sightseeing. The last couplet contrasted his own happy experience of moving the emperor with three *Fu* essays and taking the examination held by the prime minister in Jixian Academy, with his present condition of being old and infirm. In this way, he concluded the group of poems with an insightful contrast.

Though still in Kuizhou, the poet's mind often went to Chang'an, which became the primary emotional link for the whole group of "Eight Poems on Autumn Sentiments." The first three poems described Du Fu's longing for Chang'an while in Kuizhou, concentrating more on Kuizhou than on Chang'an, while the last five poems mainly centered on Chang'an. The fourth poem can be seen as the transition between the two groups. Thus we see the connecting tissue between the poems, which together formed an organic whole. The first three poems were organized chronologically: The first poem went from daytime to dusk, the second poem from dusk to midnight, the third poem from early morning to daytime. Therefore, the time in the three poems constituted one whole day. The last five poems were organized spatially, with

石鲸的鳞片仿佛在秋风中飘动，岸上是郁黑的菰米，水中是沾露的红莲，而这一切全在回忆之中，如今诗人困居重关阻隔的夔州，十多年来到处流落，身世飘零。两相对照，无限凄苦。

第八首：

> 昆吾御宿自逶迤，紫阁峰阴入渼陂。
>
> 香稻啄馀鹦鹉粒，碧梧栖老凤凰枝。
>
> 佳人拾翠春相问，仙侣同舟晚更移。
>
> 彩笔昔曾干气象，白头吟望苦低垂。

这最后一首，回忆渼陂的旧游，哀叹垂老飘零。首联写渼陂一带的山川形势和美好景致。颔联用倒装的句式，写了渼陂丰饶的物产。颈联写长安贵妇人游赏的情景。尾联把自己曾经用三大礼赋打动皇帝并在集贤院接受宰相考试的盛况，同老病苦吟的现状进行对比，在反差极其强烈的对比中收束整组诗，引起读者无尽的沉思。

身在夔州而心向长安，这是《秋兴八首》整组诗的感情主线。其中前三首写在夔州思念长安，主要写夔州而兼写长安，后五首主要写长安而照应在夔州的处境，第四首又是这两者之间的过渡。各首之间脉络相承，形成一个有机的整体。前三首依时间顺序：第一首由白天而至薄暮，第二首由黄昏而至深夜，第三首由清晨写到白天，三首诗在时间向度上构成了完整的一

the poet's thoughts traveling from far to near and moving back and forth between Chang'an and Kuizhou: The fourth poem described the present Chang'an under Emperor Daizong's rule; the fifth was about Chang'an in Emperor Suzong's time; the sixth was about Chang'an in Emperor Xuanzong's time; the seventh was about Kunming Pond in Emperor Xuanzong's time; the eighth was about his own traveling experience in Meipo of Chang'an. In terms of the structure of the whole group of poems, the closing line of the eighth poem came back to the poet himself who painfully recited poems by the riverside, echoing the night scene of Wu Gorge in the first poem. From this discussion we see the brilliant organization of this group of poems.

This group of poems employed the striking technique of contrast: Kuizhou and Chang'an, past and present, prosperity and decline of the country, individual honor and failure, ideal and reality, joy and grief, the poet and his "classmates," lively and gloomy atmosphere, bright and dark colors, and high and low sound, all of these formed sharp contrasts. However, the most important contrast was between prosperity and decline of the country, revealing the poet's patriotism and concern for his country. In terms of the poet himself, the contrast between "writing poems full of power and grandeur in my youth" and "chanting poems and longing for Chang'an painfully in my old age, hanging my head and allowing my tears to stream down," revealed the difficulties Du Fu passed through during his life.

In terms of artistic technique, the eight poems were written in magnificent language, pleasant to the ear, and employed sharp images and gorgeous color, reflecting a magnificent and gloomy style, thus revealing their artistic uniqueness. Because of this, these poems can be considered the best of Du Fu's seven-character regular verses.

Of all the various poetic forms, Du Fu contributed most to seven-character regular verses. Ancient verse matured after the Han and Wei periods and fine works were produced in the five-character regular verse style at the beginning of the Tang Dynasty, but the perfection of seven-character regular verses was accomplished by Du Fu, especially after he came to Shu. Altogether, Du Fu composed a hundred and fifty seven-character regular verses, exceeding the total number of such poems composed by poets at the beginning and height of the Tang Dynasty, with about a hundred and thirty of these verses coming after he went to Shu. Du Fu reformed the practice of writing seven-character regular verses upon the emperor's order, instilling realistic and political nature into them. In terms of art, he was keen on polishing the wording and the sentences

天。后五首以空间为序，诗人的思绪由远及近，在长安与夔州之间反复跳荡：第四首写唐代宗当前的长安，第五首写唐肃宗时的长安，第六首写唐玄宗时的长安，第七首写唐玄宗时代的昆明池，第八首写诗人自己在长安渼陂的游历。从全组诗的结构而言，则第八首的结句又落到江边苦吟的诗人自身，与第一首的巫峡暮景前后呼应，结构十分严谨。

这组诗突出地运用了对比手法：夔州和长安，过去和现在，国家的盛与衰，个人的荣与枯，理想与现实，欢乐与悲哀，诗人与"同学少年"，气氛的热闹与凄冷，色彩的明丽与暗淡，声响的高昂与低沉，都形成了鲜明的对比。而最重要的对比，则是国家的繁盛与衰败，表现出忧国伤时的爱国精神。在个人方面，则主要是"彩笔昔曾干气象"和"白头吟望苦低垂"的对比，反映了诗人一生的不幸遭遇。

从艺术表现上说，这八首诗语言华美，声韵铿锵，形象鲜明，色彩绚丽，气象雄伟，风格沉郁，表现了极强的艺术独特性，不愧为杜甫七律艺术的最高峰。

在各种诗体中，七律是杜甫独创最多、贡献也最大的一种。中国古代的诗歌，古诗在汉魏之后已成熟，五律在初唐也已产生佳作，而七律的成熟与完美，则是由杜甫完成的，尤其是在杜甫入蜀以后完成的。杜甫的七律共有一百五十首，超过他以前的初唐和盛唐诗人所作七律诗的总和，其中约一百三十首在入蜀以后写成。杜甫改造了七律诗的应制性质，赋予它现实性和政治性。在艺术上，他精于炼字、炼句，并兼采口语，善用

of his works, and he also employed oral language and reiterative locution, evolving his unique style of language use. In addition, he deliberately violated the rules and forms of verse composition: He created a new form of seven-character regular verses which allowed the use of lines which did not conform to standard tonal patterns, seperating his own poems from the natural, smooth verses composed in the prosperous era of Tang. At the same time, he created something completely new by writing several large groups of seven-character regular verses, greatly expanding the amount of content expressed by his poems and overcoming the limitation of verses caused by limited number of lines.

"From choosing the location to moving into the new house at the Red Cliff / I have seen spring views in Kuizhou twice" ("The Red Cliff"). At the beginning of the second year of the Dali reign (767 A.D.), Du Fu moved to the Red Cliff Mountain in the east of the city. The mountain, also called Flaming Mountain, was situated to the opposite side of the White Salt Mountain. There was a hundred *qing* of public field on both banks of the Rangxi River near the Red Cliff Mountain, which was said to have been the field opened by Gongsun Shu, thus earning the name East Village. Du Fu was asked to take charge of this public field. Since the Red Cliff Mountain was close to the East Village, he moved there so as to better take care of the field. His residence was built at a dangerous location, as described in the lines: "My house leaned against the Red Cliff / Which directly faces the White Sand Mountain" ("Three Poems on Moving into My New House").

In March, he moved again to a cottage in Rangxi, the western part of the city that was more densely inhabited in the Tang Dynasty. At this time, Du Fu lived a comfortable life, with an orchard of forty *mu* which yielded various kinds of fruits. Though he was still responsible for the field in the East Village, a petty official named Zhang Wang did most of the work taking care of it. There were still some male and female servants at home such as Aduan and Aji. Du Fu would send Zhang Wang to irrigate after the transplanting of rice seedlings, and he would send Zhang Wang to supervise the reaping of rice at harvest time in autumn.

He also sent Zongwen and Zongwu to gather cocklebur to treat his arthritis. The difficulty in gathering cocklebur reminded him of the poverty of the people and the extravagance of the rich in troubled times.

> Heavy taxes are urgently collected in wartime
> So that the people do not even have enough chaff to eat.
> How could they have the heart to be sated with food,

叠字，语言上具有独特的风格。他还故意打破律诗的格律限制，创造了拗体七律，在流畅自然的盛唐诗歌中独树一帜。同时，他还发挥独创精神，写了几组大型的七律组诗，大大扩展了律诗的内容含量，弥补了律诗句数有限的局限性。

"卜居赤甲迁新居，两见巫山楚水春。"（《赤甲》）大历二年（767）初，杜甫搬家到城东的赤甲山。山又名火焰山，位于白盐山的对面。赤甲山附近的瀼溪两岸，有一百顷公田，传说公孙述当年在此屯田，名东屯。杜甫当上了这些公田的管理官。由于赤甲山与东屯邻近，他搬到这里便于照料田亩。他的住宅正在形势险要之处："奔峭背赤甲，断崖当白盐。"（《入宅三首》）

三月，他又迁居瀼西草堂。瀼西在唐朝是人烟较稠密的西市。这时，杜甫的生活比较宽裕，他置有四十亩果园，园里种有各种果子。东屯的田，他是"主守"，另有"行官"张望负责照料。家里还有阿段、阿稽等男女仆人。插秧以后，杜甫派张望去补水，秋收季节，又派他到东屯去督促割稻。

他还打发宗文、宗武去采苍耳，以治疗风痹。从采苍耳的艰难，联想到乱世中人民的贫穷和富家的豪奢：

乱世诛求急，黎民糠粃窄。

饱食亦何心？荒哉膏粱客。

The rich men who are so ridiculous?
Wasted meat in rich men's kitchens rots
While battle fields are covered with white bones.
I sincerely want to offer these young rich men my advice
That they shouldn't squander away gold like this.
                ("Ordering My Sons to Pick up Cocklebur")

That year, Du Fu and his family spent the Cold Food Festival together, which made him even more homesick for his hometown and his younger brothers and sister. It seemed as if Heaven wanted to ease Du Fu's yearning. Before long, he heard from his younger brother Du Guan, who said that he had set out from Chang'an to come to Jiangling to visit Du Fu. Du Fu was overjoyed, climbing on top of the river tower each day to watch for the arrival of the ship, imagining the moment where he would meet and talk with his brother again. "After anchoring the boat and meeting with grief and joy / We would take our time to talk about returning to Chang'an" ("Two More Short Poems Written out of Joy That Du Guan is to Arrive" No. One). On a summer day, Du Guan finally arrived at Kuizhou, and the two brothers saw each other for the first time after years of long separation. Du Guan stayed for some time and then returned to Lantian to pick up his wife. Du Fu wrote a poem to see his brother off, and the two of them promised to meet again in Jiangling in autumn.

In the second year of the Dali reign (767 A.D.), several governors came to the Imperial court, too and then rumors began to fly that all the governors in Hebei were coming to court, too. After the An Shi Rebellion, many governors established separatist regimes in their own provinces. At the time if a governor went to the court, it meant that he was submitting to the Emperor. Hearing this, Du Fu was extremely happy, and then he wrote a group of quatrains entitled "Twelve Quatrains Written to Show My Great Joy, When Hearing the News That All Governors in Hebei Had Entered the Court."

The first started with the murder of An Lushan and Shi Siming, raising a warning to all governors.

An Lushan was killed as a punishment from heaven for staging rebellion;
Shi Siming has also rotted into dirt for the same reason.
Peace and tranquility haven't been restored to the country yet.
What on earth is on the minds of those who provoke wars?

　　富家厨肉臭，战地骸骨白！

　　寄语恶少年，黄金且休掷。

　　　　——《驱竖子摘苍耳》

　　寒食节杜甫全家一起度过，却使他更思念故乡，怀念弟妹。上天好像要抚慰杜甫的思念，不久，他竟突然接到弟弟杜观来书，说已从长安出发到达江陵，要前来看望杜甫。杜甫真是喜出望外，此后便天天登上江楼去眺望航船，想象着兄弟相见畅谈的情景是："泊船悲喜后，款款话归秦。"（《喜观即到复题短篇二首》其一）在一个夏日，等待中的杜观终于到了夔州，兄弟二人久别重逢，格外亲近。杜观住了一段时间，于八月份又回到蓝田去接妻子，杜甫写诗相送，兄弟俩约定秋天在江陵相会。

　　大历二年（767）年，有几位节度使入朝，并有谣传说河北诸节度使也入朝了。在安史之乱后，藩镇割据的情况下，各节度使入朝就意味着臣服朝廷。杜甫非常高兴，写了绝句组诗《承闻河北诸道节度入朝欢喜口号绝句十二首》。

　　第一首以安、史被杀作开头，对诸路节度使提出警戒：

　　禄山作逆降天诛，更有思明亦已无。

　　汹汹人寰犹不定，时时战斗欲何须。

The third poem celebrated the coming of all the governors in Hebei to court, expressing Du Fu's regret that he was unable to take part in this great celebration, as he was leading a wandering life in poverty. It also revealed the poet's patriotic zeal in advocating unification of the country and opposing separatism.

> Folk rhymes spread far and wide
> That the generals in Hebei are to be presented at court.
> From now on, the world and the court will turn the corner,
> But I feel filled with grief that I cannot return to my hometown.

To celebrate the birthday of Emperor Daizong, all the governors paid tribute of as many as two hundred and forty thousand strings of coins. Chang Gun, a mid-level official at the legislative bureau, said to the emperor, "The governors cannot farm or weave, so what they paid must be taken from others. It was incorrect for the governors to grab money and belongings from the people regardless of their resentment just to please you. Please refuse their offerings." But Emperor Daizong would not listen to him, so Du Fu said the following words of rebuke in the sixth poem:

> Though heroes make correct judgement like gods,
> Men are always insignificant in the mind of saints.
> Yan and Zhao shouldn't be proud that they could produce beauties,
> For the court has no plan for finding gifted ladies for the emperor.

There are still more than a hundred and thirty of Du Fu's quatrains in existence today, among which pentasyllabic quatrains accounted for thirty and heptasyllabic quatrains added up to over a hundred. Most of these poems were written in Chengdu and Kuizhou. Du Fu used quatrains to write about current events, to replace letters, and to comment on literature and art, thus expanding the range of subject matters and the usage of quatrains. In terms of art, he deliberately violated the rhyme pattern to create a new form of quatrains which allowed the use of lines not up to standard tonal patterns. He was also influenced by folk songs such as "Words on Bamboo Leaves" and integrated dialect and oral language into his poems, developing a unique style of his own. In addition, he wrote many groups of quatrains according to content. The quatrains he wrote blazed a new trail, developing a new school of his own, on par with those written by Li Bai and Wang Changling.

In autumn of that year, Du Fu wrote two long five-character regulated verses in Rangxi as gifts to friends. "A Poem of Forty Rhymes to Governor Liu

第三首庆祝河北诸节度使入朝,并自伤流落未能躬逢其盛,表现了诗人维护统一、反对割据的爱国热忱:

喧喧道路多歌谣,河北将军尽入朝。

始是乾坤王室正,却教江汉客魂销。

为了给唐代宗祝寿,各节度使进贡达二十四万缗之多。中书舍人常衮上言:"节度使非能男耕女织,必取之于人。敛怨求媚,不可长也。请却之。"但代宗不从,杜甫在组诗的第六首,委婉地讽刺说:

英雄见事若通神,圣哲为心小一身。

燕赵休矜出佳丽,宫闱不拟选才人。

杜甫的绝句今存一百三十余首,其中五绝约三十首,七绝一百余首,绝大部分作于成都和夔州。杜甫用绝句写时事,以绝句代书信,并用绝句评论文艺,扩大了绝句的题材范围和用途。在艺术上,他故意打破声韵格律,创为拗体绝句,并吸收《竹枝词》等民歌养料,以方言和口语入诗,形成独特的风格。此外,他还根据内容需要,写了不少绝句组诗。他的绝句另辟蹊径,自成一家,在李白、王昌龄之外别开生面。

这年秋天,杜甫还在瀼西写了两首很长的五言排律送给朋友。《寄峡州刘伯华使君四十韵》长达四百字,而《秋日夔

Bohua of Xiazhou" was four hundred characters long, while "A Poem of a Hundred Rhymes to Zheng Shen and Li Zhifang, Written in Kuizhou to Express My Feelings in Autumn" was a thousand characters long, the longest five-character regulated verse Du Fu ever wrote. In regulated verses, each two lines except the four beginning and ending lines match in both tonal patterns as well as the arrangement of functional and notional words, allusions were very much preferred, and all the lines rhymed. In this case, the longer the poem was, the more difficult it became to write. Du Fu was especially skilled at this form of poetry, which can be attributed to his grandfather Du Shenyan's innovative tradition in poem composition.

As Du Fu was in charge of taking care of the public field in the East Village, he often needed to travel between Rangxi and the East Village. But it was a rather long distance between the two places, so in autumn of the second year of the Dali reign (767 A.D.), Du Fu simply moved to the East Village temporarily in order to supervise the harvesting of rice.

Kuizhou was surrounded by high mountains and valleys on all sides, but the East Village was a piece of level land in the middle of high mountains. It had been a public field from the Han Dynasty till the Tang Dynasty. While living in the cottage in the East Village, Du Fu had a neighbor who was a minor official surnamed Feng, from whose highly positioned home, one could view all the way to the distant mountains. Du Fu was rather fond of this neighbor and the view from his home.

By that time, Du Fu had already caught many diseases, even losing half his teeth. After moving to the East Village, his left ear became deaf as well. Under these circumstances, all the nature around him aroused Du Fu's homesickness, whether it was cold river in autumn rain, yellow chrysanthemums blooming on the day of White Dew, doors flapping in wind or the light of fireflies filtering through thin curtains. On the Double Ninth Festival on the ninth day of the ninth lunar month, Du Fu drank a couple of cups of wine and then climbed on top of the river tower again. His despondent mood can be seen in the following lines: "Drinking alone in illness is no fun, I don't feel like drinking / As I have no mood, there's no need for chrysanthemums to bloom again" ("Five Poems Written on the Ninth Day of the Ninth Lunar Month" No. One). He also thought, "Where are my brothers and sister living in such sad times / While I'm suffering from war and old age" (ibid).

One day, he climbed onto a high position alone. Looking at the bleak autumn view with his own eyes, he sighed with regret and wrote a sad poem on autumn.

府咏怀奉寄郑监审李宾客之芳一百韵》则长达一千字，是杜诗中最长的一首五言排律。排律除首尾四句外，其余都须对仗，又讲究用典，还要一韵到底，因此越长越难作好。杜甫专擅此体，这与他继承了乃祖杜审言的作诗家法是分不开的。

因为要管理东屯的公田，杜甫时常要往来于瀼西和东屯之间。但是两地颇有距离，所以大历二年（767）秋天，为了督收稻谷，杜甫干脆搬到东屯居住。

夔州四面都是高山峡谷，东屯却是四面高山中间的一块平地，从汉至唐，都是官田。他在东屯草堂，有一个邻居是都使，姓冯。从冯都使建在高处的书房，可以远望山川风物。杜甫对这个邻居和他的书房，颇有好感。

杜甫本来患有多种疾病，牙齿落了一半，搬到东屯后，左耳也聋了。他身边的景物，不论是秋雨寒江、白露黄菊，还是风扉不定、疏帘萤火，都会引发诗人的思乡之情。九月九日重阳节，他喝了两杯酒，又抱病登临江上台，在"竹叶于人既无分，菊花从此不须开"（《九日五首》其一）的情绪下，他又想到"弟妹萧条各何在，干戈衰谢两相催。"（同上）

一天，他独自登上高处，目睹萧瑟的秋景，生发感慨，写出一首秋天的悲歌：

Apes are crying sadly under the violent wind of the high sky;

Birds are flying to and fro over clear water and white sand.

The leaves of boundless forest are falling in the whistling wind;

The endless Yangtze River flows on and on.

I have been wandering in grief far away from home.

Being ill most of my life, I can only climb the tower alone.

My hair has turned white after leading a hard and miserable life for many years.

Overwhelmed by misery after illness, I've stopped drinking unstrained liquor.

("Climbing a Height")

This poem created a deep mood, conveying dark feelings in a powerful style, causing Hu Yinglin, a literary theorist of the Ming Dynasty, to call it "the best seven-character regular verse in all history."

One winter night, Du Fu took part in an evening banquet that Su Ying held in the river tower to entertain Judge Cui and County Magistrate Wei. As all of these three men were from Luoyang, this banquet aroused deep homesickness in Du Fu's heart, which can be inferred from the following lines: "Men from the same place gathered tonight / Arousing profound longing for my hometown" ("Three Poems Written on the Night Banquet in the River Tower in Autumn" No. One). When Meng Cangcao went to Luoyang to take an exam, Du Fu charged him with examining Luhun Village in Yanshi for his sake.

His hometown was remote. He sometimes thought that he might as well stay there as a recluse, but his homesickness and old age made it too difficult. Besides, he did not like the customs and people in Kuizhou, believing that it was a place where "the nature is beautiful but the customs are bad" ("Sightseeing in the Gorges"). Therefore, after Du Guan returned to Lantian, he hastened to make preparations for leaving the gorges region. He was counting the days for news of Du Guan, but even when the agreed upon deadline came and past, he heard nothing; this made Du Fu feel even more abandoned.

In the third year of the Dali reign (768 A.D.), the poet was fifty-seven years old. On New Year's Day, when the whole family gathered together and celebrated the occasion with wine and cheers, the poet remembered his younger brother Du Feng who had been "Wandering east of the river / And sending no message these days" and exclaimed, "Having not seen my brother living east of the river / I shed streams of tears while singing songs aloud"

　　风急天高猿啸哀，渚清沙白鸟飞回。

　　无边落木萧萧下，不尽长江滚滚来。

　　万里悲秋常作客，百年多病独登台。

　　艰难苦恨繁霜鬓，潦倒新停浊酒杯。

——《登高》

　　这首诗意境深邃，感情沉郁，风格遒劲，明代的文学理论家胡应麟称其为"古今七言律第一"。

　　冬天的一个晚上，他参加苏缨在江楼招待崔评事、韦少府的夜宴，因为这三人都是洛阳人，所以勾起了诗人深深的乡思："一时今夕会，万里故乡情。"（《秋季江楼夜宴三首》其一）孟仓曹去洛阳应试，杜甫也托他去看看偃师的陆浑庄。

　　故乡渺渺。他有时也想，自己就隐居在这里算了，但是老来思乡之情实在太强烈了，加之他不喜欢夔州的风土人情，认为这里"形胜有余风土恶"（《峡中览物》），所以自杜观返回蓝田以后，他便加紧做着出峡的准备。他一天天地数着日子等待杜观的消息，可是约定的期限到了，杜观的消息却迟迟不来，这更增添了杜甫的飘零之感。

　　大历三年（768），诗人已经五十七岁了。元旦这天，在全家团聚、举杯祝贺的欢乐声中，诗人想起"漂泊江左，近无消息"的弟弟杜丰，叹息："不见江东弟，高歌泪数行。"《元旦

("Giving Instruction to Zongwu on New Year's Day").

News of Du Guan finally arrived, and Du Fu learned that Du Guan had returned to Jiangling with his wife. This was heartening for Du Fu to hear, who suddenly felt that the Xiajiang River had never been so narrow as to make him eager to set sail at once. Before long, Du Guan sent a letter again, saying that he had found a place to live in Dangyang (now Dangyang in Hubei) to the northwest of Jiangling, and hoped that Du Fu would come there with his family. Therefore, Du Fu decided to leave the Three Gorges in the middle of the first lunar month.

示宗武》

　　总算得到了杜观的消息，他已经带着妻子回到了江陵。这让诗人感到振奋，顿时觉得峡江从来没有如此狭小过，恨不得立即扬帆而去。不多时，杜观又来信说他在江陵西北边的当阳（今湖北当阳）找到住处，希望他带着家人一同前往，于是杜甫便决定正月中旬出三峡。

杜甫诗意画──无边落木萧萧下
Painting according to Du Fu's poem "The leaves of boundless forest
are falling in the whistling wind"

八　漂泊湖湘

Chapter Ⅷ　Wandering in Hunan

The planned time of departure soon arrived, so Du Fu gave his orchard in Rangxi to a "Mr. Nan." He then bid farewell to Kuizhou. He was to set out from Baidi City through Qutang Gorge and then make his way eastward to Jiangling. When it came time to sail, his feelings were mixed. In an eighty-line poem that recorded this journey, he described himself, writing, "I couldn't cheer myself up after boarding the boat / I couldn't help uttering sighs after it set sail" ("A Forty-Rhyme Poem Written When Taking a Boat from Baidi City to Sail out of Qutang Gorge and Head for Jiangling in the Spring of the Third Year of the Dali Reign after Living in Kuizhou for a Long Time").

Located in the upper middle region of the Yangtze River, Jiangling was a place that one had to pass by when coming in or out of the gorges, so it became an important transportation hub. At that time, a younger brother in Du Fu's family named Du Wei was an official of war in the office of Wei Boyu, Governor of Jiangling. He had always maintained correspondence with Du Fu. It was a gloomy and rainy March day when Du Fu arrived in Jiangling, so he went to Du Wei's home directly as soon as he got off board.

Life in Jiangling was not as comfortable as Du Fu had expected. He had to temporarily install his family in his brother's home in Dangyang while he traveled first to Jiangling to make a living. He had sent poems to Wei Boyu, Governor of Jiangling, while staying in Kuizhou. Du Fu also visited Wei Boyu and took part in his banquet after arriving at Jiangling. However, Wei Boyu only entertained Du Fu as a guest. Du Fu then went sightseeing, took part in banquets and recited poems with Li Zhifang, minister of rites and Adviser to the crown prince, as well as Zheng Shen, assistant governor of Jiangling.

Du Fu received continuous letters from his family, saying that they couldn't even find chaff and wild herbs to eat. He was left with no choice but to ask around for loans and aid. That summer, excessive rain caused the river water to go up, making the weather both damp and humid. On his way to Wuling (now Changde in Hunan) to get help, the boat he was taking became grounded. He could do nothing but get off the boat and stay overnight on the dyke. That night, looking far into the distance at the moon and the stars in the sky and listening to the mournful sounds of reed pipes and drums, his journeys at an old age weighed down on his heart. His life was growing more and more difficult and getting help from others was a great humiliation to him. Du Fu expressed his feelings about this period of life in the following poem:

Having to ask others for help in this time of suffering,

计划中出峡的日子到了，他把瀼西果园送给了一位"南卿兄"，告别夔州，从白帝城出瞿塘峡，东下江陵。行船之际，颇多感慨，在记录此行的一首长达八十句的诗里，他说自己是："入舟翻不乐，解缆独长吁。"（《大历三年春白帝城放船出瞿塘峡久居夔府将适江陵漂泊有诗凡四十韵》）

江陵地处长江中上游，是出峡入峡的必经之处，为东南西北的交通枢纽，地理位置很重要。杜甫的族弟杜位这时在江陵节度使卫伯玉的使府里任行军司马，早先一直和杜甫互通音信。杜甫到达江陵那天，是三月里一个阴雨霏霏的日子，所以他一上岸，便直接投奔杜位家去。

江陵的生活并不如原来所想的宽裕，为了生计，诗人将家人寄居在当阳弟弟家，本人则打算先在江陵谋生。他在夔州曾寄诗给江陵节度使卫伯玉，到江陵后又去拜会过他，还参加过他的宴会，可是卫只以客礼待他。他还和礼部尚书改太子宾客李之芳、江陵少尹郑审等人游宴酬唱。

杜甫在江陵不断接到家人寄来的书信，说连糠菜粥也喝不上了，他很无奈，只好到附近去告贷求援。这里的夏季雨多水涨，潮湿闷热，在前往武陵（今湖南常德）求援的途中，所乘之船又不巧搁浅了，没有办法，只好下船在长堤上过了一夜。在这样一个夜晚，遥望着夜空中的星月，听着城头箛鼓的悲鸣声，想到自己暮年漂泊生活中的种种悲凉境遇，不由得伤心痛苦起来。生活是一天比一天恶劣，求人周济又使他备尝屈辱，杜甫对于这一段生活的感受是：

苦摇求食尾，常曝报恩鳃。

I am unable to realize my aspirations and repay my debt to my
country.

I shut my mouth so as not to provide others with grounds for
defaming me,

For placing too much confidence in others is usually the cause of ruin.

Like Yuan Ji, I return crying when I get lost in the wilderness;

Like Wang Can, I toss about and feel uneasy in wartime.

When in hunger, I go to every household for food;

When in grief, I search everywhere for drink.

I don't have to pity for other poor scholars,

And I allow all to laugh at me.

("A Thirty-Rhyme Poem on My Feelings While Staying in Jingnan
on an Autumn Day")

It seemed that Jiangling was no longer the place for him, but he had no
money to buy a boat to sail south, and couldn't return north as the social unrest
was not yet over. Where could he go? Du Fu was lost and confused.

Despite these difficulties, he left Jiangling at last, taking a boat along the
Yangtze River. He arrived at Gong'an (now in Hubei) after sailing for almost a
hundred *li*. It was already late autumn then, with a cold and lifeless wind
blowing. In such troubled times, Du Fu did not expect to find a peaceful place
to stay, so he made do with a countryside tavern. As soon as he arrived at
Gong'an, he heard the news that Li Zhifang had died of illness, writing two
poems to mourn for him. Several of Du Fu's relatives and friends were
delighted to know of his arrival, so they prepared wine and a welcome dinner
for him and Du Fu wrote several poems for it. But the problem of finding
lodging for his family had still not been solved. After a short period of time, he
was wronged by some petty officials. Feeling inconsistancy of human
relationship, he had to leave Gong'an and search for the next place to live.

One winter morning, the family set out eastward by boat along the
Yangtze River. The north wind blew violently for over ten days straight. As a
result, every day was pitch-dark and the sun was covered even at noon. The
boats in the river were covered with sand and dirt, and tigers and wolves
prowled in the empty villages on the bank.

At the end of the year, Du Fu came to Yueyang. His experiences on the
way made him further understood the poverty and hardships from which the
people suffered, prompting him to compose a poem entitled "Traveling at the
End of the Year." He saw fishermen dragging frozen nets to catch fish on
Dongting Lake in a blowing north wind and heavy snow; he also saw hunters

结舌防谗柄，探肠有祸胎。

苍茫步兵哭，辗转仲宣衰。

饥藉家家米，愁征处处杯。

休为贫士叹，任受众人咍。

——《秋日荆南述怀三十韵》

江陵看来是呆不下去了，可是想要南渡又没钱买船，想要北归而世乱未平。能到哪里去呢？诗人茫茫然。

不过他最终还是离开了江陵，小船沿长江漂流而下，行近百里，到了公安（今属湖北）。时已深秋，天风肃杀。在这乱世里，杜甫不再希求能得到一处安稳的居所，暂时寄住在一处山野小店里。刚到公安，就听到李之芳病死的消息，他写了两首诗哀悼。公安的几个亲朋好友听到杜甫来了，很高兴，备了水酒为他接风，杜甫也为此写了几首应酬诗。可是一家人的生活问题并没有解决。住了一段日子，生计无着的他便受到一些世俗小吏的轻慢。这让诗人深感世态炎凉。于是不得不离开公安，继续寻找下一个落脚点。

冬天的一个早晨，一家人乘船启程，沿长江东下。路上一连刮了十多天大北风，昏天黑地，连中午都不见日光。行在江中的船里吹满了沙尘，岸上空无人烟的村落里虎狼出没。

年底，诗人来到岳阳。一路的所见所闻，使诗人进一步体念到人民的贫穷痛苦，于是写了一首《岁晏行》：他看到在北风呼啸、大雪纷飞的洞庭湖上，渔夫拖着结冰的网在捕鱼，猎

searching for game in spite of the severe cold. He mourned that food had been so rare last year that even the soldiers did not have enough to eat; he mourned that food was so cheap this year that the peasants suffered great losses, while high dignitaries were wantonly wasted the gifts of Heaven. He heard that everywhere there were people who had no choice but to sell their children to pay taxes. He was worried about the current situation that private money was circulating unchecked, and that quality products were substituted by shoddy goods. What's more the government did nothing to prevent it. At the end of the poem, he echoed the grieving horn from the gate tower to express his boundless sadness. This poem revealed Du Fu's deep grief and indignation over "the hard life suffered by the people," and was a masterpiece of practical significance written in his old age.

Anchoring the boat by the city wall, Du Fu scaled the magnificent Yueyang Tower and composed the famous poem "Climbing onto Yueyang Tower" :

> I had heard of Dongting Lake,
> But today I climbed Yueyang Tower.
> The lake divides Wu and Chu through the center,
> While the sun and the moon float over it by night and by day.
> I haven't heard from my family or friends for long.
> Old and sick, I only have a lonely boat in which to stay.
> War broke again in the northern fortresses and mountains.
> I can do nothing but shed tears, leaning against the railing of my boat.

On Yueyang Tower, Du Fu felt that Dongting Lake, which divided the two regions of Wu and Chu, was so vast that all of heaven, earth, the sun, the moon and the stars all seemed to be floating on its surface. Compared with this, his own fate seemed so trivial. With this grand celestial scene serving as a backdrop to his lonely fate, the circumstances of his life seemed even more dismal. But besides his own fate, the poet was also worried about the state and the people, "plagued by frequent ills in all places." This poem was saturated with deep grief. Feeling and setting were artfully blended by coordinating grand scenery with profound ideas. The third and fourth lines of the poem presented the grand scene in perfect verbal parallelism, becoming the most famous description of Dongting Lake. It was remarkable that such an old and feeble man under such lonely and distressed circumstances still possessed such great writing power. One cannot help but praise his vigorous and remarkable creativity.

人冒着严寒打猎。他感叹去年的粮价太贵，军队乏食，今年的粮价又太便宜，使农民惨遭损失，而那些达官贵人却依旧暴殄天物。他听说到处都有卖儿卖女用来缴纳赋税的百姓。他忧心私钱泛滥、以次充好，而官府不加禁止的现状。最后借城头哀伤的画角之声，抒发自己无穷的忧愁。这首诗表达了杜甫"哀民生之多艰"的深广忧愤，是杜甫晚年最富现实意义的一篇力作。

泊船城下，诗人登上雄伟的岳阳楼，写下了著名的《登岳阳楼》：

> 昔闻洞庭水，今上岳阳楼。
> 吴楚东南坼，乾坤日夜浮。
> 亲朋无一字，老病有孤舟。
> 戎马关山北，凭轩涕泗流。

在岳阳楼，杜甫感到这分开了吴、楚两地的洞庭湖真是广大无边，以至于好像整个天地、日月星辰都浮在湖水之上。而回想自己的身世，却很渺小。以壮阔之景反衬孤苦之身，更显出景况的悲凉。但是除了自己的身世，诗人所忧的还有"万方多难"的国家和人民。这首诗感情极为沉痛，壮阔的图景和宽广的胸怀相配合，达到了情景交融的佳境。三、四两句，气象雄阔，且对仗工稳，成为描写洞庭湖的名句。一个年老体病的人，在孤独愁苦的境遇中，能有这样雄强的笔力，不能不让人对他旺盛非凡的创造力发出赞叹。

Spending the remaining winter days of the third year of the Dali reign (768 A.D.) in Yueyang, the poet left for the south in the first lunar month of the fourth year of the Dali reign (769 A.D.). South of Dongting Lake was the Xiaoxiang River Valley, the setting of many folktales. Legend had it that since Emperor Shun died in Cangwu Mountain (now Jiuyi Mountain in Hunan) on his inspection tour to the south, his two concubines, Tangyao's two daughters Ehuang and Nvying, came to the banks of the Xiangjiang River to weep in sorrow, leaving tear stains on the bamboo leaves. These bamboos then became the mottled bamboos in existence today, also called Xiangfei Bamboos. Ehuang and Nvying became the goddesses of the Xiangjiang River after death. Qu Yuan of the Warring States Period was exiled around here upon false accusations, and he composed the poem "Ladies of the Xiangjiang River" in their honor. Du Fu visited the Temple of the Ladies of the Xiangjiang River, a memorial temple to Ehuang and Nvying, composing another poem in their memory.

The Xiangjiang River flowed south to north into Dongting Lake. Sailing southward against the current, Du Fu arrived at Tanzhou (now Changsha in Hunan). He visited Yuelu Mountain, as well as Daolin Temple which lay at its foot. Soon he left Tanzhou, traveling southward towards Hengzhou (now Hengyang in Hunan). The governor of Hengzhou, Wei Zhijin, was Du Fu's friend. He had met Du Fu in Kuizhou on his way to take office in Hunan. This time, Du Fu went to him to seek his aid. However, when Du Fu arrived at Hengzhou, he found that Wei Zhijin had been transferred to Tanzhou to be the governor there. Having neither friends nor relatives in Hengzhou, Du Fu and his family turned back to Tanzhou, only to find that Wei Zhijin had died of illness in Tanzhou. At this news, Du Fu was heartbroken, so he wrote a poem to mourn Wei Zhijin's passing. From that time till winter, Du Fu and his family stayed on a small boat anchored in Tanzhou, spending the interminable days in hunger.

Tanzhou was situated on the vital communication line between south and north, so officials often passed by there. In Tanzhou, Du Fu became acquainted with Wei Tiao, Su Huan and others. Wei Tiao was the newly appointed governor of Shaozhou (the local authority is now located in the southwest of Shaoguan in Guangdong) and was just passing by Tanzhou on his way to take office there. He paid a special visit to Du Fu, who was ill in bed, and exchanged poems with him as gifts. Su Huan was a legendary man, who had loved looting in his youth. Since he used a white bow and crossbow, merchants around Bashu were all afraid of him, calling him "Baizhi," meaning the white

在岳阳送走了大历三年（768）的残冬，大历四年（769）正月，诗人便离开此处南行。洞庭湖南面是充满神话色彩的潇湘流域。传说舜帝南巡，死于苍梧山（今湖南九嶷山），他的两个妃子，即唐尧的两个女儿娥皇和女英，闻讯赶到湘水之滨痛哭，竹上留下斑斑泪痕，形成了今天的斑竹，又叫湘妃竹。娥皇、女英死后，成为湘水之神。战国时代的屈原受谗而被放逐在这一带，写下了《湘夫人》以歌咏她们，屈原后来也投入附近的汨罗江而死。杜甫到这里后游览了娥皇、女英的祠堂——湘夫人祠，并写诗纪之。

湘江由南向北流入洞庭湖，杜甫逆着江水南行，到达潭州（今湖南长沙），游览了岳麓山和山下的道林寺。不久，又离开潭州，继续逆湘水南行，前往衡州（今湖南衡阳）。衡州刺史韦之晋是杜甫的朋友，他在调往湖南途中，曾在夔州和杜甫相见过。杜甫此行是前往投奔他的。可是当他到达衡州时，韦之晋已经调任潭州刺史。杜甫一家在衡州举目无亲，只好折回潭州，却没有想到韦之晋已在潭州病卒，杜甫闻听噩耗，十分伤心，写诗悼念他。此后直到冬天，杜甫一家只好住在停泊于潭州的一叶扁舟之中，在饥饿中度日如年。

潭州处在南北交通要道上，官绅来往经过的不少。杜甫在这里认识了韦迢、苏涣等人。韦迢新任韶州（治所在今广东韶关西南）刺史，经过潭州，特来看望卧病的杜甫，并与杜甫互相作诗赠答。苏涣是一个很有传奇色彩的人物，他少年时代喜欢剽盗，使一副白色的弓弩，巴蜀一带的商人都怕他，称他为

robber. He later turned his life around and started to study, being as a successful candidate in the highest imperial examination and finally becoming an official. After arriving at Tanzhou, he came by sedan to visit Du Fu in Du's small boat, and talked with Du Fu about poetry. Du Fu was quite appreciative of this new friend.

The fifth year of the Dali reign (770 A.D.) arrived. It was to be the last year of Du Fu's life. When the poet reviewed his old poems on the twentieth of the first lunar month, he found a poem that the deceased Gao Shi had written to him ten years prior. Reflecting that most of his friends had passed away while the country was still in turmoil, deep regret welled up in him, and he wrote a poem as a gift to two friends who were still alive. He said that he was so deeply worried about the ceaseless internal disturbance within the country and foreign invasions from out, that he simply wanted to turn the East Sea over to wash the world clean.

The spring that year was a season of singing birds and fragrant flowers. Watching the beautiful spring view from the river, Du Fu felt at peace, composing several new poems. One day, a swallow flew to Du Fu's boat, arousing his deep homesickness. Perhaps he thought it was the swallow which had built its nest in his old home and then come to visit him. On Tomb-Sweeping Day, it was warm and sunny with all the brightness and charm of spring, prompting many people to go outdoors. Du Fu was surprised to see that some officers were also frolicking in the crowd, negligent of their military duty. He watched them on the river, and found that when all the other tourists left at sunset, these officers didn't return to their camp, but took beautiful prostitutes to whore-houses. Recalling the ancient times, Du Fu knew that such depravity always appeared before the collapse of a country; he just hadn't imagined that it would happen in his lifetime.

In late spring, Du Fu saw Li Guinian again, the famous musician he often met in his youth. It had been forty years since they last saw each other, and they had not expected to ever meet again, as both of them led wandering lives. In his sadness, Du Fu composed a poem entitled "Meeting Li Guinian in the South of the Yangtze River."

> I often saw you at the residence of Prince Qi
> And on several occasions heard your music in Mr. Cui's house.
> It was the best season in the south of the Yangtze River,
> When I met you again at the time of falling flowers.

Because this poem was written in simple and plain language, but loaded

"白跖"。他后来折节读书，中了进士，做了官。他到潭州后，也坐着轿子来杜甫的小舟中探望，与杜甫谈论诗艺，杜甫对这个新结识的朋友十分欣赏。

大历五年（770）到来了，这是杜甫生命中的最后一年。正月二十日，诗人翻检旧诗，发现已故的高适十年前赠给自己的一首诗，想到老友大半凋零，而国家仍在乱中，因而十分感慨，就写了一首和诗，赠给还在世的两位友人。他说自己深感国家外患内乱不断，恨不得翻倒东海来冲洗乾坤。

今年的春天仍然是一个鸟语花香的季节，江上美丽的春景使诗人高兴起来，写了几首清新的诗歌。一天，一只小燕子飞到杜甫的船上来，勾起了杜甫的思乡之情，他想这就是以前常在自己故园里筑巢的那只燕子来看他了吧。清明节那天风和日丽，春光明媚，男女老少都出来游春。杜甫惊讶地看到，一些将军们竟也不管军务，带着部将在人群中嬉玩。杜甫在江上瞅着他们，当夕阳西下，游人散去时，这些将军竟然不回军营，而是携带美妓，向青楼而去。杜甫回想古代，每当国家覆灭前，总会有这样的乱象出现，不料如今又被自己遭逢。

暮春时节，杜甫见到了年少时曾多次见过的著名音乐家李龟年，这是相隔四十多年后两人的再次相逢，想不到两人竟都是在流落天涯的状态之下。诗人感慨万千，写了一首《江南逢李龟年》：

　　岐王宅里寻常见，崔九堂前几度闻。

　　正是江南好风景，落花时节又逢君。

这首诗语言浅近而感情深远，千百年来感动了无数读者的

with profound emotion, it has moved numerous readers over the ages. "The best season in the south of the Yangtze River" contrasted sharply with their reduced circumstances, while "the time of falling flowers" echoed his personal decline as well as the decline of Tang, highlighting the differences between the prosperity of the past and the decline of the present.

At that time, the court was especially weak, with warlords fighting endlessly amongst themselves. On the night of April the eighth, Tanzhou city was suddenly filled with flames which lit up the sky, and the noises of killing seemed to shake the earth. Zang Jie, commander of the Hunan forces, had raised a revolt, killing his superior and seizing Tanzhou for himself. During this time of war, Du Fu took his wife and children and fled southward, against the current of the Xiangjiang River. They arrived at Hengzhou and were received by Yang Ji, Governor of Hengzhou.

Du Fu's uncle Cui Wei was Governor of Chenzhou (now in Hunan), so he took his family to seek refuge with Cui Wei after staying in Hengyang for a short period of time. Sailing on southward against the current of the Leijiang River, a branch of the Xiangjiang River, he arrived in Leiyang (now in Hunan). As it was flood season, he had to anchor his boat at Fangtian Station, where they were surrounded by a vast expanse of water and couldn't find anything to eat for five days. Fortunately, the county magistrate Nie of Leiyang heard the news. He immediately wrote a letter to convey his greetings, and sent the family beef and liquor to save them from starvation. Since the flood made it impossible to travel on to Chenzhou, they had to turn around to return to the north.

After that, little can be traced about the experience of Du Fu and his family, or about the poems he wrote from that summer and winter. Opinions vary, making it impossible to decide which is right. We only know that the poet fell ill on a small boat sailing to Yueyang in winter. He devoted the last moments of his life to poetry, writing the last poem in his life entitled "A Poem of Thirty-Six Rhymes Given to My Relatives and Friends in Hunan, Written While Lying on the Pillow in a Swift Boat Traveling in the Wind." In the persistent fog and fine drizzle of the southern winter, with admiration for the ancient sages and while yearning for the capital and his hometown, he recalled his own miserable experience with a heavy heart. Starting from the time when he held the office of Commissioner of the Left and irritated Emperor Suzong for his attempt to rescue Fang Guan, the poet recalled the long wandering hard life he had led after being convicted and banished, with emphasis on his time in Hunan. Nevertheless, at the very end of life, he still couldn't forget the disaster of the state and the miserable fate of the people. He lamented that

心灵。"江南好风景"与彼此沦落的身世构成强烈反差，"落花时节"与个人的衰老和国势的衰败相互映衬，寄寓了浓重的今昔盛衰之感。

这时的朝廷非常软弱，地方军阀相互攻杀，战乱不断。四月八日夜里，潭州城内忽然火光冲天，杀声动地。湖南兵马使臧玠叛乱了，他杀死上级，自己占据了潭州。在这兵荒马乱之中，杜甫带着妻子儿女，又逆湘水向南逃难，匆匆忙忙地来到衡州，衡州刺史阳济接待了他。

杜甫的舅舅崔玮任郴州（今属湖南）刺史，杜甫在衡阳暂住了一段时间，便携家眷前去投奔他。他逆着湘江的支流耒水继续向南，到达耒阳（今属湖南）境内时，正值江水大涨，只得泊舟于方田驿。这里四周一片汪洋，诗人一家竟有五日没有食物。幸亏耒阳聂县令闻讯，立即写了一封书信慰问他，并送来了牛肉白酒，一家人方免于饿死。因阻水不能前行，郴州是去不了了，只好又回棹北归。

此后，从夏到冬，关于杜甫一家的经历，关于杜甫所写的诗歌，就线索不清了。后人们众说纷纭，莫衷一是。我们只知道冬天的时候，诗人是病倒在驶往岳阳的一艘小船上。他把自己生命的最后一刻献给诗歌，作了绝笔诗《风疾舟中伏枕书怀三十六韵奉承湖南诸亲友》。在严冬依然不散的南方瘴气里，在蒙蒙的细雨之中，伴随着对古代先贤的追慕，对京城和故乡的怀念，他怀着沉痛的心情回顾了自己悲惨的经历。诗人以自己任左拾遗时因疏救房琯而触怒肃宗这一件事为起点，追述了获罪贬官而长期漂泊的苦难历程，重点叙述了进入湖南以后的痛苦生活。但是在这生命垂危之际，他仍然没有忘怀国家的灾难和民生的凄惨，他感叹像汉代公孙述那样的军阀仍在恃险割

warlords like Gongsun Shu of the Han Dynasty still relied on the strength of strategic position to establish separatist regimes, and that rebel leaders like Hou Jing of the Liang Dynasty were still arrogant and domineering. Correspondence with the Central Plains had been cut off for a long time, and Chang'an still faced the threat posed by Tubo. He uttered a long sigh of grief, "The soldiers' blood has been flowing / And the din of combat has been going on till now." Du Fu watched the war-torn and calamity-stricken land with tearful eyes, bidding a silent farewell to the country and the people that had been plagued by so many misfortunes.

The heart of this great soul stopped beating, and a great man thus passed away in boundless loneliness.

After Du Fu's death, his family had no means to carry his coffin back to his hometown, so he had to be buried in Yueyang. Forty-three years later, his grandson Du Siye moved his coffin to Shouyang Mountain in the northwest of Yanshi to be buried there. At last, the poet's dream of returning to his hometown was fulfilled, many years after his death.

据，像梁代侯景那样的叛将仍在飞扬跋扈。中原的书信长久断绝，长安仍处在吐蕃的威胁之中。他痛苦地长叹："战血流依旧，军声动至今。"诗人用饱含着泪水的双眼望着满目疮痍的山河，默默告别多灾多难的祖国和人民。

一颗伟大的心灵就这样停止了跳动，一颗巨星就在这无限的孤独、寂寞中陨落了。

杜甫死后，家人无力将他的灵柩运回故乡，只得停放在岳阳。四十三年之后，他的孙子杜嗣业将灵柩迁葬于偃师西北的首阳山下。诗人回归故乡的愿望，死后多年才得以实现。

杜甫画像
Portrait of Du Fu

九 诗人和诗歌的双重楷模

Chapter Ⅸ A Standard of Excellence for Poets and
Poems

Who is the greatest poet in the history of Chinese poetry?

Such a seemingly unanswerable question has been asked and answered by countless scholars over thousands of years. Yuan Zhen, a poet towards the middle of the Tang Dynasty had been entrusted by Du Fu's grandson Du Siye to write an epitaph for Du Fu. The line he proposed was: "Among all the poets of history, never has there been one to match Du Fu."

This line caused a disagreement between supporters of Li Bai and Du Fu in later generations. In fact, Li Bai and Du Fu can both be considered masters of poetry. As their writing techniques and artistic styles differed, it is impossible to say which is superior or inferior. However, considering the depth and breadth of social life depicted in the poems, considering the writer's concern for the state and people and sympathy for the unfortunate, considering the achievements and originality in various poetic forms, Du Fu fully deserves to be honored as the greatest Chinese poet.

Coming from the Tang society where Confucianism, Buddhism and Taoism were of equal importance, Du Fu visited the Taoist monk Huagai with Li Bai in his youth, and also made pills of immortality and prayed to Buddha when he suffered from frustration and hardships. These actions did not represent his deepest beliefs, however, because he was merely acting on the impulse of the moment. If we take a broader view of his service in office and his political integrity, we'll find that his main ideology was always Confucianism.

Du Fu carried on the early tradition of Confucian ideas, based on the philosophy of Confucius and Mencius. He inherited the positive elements of the doctrines of Confucius and Mencius. In general, these include the following aspects.

I. Thoughts on Benevolence and Humanitarianism

Throughout his life, Du Fu had always promoted the Confucian value of benevolence, evidenced by the abundance of humanitarian emotions to be found in his poetry. He hoped that rulers would implement benevolent policies, satirizing the unjust war Emperor Xuanzong launched against the nomadic tribes in neighboring regions. He harshly condemned the inequality between the rich and the poor, criticizing the extravagant life led by all levels of the ruling class, as well as their exorbitant demands on the people. "I worry for the people all the time / So that I am filled with anxiety in my heart." He had great sympathy for the sufferings of the people, revealing the common

谁是中国诗歌史上最伟大的诗人？

这个看似不可回答的问题，千百年来却被无数人提出并且回答过。中唐诗人元稹曾经受杜甫的孙子杜嗣业之托，为杜甫作墓志铭，他给出的答案是："诗人以来，未有如子美者。"

这句话在后代引起一场李杜之争。其实，李白和杜甫二人作为中国诗歌史上的双子星座，都占据着诗坛最高峰的地位。因其创作方法和艺术风格的不同，不宜强分优劣。但是若论作品反映社会生活的深广，作家对国家和人民的关切、对弱小生命的同情以及在各种诗体上的造诣和创新等诸多方面，杜甫则是当之无愧的千古诗坛第一人。

在儒、释、道并重的唐代社会，杜甫虽在年轻时曾和李白一道拜访过道士华盖君，后来在失意和困苦中也说过要炼丹、求禅的话，但那都只是一时的冲动之举和兴到之言。纵观其一生的出处大节，他的主要思想一直坚守着儒家思想的阵营。

杜甫继承的是以孔孟学说为核心的早期儒家思想传统。他全面继承了孔孟之道的积极因素。大致说来，主要有以下几个方面：

（一） 仁爱思想和人道主义

杜甫一生奉行儒家的仁爱思想，他的诗歌里充满着人道主义的感情。他希望统治者施行仁政，讽刺唐玄宗发动的对周边少数民族的不义战争。他愤怒地控诉贫富不均的社会现实，鞭挞了从皇帝到地方官员的各级统治者穷奢极欲的生活和对老百姓敲骨吸髓的诛求。"穷年忧黎元，叹息肠内热！"他对人民所遭受的苦难给予了极大的同情，用满含泪水的笔墨反映民生

people's hard life with a tear soaked pen, vividly describing the pains they suffered from military service and heavy taxes. His poems skillfully painted the social landscape of the times: endless war and devastating taxes leaving desolate villages and peasants fleeing for their lives. His life was full of frustration, but he could put himself in the place of others, integrating his own misfortune into the calamities befalling the state and the misfortunes of the people. When his youngest son died of starvation, he thought of the peasants who had lost their land and the soldiers who were guarding the frontiers; when his cottage was destroyed by wind, he thought of all the people who suffered from the cold. He was willing to offer what he could help: He planted wild herbs and allowed his neighbors to gather them; He planted date trees and then allowed his neighbors to pick the fruit; he planted rice in the East Village in Kuizhou and gave some to the poor peasants; his great writing power could have described whales in the deep sea, but he often used it to describe the weak animals and plants in a compassionate tone. All this shows that a benevolent spirit, humanitarianism and consideration of the common folk as the foundation of a country are not only themes in his poems, but also reflected in his actions. Du Fu's sympathy is not only directed towards human beings, but also to all creatures in nature.

II. Patriotism and Sense of Anxiety

Confucianism places great importance on proper respect for the monarch, advocates the unification of the country, and is opposed to foreign invasion. Du Fu exemplified this doctrine. From the time he was young, he showed anxious concern for the fate of the state and the people. As social and national conflicts became worse day by day, this concern and sense of anxiety which it caused grew ever stronger. Each incident of unrest, each military action and its consequence, were all depicted in his poems. Major turmoil, such as the An Shi Rebellion and Tubo's capture of the capital, as well as minor unrest, such as the battle of Chentao and Qingban and local warlords' revolts, can all be found in Du Fu's poems, with some poems even correcting errors found in history books. "I have always been worried about my country / So my tears often wet my clothes" ("Paying Homage at the Ancestral Temple"). It was because of his concern for the national fate that he could often put forward some rational suggestions and ideas, such as tenaciously defending Tongguan Pass, strengthening the garrison of Luzi Pass, restricting the forces of Huihe, and properly deploying court personnel. The best moment to test one's

疾苦，描写了人民遭受的兵役之苦和赋敛之苦。他生动地刻画了在长期战乱破坏和沉重赋税压迫下农村荒废、农民逃亡的时代画卷。他的一生历经坎坷，但他却能推己及人，由自己的不幸想到人民的不幸，把自己的不幸放在国家的危难和人民的不幸中加以反映。当自己的小儿子饿死时，他想到的是失去土地的农民和戍守边疆的战士；当自己的茅屋被风吹破时，他想到的是天下的寒士。他还愿意给别人提供一些力所能及的帮助：他种有草药，就让邻人来采药；他种了棵枣树，就任邻人来扑打；他在夔州东屯种了水稻，就把稻米分一些给贫苦的农民；他雄劲的笔力可以掣鲸碧海，但却常以悲悯的语气描写那些弱小的动植物。这说明，仁爱精神、人道主义、民本思想，不仅渗透在他的诗歌中，还反映在他的行动中。杜甫的恻隐之心，不仅针对人，甚至推广到自然界的万事万物。

（二） 爱国主义和忧患意识

儒家重视尊王，主张维护国家的统一，反对外族入侵。杜甫很好地继承了这一点。他从青年时代开始，就对国家和人民的命运给予密切的关注，随着社会矛盾和民族矛盾的日益激化，这种关注及由之而形成的忧患精神表现得愈加强烈。国家时局的每一次动荡，军事上的每一次行动及后果，都在他的诗中留下了印记。大到安史之乱、吐蕃陷京，小至陈陶、青坂之役以及地方军阀作乱，无不反映于杜诗中，一些作品还能弥补史书之阙。"向来忧国泪，寂寞洒衣巾。"（《谒先主庙》）正是由于他对国家命运的关切和思考，才能常常提出一些合理的建议和主张，如固守潼关、增防芦子关、限制回纥兵力、朝廷合理用人等。面临危险时最能考验一个人的爱国精神，当被安史叛军

patriotism is when one's life is in peril. When being taken to the captured Chang'an by the An Shi rebels, many officials in important positions and a lot of members of the royal family all surrendered, accepting appointments from the rebels. However, Du Fu, though an official in a minor position, risked his life to escape, fleeing alone to the emperor's residence. The emperor and the court were the symbol of the state in feudal society, so Du Fu always yearned for the emperor and the court. However, when the court implemented corrupt policies that caused serious harm to the state and the people, he mercilessly satirized and condemned them. Du Fu admonished, mocked, or condemned treacherous court officials, power abusing eunuchs, local officials who oppressed the people, as well as arrogant and rebellious officers and warlords; Du Fu was often moved to tears, never forgetting to write poems in honor of those loyal officials, righteous people, and virtuous and talented ministers who sacrificed their lives for the state. This great patriotism has been a lesson for generations after, and it has been the spiritual power that has maintained the unification and enhanced the development of the Chinese nation.

Ⅲ. A Broad-Minded, Strong-Willed Personality and a Persevering Spirit

Du Fu embodied the ideal personality traits of a Confucian scholar. Even in his boyhood, he cherished the ideal of "Causing the return of Yao and Shun / So as to restore simple customs" ("A Twenty-Two Rhyme Poem to Wei Ji"). After living ten miserable years in Chang'an, he did not give up his original dream, writing, "I thought I could match Ji and Qi" ("Feelings Expressed in Five Hundred Words after Traveling from the Capital to Fengxian County"). Even though he stayed far away from the court and suffered from both poverty and sickness in his old age, his heart still went out to all people under heaven, ashamed that he was unable to devote himself more to his country, showing his thoughts and feelings by praising others. "I wish that I could become an immortal star / As I'm determined to bring back such wise monarchs as Yao and Shun" ("Regret"). It was this lofty aspiration that one's responsibility should be the betterment of one's country as well as this sense of duty that granted him such broad perspective and indomitable courage. So when he held the post of Commissioner of the Left, he dared to challenge the emperor's order to rescue Fang Guan. He was also a man of unyielding character and steadfast will. "Though my teeth have gone, I'm not a man without heart / Though my tongue is still with me, I feel ashamed to cry when my heart changes" ("A Reply

押解在沦陷后的长安时，许多身居要职的官员、皇亲国戚纷纷投降，接受伪职。官职低微的杜甫却冒死逃出并只身投奔皇帝的行在。封建社会的皇帝和朝廷就是国家的象征，所以杜甫一生始终心系君王、依恋朝廷，但是当朝廷施行祸国殃民的败政时，他就毫不留情地予以讽刺和批判。对于朝廷中的奸臣、宫中弄权的宦官、鱼肉百姓的地方官、骄奢无能的军官、恃险作乱的军阀，杜甫总能站在国事的高度予以规劝、讽刺或者谴责。而对那些为国牺牲的忠臣义士和被奸邪所残害的贤能大臣，杜甫则从未忘记作诗悼念，而且常常为之老泪纵横。这种伟大的爱国思想，曾经激励和教育了一代代后来者，这正是维系中华民族统一并促其发展的强大精神力量。

（三） 弘毅的人格和笃行精神

杜甫具有典型的儒家"士"的品格。他青年时代即有"致君尧舜上，再使风俗淳"（《奉赠韦左丞丈二十二韵》）的远大理想。经过长安十年穷愁潦倒的境遇后，并没有放弃"窃比稷与契"（《自京赴奉先县咏怀五百字》）的初衷。即使到了晚年远离朝廷、贫病交加时，他仍然心怀天下苍生，为自己无法为国出力而惭愧，并借赞扬别人以表明自己的情怀："死为星辰终不灭，致君尧舜焉肯朽？"（《可叹》）正是这种以天下为己任的远大抱负和责任感，使他具有了宽广的胸怀和大无畏的勇气，因而在任左拾遗时，他敢于挑战皇帝的命令，营救房琯。他还具有刚强的品格和坚忍不拔的毅力，"齿落未是无心人，舌存耻作穷途哭。"（《暮秋枉裴道州手札，率尔遣兴，寄近呈

Containing My Heartfelt Feelings to Governor Pei's Letter That Had Arrived in the Late Autumn, a Poem also Presented to Su Huan"). His life was full of frustration, but he never ceased to improve himself and had never been afraid to face both good times and bad ones. He never gave up his pursuit of moral integrity and literary creation, even when he was in great tribulation.

IV. Value Placed on Harmony and Loyalty

Du Fu carried on the Confucian ideal of harmony, advocating the peaceful coexistence of people and the harmonious relationship between man and nature. He was kind and faithful toward friends, befriending princes, dukes and aristocrats from the upper class, as well as peasants from the laboring class. He often felt grateful when others sent him bundles of chives, or when they let him have a hot bath. He would write poems to show his gratitude for such favors. His friendship did not fade, even if his friends fell upon difficult times. When old friends such as Zheng Qian, Li Bai and Fang Guan were convicted and banished, he did not distance himself from them, but rather felt more worried for them. Even when his friends had long since passed away, he would still write poems to mourn for them. He never did assume the haughty air of a scholar or official; he was always able to make friends with peasants and participate in physical labor. He also advocated the spirit of benevolence, love, faithfulness and forgiveness towards the relationship between man and nature. "Hills that complement one another are like my lungs / Birds and flowers in the mountains are like my friends" ("A Trip to Yuelu Mountain Temple and Daolin Temple"). This demonstrates that he was a faithful advocate and practitioner of the Confucian ideals of loyalty and consideration.

Du Fu not only carried on the positive elements of early Confucian thought but also overcame its negative elements. For example, Confucianism advocates that "one should pay attention to one's own moral progress without thinking of others while poor and should do good to others when he is rich." Du Fu was always concerned for the people whether he was poor or rich; Confucianism advocates "universal love for all people" but also emphasizes the difference between intelligent men and stupid men, showing contempt for the laboring people, while Du Fu befriended peasants.

As the leading figure of Chinese poetry, Du Fu's artistic achievements in poetry were brilliant.

First, he carried on and developed the tradition of realism passed down from *The Book of Poetry*. His poems faithfully and comprehensively reflected

苏涣侍御》）他的一生历经坎坷，但却始终自强不息，始终直面人生的顺境逆境，即使在最艰难的状况下也没有停止他的人格追求和文学创作。

（四） 以和为贵的忠恕思想

杜甫继承了儒家以和为贵的思想，主张人与人之间的和平共处以及人与自然之间的和谐关系。他善待朋友，忠于友谊，因而上至王公贵族、下至田父野老都有他的朋友。他常怀感恩之心，别人送他几束韭菜，或者让他洗了一个热水澡，他都会郑重地写诗感谢。他的友谊不因朋友境遇的改变而褪色，当老朋友郑虔、李白和房琯等人因罪被贬或被流放时，他不但没有疏远，反而更加牵挂他们。在朋友死去多年后，他还写诗沉痛地怀念。他不摆读书人和官老爷的架子，能与农民很好地交往，并且亲自参加劳动。他还把这种仁爱忠恕的精神推广到人与自然之间，"一重一掩吾肺腑，山鸟山花吾友于。"（《岳麓山道林二寺行》）他是儒家忠恕精神的忠实倡导和践行者。

杜甫不仅继承了早期儒家思想中的积极因素，还能突破它的消极方面。比如儒家提倡"穷则独善其身，达则兼济天下"，杜甫则不论穷达，都心怀天下；儒家虽提倡"泛爱众"，但又认为"上智下愚"，看不起体力劳动者，杜甫则能和农民很好地交往等等。

作为中国诗歌王国顶峰上的人物，杜甫的诗歌艺术成就是巨大的。

首先，他继承并发展了《诗经》以来的现实主义传统，他

the process of decline of the Tang Empire, so they were praised as "poetic history." He infused *Yuefu* folk songs with new subject matters, by naming the songs for their contents, enabling *Yuefu* folk songs to better reflect reality. He freed seven-character regular verses, which could previously only be written upon the emperor's order, and used them to reflect reality, helping this kind of poetic form achieve its maturity. He also created the new style of "poem groups linked by related subject matters," which greatly expanded the contents of poetry. He composed a great many regulated verses and long ancient verses with rich content, grand scale and great expressive power.

Furthermore, he carried on and absorbed a wide range of literary achievements from preceding poets, believing that "one should learn from both contemporary men and the ancient men." He also composed over a thousand four hundred poems with the attitude that "one should never give up until one's words leave people gasping with wonder." These poems were imbued with rich and vibrant emotion, integrated and profound conception, objective and well-knit content, and unique and powerful language, forming a uniquely morose artistic style.

Last, his poetry takes many different poetic forms, all of which he mastered. Among these, his greatest achievements came in regular verse, so that his poetry has always been considered as the model for regular verse composition. In terms of metrical techniques and verbal parallelism in regular verse composition, he made detailed studies and did intensive exercises on his way to achieving perfection.

Due to his broad thinking, sincere emotions, steadfast personality, and brilliant poetic achievements, Du Fu was praised as a "poet sage" as well as the greatest of poets, both of which were titles he richly deserved.

Du Fu's poetry has always been considered as a model for later generations. Yuan Zhen and Bai Juyi, and Han Yu and Meng Haoran towards the middle of the Tang Dynasty represented two totally different schools of poetry, but both of them were inspired by Du Fu's poetry. Even poets of the latter years of the Tang Dynasty were influenced by Du Fu; Li Shangyin especially understood the essence of Du Fu's poetry, and was able to build upon it.

Du Fu's value and significance was reestablished in the Song Dynasty, with his poetry gaining wider influence at that time. Wang Anshi, Su Shi, Huang Tingjian, Chen Shidao and others praised Du Fu and emphasized the necessity of learning from Du Fu's poetry. Since the middle years of the Northern Song Dynasty, learning from and respecting Du Fu was no longer a characteristic of the minority of poets, but had become accepted understanding

的诗歌忠实全面地反映了唐王朝由盛转衰过程中的历史面貌，被誉为"诗史"。他所开创的"即事名篇"的新题乐府，使乐府诗能更好地反映现实。他把七律从应制、应酬的藩篱中解放出来，用以反映现实，使这种诗歌体式完全成熟。他还开创了"联章组诗"的新形式，扩大了诗歌的表现内容。他创作的大量排律和长篇古诗内容丰富、规模宏大，具有强大的表现力。

其次，他以"不薄今人爱古人"的宽广胸襟，广泛继承和吸收前代诗人的创作成就，并以"语不惊人死不休"的认真态度，创作出一千四百多首诗歌。这些诗感情丰富饱满，意境完整深厚，内容客观严谨，语言奇拔雄劲，形成了沉郁顿挫的独特艺术风格。

再次，他的诗各体皆备，各体皆善，尤其以律诗成就最高，一直被后人奉为创作上的典范。在律诗的声律技巧和对仗等方面，精于研炼，使其达到完美的境地。

因其丰富的思想、真挚的感情、坚定踏实的人格和巨大的诗歌艺术成就，杜甫被后人誉为"诗圣"，誉为诗国中的集大成者，他是无愧于这一称号的。

杜诗在后代一向被视为典范。中唐的元白和韩孟是风格截然不同的两大诗派，但是两派诗人都从杜诗中吸取营养。晚唐诗人也受杜甫影响，其中李商隐更是得杜诗真髓，并且能对其推陈出新。

宋人进一步发现了杜甫的价值和意义，杜诗也因此在宋代产生了更为广泛的影响。王安石、苏轼、黄庭坚、陈师道等人都竭力推崇杜甫，并且指出了在诗歌创作上学杜的必要性。北宋中叶开始，学杜、尊杜的倾向已经不是少数诗坛巨子的个人

among poets. At the same time, discussing Du Fu's poetry also became common practice. During the Southern Song Dynasty, the Jingkang Incident erupted, which damaged the country and brought about social unrest. Under these circumstances, it was much easier for poets to relate to the themes of worry for the state and concern for the people found in Du Fu's poetry. Lv Benzhong and Chen Yuyi were both influenced by Du Fu's gloomy poetic style. With his concern for the state and his loyal indignation that he had no opportunity to serve the state, Lu You was very similar to Du Fu, and a gloomy, reflective mood was also characteristic of his poetic style. Before and after the collapse of the Southern Song Dynasty, Wen Tianxiang, Wang Yuanliang, Lin Jingxi and others had all written verses that shared the same poetic style and sentiments as Du Fu's poetry.

With the new understanding and evaluation gained in the Song Dynasty, Du Fu's position as a model of moral uprightness has been established. When the nation's existence was in peril, Du Fu's spirit was especially inspiring.

Du Fu is the writer whose works have been studied the most in Chinese history. In Chinese literary history, no other writer's works have been interpreted in as many different ways as Du Fu's poetry. In the Song Dynasty, there was a saying that "there are a thousand interpretations of Du Fu's poetry." From the Song Dynasty till now, there have been more and more people interpreting, selecting and studying Du Fu's poetry, a rare honor for a writer.

Du Fu traveled in his youth and wandered in his old age, making his way over more than half of China, and traces of his passage can still be found today. At the places where the poet built cottages, later generations built memorial temples to commemorate him, among which Du Fu's cottage in Chengdu is the most well-known. After Du Fu left Shu, the cottage had been left desolate for some time. Wei Zhuang, a poet of former Shu in the Five Dynasties era, found the former site and rebuilt the cottage, preserving it to this day. The cottage was renovated during the Song, Yuan, Ming and Qing dynasties and has been preserved to this day. After the founding of the People's Republic of China, the cottage was opened as the Du Fu Memorial Hall, and its name was changed to the Du Fu Cottage Museum in 1985. In addition, there are also memorial buildings including Du Fu's cottages and memorial temples, in Yan'an of Shaanxi, Tianshui and Chengxian County of Gansu, Santai of Sichuan and so on. Some places even have more than one memorial building (for example, Tianshui), and those buildings have been destroyed and rebuilt many times, so that sacrifices for Du Fu have never ceased. In Southern Yaowan Village of

选择了，而是整个诗坛的共识，同时讨论杜诗也蔚然成风。南宋靖康事变发生，山河破碎，社会动荡，许多诗人更容易在杜诗中找到忧国忧民的感情共鸣。吕本中、陈与义接受杜甫沉郁诗风的影响，陆游的忧国情怀和报国无路的忠愤堪称杜甫的异代知己，其创作也以沉郁顿挫为主导诗风。南宋灭亡前后，文天祥、汪元量、林景熙等都有与杜诗风格、情怀极为一致的诗歌作品。

经过宋人的重新认识和评价，杜甫的人格典范已被确立起来。特别是在民族危亡之际，杜甫的精神更加富于感召力。

杜甫也成为中国历代被研究最多的作家。在中国文学史上，没有哪位作家的作品能拥有像杜诗那么多的注本。宋代就有"千家注杜"的说法，自宋迄今，杜诗的注家、选家和研究者不断增加，成为文学史上罕见的壮观。

杜甫早年壮游、晚年漂泊，行踪所到之处遍布大半个中国，各地也都保留了他的遗迹。在诗人曾结庐居住的地方，后人修建了许多祠宇以纪念他，其中最著名的是成都的杜甫草堂。杜甫离蜀后，草堂一度荒芜，五代前蜀诗人韦庄觅得旧址重结茅屋，草堂胜迹得以保存下来。宋、元、明、清各代，草堂经过多次修葺，保存至今。建国后辟为杜甫纪念馆，1985年更名为杜甫草堂博物馆。此外，陕西延安、甘肃天水与成县、四川三台等地也建有杜甫草堂或祠堂等纪念性建筑物，有的地方（如天水）还不止一处，而且屡毁屡建，祭祀不绝。杜甫的诞生地

Gongxian County in Henan where Du Fu was born, the Du Fu Hometown Memorial Hall was constructed. There are tombs constructed in Du Fu's honor in Leiyang and Pingjiang in Hunan, Gongxian County and Yanshi in Henan.

Famous calligraphers of all dynasties loved writing Du Fu's poetry, and well-known painters also painted their renditions of Du Fu's poems. Du Fu's influence also expanded into other popular literary fields. Since the appearance of the dramatic script of the *Yuanben* in Jin ❶ period entitled *Du Fu's Spring Tour*, Du Fu has become a character in plays, who often appeared in the dramatic works of the Yuan, Ming and Qing dynasties. There were as many as eight kinds of such drama in which Du Fu's stories were played, showing the love of the common people for Du Fu.

As Chinese culture has spread overseas, Du Fu's influence has crossed national boundaries. Since the thirteenth century, Du Fu's poetry has been popular in Japan, Korea, Vietnam and other countries. Since the nineteenth century, Du Fu's poetry has been translated into different languages and introduced to westerners, attracting more and more attention from Western scholars of Sinology. On the Presidium Conference of Universal Peace Council held in Stockholm in 1961, it was decided that Du Fu would be named a Cultural Personage of the World, and would be commemorated the next year. In 1962, at the 1250th anniversary of Du Fu's birth, a wide range of commemorative activities were held in various places of the world. Du Fu is not only a brilliant representative of the Chinese culture but a great poet who has gained international fame.

Du Fu's widespread influence is felt not only in China, but also in foreign countries; not only in the fields of poetry and literature, but also in virtually all domains of Chinese culture. What is the most important is that Du Fu has exerted a subtle but formative influence on the building of the Chinese national character. Du Fu's strong-minded and reliable attitude towards life, his benevolence that enabled him to put himself in the place of others, his loyalty and consideration for others that showed he valued harmony, his sense of duty that made him feel responsible for the betterment of his country, and his sense of anxiety that made him worry for the state and the people are all laudable aspects of the Chinese national character. Though the building of such national character should not be attributed to one individual person, Du Fu's influence is undoubtedly an indispensable part. In addition, in the fields of traditional culture, it is Chinese literature, especially poetry, that has become the most widespread and inspiring. Because of this, Du Fu occupies a very prominent position in Chinese cultural history and has had a profound impact on the

河南巩县南瑶湾村，建有杜甫故里纪念馆。湖南耒阳、平江，河南巩县、偃师等地都保存有杜甫墓。

历代书法家多喜爱书写杜诗，画家也有杜甫诗意图传世，各代收藏颇富，且多出名家之手。杜甫的影响还进入了通俗文学领域，从金院本❶《杜甫游春》开始，杜甫成为戏剧人物，元杂剧、明清传奇等都有反映杜甫故事的剧作，共有八种之多，反映了广大群众对杜甫的喜爱。

随着中华文化在海外的传播，杜甫的影响早已超出了国界。从十三世纪开始，杜诗就在日本、朝鲜、越南等国广泛流传，受到各国人民的喜爱。从十九世纪起，杜诗又被译成了各种文字介绍给西方人民，并受到了西方汉学家越来越多的关注。1961年在斯德哥尔摩举行的世界和平理事会主席团会议上，决定将杜甫列为次年纪念的世界文化名人。1962年，在杜甫诞辰1250周年之际，世界各地举行了广泛的纪念活动。杜甫不仅是中华文化的杰出代表，而且也是一位赢得国际声誉的伟大诗人。

杜甫不仅在国内，而且在国外产生了极为广泛的影响；不仅在诗歌和文学的领域，而且在中华民族文化形态的各个领域中，都产生了极为深远的影响。尤其重要的是，杜甫对中华民族的性格塑造也具有潜移默化的作用。杜甫坚定踏实的人生态度、推己及人的仁爱精神、以和为贵的忠恕思想、以天下为己任的责任感以及忧国忧民的忧患意识，正是中华民族性格中最光辉的部分。虽说这种民族性格的陶铸不能归因于个人，但其中杜甫的影响无疑是不可或缺的。而且，在传统文化领域中，中国文学，特别是诗歌又是传播最为广泛、感召力最为巨大的一种。因此杜甫在中国传统文化史上占有极为显著的地位，在

---

❶ 译者注：金朝时一种戏曲脚本。

❶ Translator's note: a representative form of operas in Jin period.

formation of Chinese culture. As Wen Yiduo said, Du Fu was "the most dignified, the most magnificent and the most enduring beam of brilliant light in the four thousand years of Chinese cultural history."

中国文化的建构上具有十分突出的文化意义，诚如闻一多先生所云，杜甫是"四千年文化史中最庄严、最瑰丽、最永久的一道光彩"！

杜甫画像
Portrait of Du Fu

杜甫诗意画
Painting according to Du Fu's poem

References and Further Reading

1. Chen Yixin. *The Critical Biography of Du Fu*. Beijing: Beijing University Press, 2003.

2. Du Fu's Cottage Museum in Chengdu, and Research Association on Du Fu in Sichuan. *The Complete Collection of Du Fu's Poetry with Modern Annotation*. Chengdu: Heaven and Earth Publishing House, 1999.

3. Han Chengwu. *Poet Sage: Du Fu Living in the World of Misery*. Baoding: Hebei University Press, 2000.

4. Jin Qihua, and Hu Wentao. *The Critical Biography of Du Fu*. Xi'an: Shaanxi People's Publishing House, 1984.

5. Liu Xu, et al. (Latter Jin Dynasty). *Book on Literature*. in *The Old Book of Tang*, vol. 190. (Book II) Beijing: Zhonghua Book Company, 1975.

6. Mo Lifeng. *The Critical Biography of Du Fu*. Nanjing: Nanjing University Press, 1993.

7. Mo Lifeng, and Tong Qiang. *The Biography of Du Fu: A Benevolent Man's Pursuit in Hardships*. Tianjin: Tianjin People's Publishing House, 2001.

8. Nie Shiqiao, and Han Zhaoqi. *Selected Works of Du Fu's Poetry*. Haikou: Nanhai Publishing House, 2005.

9. Qiu Zhaoao (Qing Dynasty). *Detailed Annotation of Du Fu's Poetry*. Beijing: Zhonghua Book Company, 1979.

10. Song Qi, Ouyang Xiu, et al. (Song Dynasty). *Book on Art and Literature*. in *The New Book of Tang*, vol. 201. (Book I). Beijing: Zhonghua Book Company, 1975.

11. Wang Sishi (Ming Dynasty). *Du Fu's Poetry Annotated by Wang Sishi*. Shanghai: Shanghai Classics Publishing House, 1983.

12. Xiao Difei. *Annotation of Selected Works of Du Fu's Poetry*. Beijing: The People's Literature Publishing House, 1979.

图书在版编目(CIP)数据

杜甫:汉英对照/莫砺锋,武国权著:潘智丹译. —南京:
南京大学出版社，2010.4
(中国思想家评传简明读本)
ISBN 978-7-305-06826-3

Ⅰ.杜… Ⅱ.①莫…②武…③潘… Ⅲ.①杜甫
(712～770)—评传—汉、英 Ⅳ.K825.6

中国版本图书馆CIP数据核字(2010)第048045号

出 版 者 南京大学出版社
社　　址 南京汉口路22号　邮　编 210093
网　　址 http://www.NjupCo.com
出 版 人 左　健

从 书 名 《中国思想家评传》简明读本(中英文版)
书　　名 杜　甫
著　　者 莫砺锋　武国权
译　　者 潘智丹
审　　校 Thomas Mitchell
审　　读 石云龙
责任编辑 李海霞　　　　编辑热线 025-83685720

照　　排 江苏凤凰制版印务中心
印　　刷 宜兴市盛世文化印刷有限公司
开　　本 787×1092　1/16　印张 18　字数 333千
版　　次 2010年4月第1版　2010年4月第1次印刷
ISBN 978-7-305-06826-3
定　　价 43.20元

发行热线 025-83594756
电子邮箱 Press@NjupCo.com
　　　　 Sales@NjupCo.com (市场部)

延伸阅读书目

一、陈贻焮《杜甫评传》，北京大学出版社2003年版。

二、成都杜甫草堂博物馆、四川杜甫研究会编《杜诗全集》（今注），天地出版社1999年版。

三、韩成武《诗圣：忧患世界中的杜甫》，河北大学出版社2000年版。

四、金启华、胡文涛《杜甫评传》，陕西人民出版社1984年版。

五、刘昫［后晋］等《旧唐书》卷一百九十（下）《文苑传》，中华书局1975年版。

六、莫砺锋《杜甫评传》，南京大学出版社1993年版。

七、莫砺锋、童强《杜甫传：仁者在苦难中的追求》，天津人民出版社2001年版。

八、聂石樵、韩兆琦《杜甫诗选》，南海出版公司2005年版。

九、仇兆鳌［清］《杜诗详注》，中华书局1979年版。

十、宋祁、欧阳修［宋］等《新唐书》卷二百零一《艺文传》上，中华书局1975年版。

十一、王嗣奭［明］《杜臆》，上海古籍出版社1983年版

十二、萧涤非《杜甫诗选注》，人民文学出版社1979年版